THE
FAMILY
CREATIVE
WORK
SHOP

THE FAMILY CREATIVE WORKSHOP

6

Embroidery, Enameling Metal
Flags and Banners, Florentine Stitch
Flowers (Artificial)
Foam Forms, Folk Art, Framing
Furniture Refinishing, Fur Recycling
Genealogy, Gingerbread

Plenary Publications International, Inc.
New York and Amsterdam

Published by Plenary Publications International Incorporated 300 East 40 Street, New York, N. Y. 10016, for the Blue Mountain Crafts Council.

Library of Congress Catalog Card Number: 73-89331. Complete set International Standard Book Number: 0-88459-021-6. Volume 6 International Standard Book Number: 0-88459-005-4. Second Printing

Manufactured in the United States of America. Printed and bound by the W. A. Krueger Company, Brookfield, Wisconsin.

Printing preparation by Lanman Lithoplate Company.

Publishers:
Plenary Publications International, Incorporated 300 East 40 Street New York, New York 10016

Allen Davenport Bragdon
EDITOR-IN-CHIEF AND PUBLISHER OF THE FAMILY CREATIVE WORKSHOP

Nancy Jackson
ADMINISTRATIVE ASSISTANT

Jerry Curcio
PRODUCTION MANAGER

Editorial preparation:
Tree Communications, Inc. 250 Park Avenue South New York, New York 10003

Rodney Friedman
EDITORIAL DIRECTOR

Ronald Gross
DESIGN DIRECTOR

Paul Levin
DIRECTOR OF PHOTOGRAPHY

Donal Dinwiddie
CONSULTING EDITOR

James Wyckoff
TEXT EDITOR

Sonja Douglas
ART DIRECTOR

Barnet Friedman
COPYREADER

Betty Friedman
ADMINISTRATIVE MANAGER

Rochelle Lapidus
ASSISTANT DESIGNER

Editors for this volume:
Frank Cogan
ENAMELING METAL
FLAGS AND BANNERS

Andrea DiNoto
GENEALOGY

Linda Hetzer
FRAMING
FURNITURE REFINISHING

Nancy Levine
EMBROIDERY
FLORENTINE STITCH

Marilyn Nierenberg
FLOWERS (ARTIFICIAL)
FOLK ART, FOAM FORMS

Marilyn Ratner
FUR RECYCLING
GINGERBREAD

Contributing illustrators:
Marina Givotovsky
Nancy Levine
Sally Shimizu
Barbara Auran-Wrenn

Contributing photographers:
Dick Frank
Benno Friedman
Paul Levin
Frank Lusk
Stephen McCarroll
John Savage

Contributing editors:
Kay Bardsley
Denise Demong
William Mulligan
Molli Nickell
Nona Remos

Acknowledgements:
EMBROIDERY: embroidered coif and matching forehead cloth, courtesy of The Metropolitan Museum of Art, gift of Irwin Untermyer, 1964. FOLK ART: birth certificate, courtesy of Philadelphia Museum of Art; dower chest, courtesy of Philadelphia Museum of Art; weather vane, courtesy of Creative Art Gallery. FRAMING: box frame, designed and built by Cliff Hetzer. FUR RECYCLING: pillows, courtesy of Seymour Winik, inc.; furs, courtesy of American Fur Industry; fling, courtesy of Reynard. GENEALOGY: illuminated family tree, courtesy of Local History and Genealogy Division, The New York Public Library, Astor, Lenox and Tilden Foundations.

The Project-Evaluation Symbols appearing in the title heading at the beginning of each project have these meanings:

Range of approximate cost:
¢ Low: under $5 or free and found natural materials

$ Medium: about $10

$$ High: above $15

Estimated time to completion for an unskilled adult:
⊠ Hours

🕐 Days

Weeks

Suggested level of experience:
Child alone

Supervised child or family project

Unskilled adult

Specialized prior training

Tools and equipment:
Small hand tools

Large hand and household tools

Specialized or powered equipment

On the cover:
Tissue and crepe paper sheets, cut, folded, fluffed and tipped with a felt pen. See the entry, Flowers (Artificial) beginning on page 688. Photograph by Paul Levin.

Contents and craftspeople for Volume 6:

EMBROIDERY
Stitch Imagery

Solweig Hedin studied textile design at the Institute of Textiles and the School of Arts and Crafts in her native Sweden. She teaches embroidery and other needlework skills in New York City and is a free-lance needlework designer, artist, and consultant. The co-author and designer of Creative Needlework, *she also exhibits her work in craft shows.*

Embroidery, the art of stitching decorative designs by hand or machine on textiles or leather, encompasses a great variety of techniques and materials. The basic materials most commonly used are cotton, linen, wool, silk, leather, and some synthetics; but unusual substances, such as gold and silver, precious stones, pearls, beads, and feathers can be employed to achieve spectacular effects.

Because there are so many kinds of embroidery techniques, it is difficult to classify them. A good deal of overlap exists, since one technique may influence another. Many of the same stitches can be used in several techniques and worked in different materials, according to the type of embroidery. For example, the satin stitch (see "Crewelwork Sampler," Volume Five) can be employed in crewelwork and hardanger, two quite dissimilar embroidery techniques.

Historically a popular craft, embroidery is rapidly coming back into favor today. It is a relaxing, creative pastime with an end product that carries the mark of the creator's personality. In fact, some men are taking up embroidery for this very reason. It is also inexpensive and easy to learn, strong factors in its appeal to children.

The following brief summary of some of the major embroidery techniques include easy ones as well as some that require a skill and patience not as much in evidence now as they were 50 or 100 years ago when people had more time. The following projects, however, help you to develop the basic skills of the craft and are within the capabilities of the modern embroiderer.

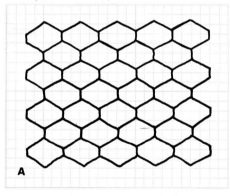 

Figure A: In this simple black work filling pattern (a repeated design used to fill in an area), each blue square equals two fabric threads.

The pattern in Figure A, left, is shown worked in backstitch on even-weave fabric. See page 648 for a description and photograph of black work.

Counted-Thread Embroidery

This technique requires an even-weave fabric (also called even-count fabric), so named because it has an equal number of horizontal and vertical threads per inch.

The stitches are worked by referring to a chart that is in the form of a grid. The squares of the blue grid in Figure A correspond to the threads of the background fabric. The embroiderer counts the squares on the chart, then makes the stitch by counting the appropriate number of threads on the fabric (photograph 1). A square may represent one, two, or more fabric threads for a variety of reasons depending on the fabric, the type of thread used, and the design. Embroidery techniques employing counted-thread principles are needlepoint, hardanger, cross stitch, black work, and most forms of white work (see page 648).

This is a portion of Solweig Hedin's 36-by-36-inch square wall hanging, worked in silk and rayon threads and fabrics. Directions and a photograph of the piece in its entirety are on page 653. The basic design idea of appliqueing and embroidering small circles within a large circle adapts well to a number of useful items. A bedspread or a tablecloth would look dramatic with this design at its center or cushions and curtains may be coordinated by applying only a few small circles.

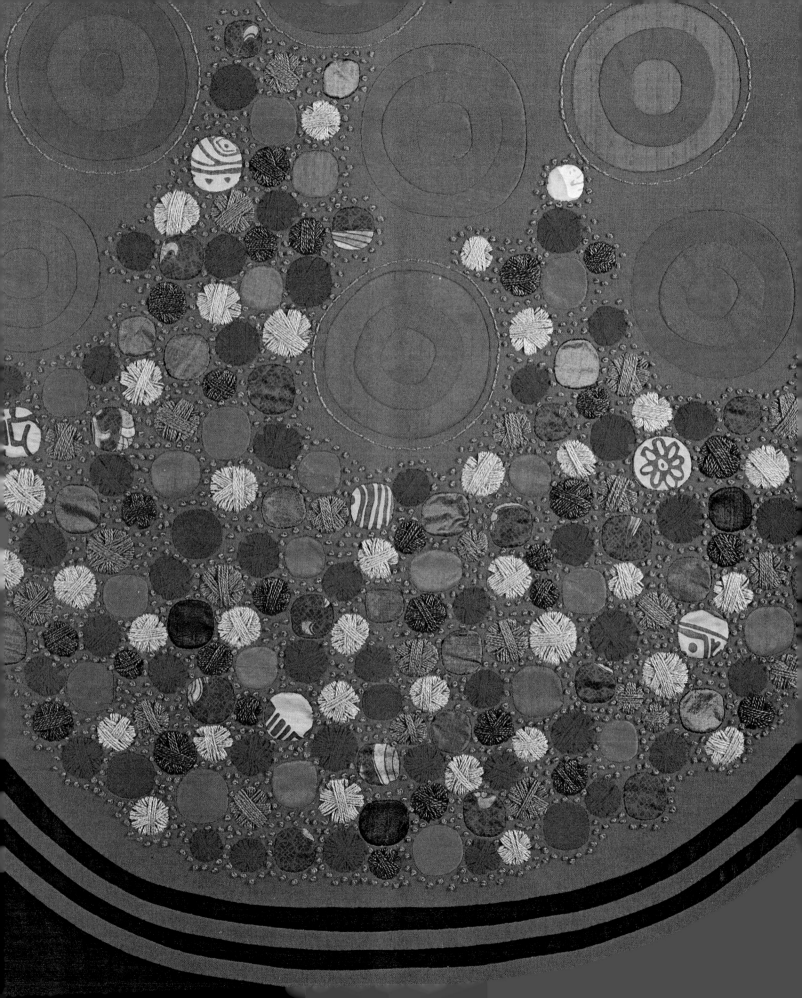

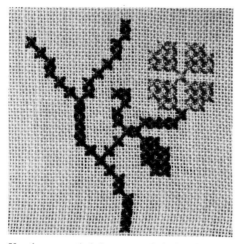

Use the cross stitch for geometric designs like this flower worked on even-weave fabric using No. 3 and No. 5 pearl cotton.

Sixteenth-century coif (top left) and matching forehead cloth were embroidered in the black work technique using black silk on white linen.

Cross Stitch Embroidery

Embroiderers usually combine the cross stitch (see "Crewelwork Sampler," Figures 9A and 9B, Volume Five) with other stitches, but you can work an entire piece of embroidery in this stitch alone. The regularity of the stitch is more easily accomplished by carrying it out on an even-weave fabric. Owing to its regular and geometric construction, cross stitching looks best if the design is rather formal or has a motif that repeats itself several times.

Black Work

As the name suggests, black work was traditionally done using black silk thread on white or natural-colored, evenly woven fabric. Black work originated in Spain and was brought to England by Catherine of Aragon in 1501. It reached its greatest popularity in Elizabethan times, when it was widely used for embroidering fine linen neck ruffs and frilled shirt cuffs. Black work, when done in a double running stitch (Holbein), is completely reversible (see Figure E, page 654), and thus it was especially suited for items on which the stitches were visible from both sides. As clothing styles changed, exposing more and more shirt, entire sleeves, stomachers (garments worn over the chest and stomach), and bodices—in addition to coifs (caps; photograph left center), gloves, and handkerchiefs—were embroidered with increasingly elaborate black work patterns. Delicate, formalized flowers and leaves, outlined and filled in with lacy geometric patterns of counted stitches, later embellished coverlets and cushions. The striking effect of black work is achieved by the weight or tone of the filling patterns and the interrelationship of dark, medium, and light patterns within a design. Black work is also known as Spanish work and Black and Gold, because of the frequent addition of metallic threads as highlights. Directions for black work projects begin on page 654.

White Work

Traditionally worked in white or off-white threads on a white or natural-colored background fabric, white work comprises a number of different stitches and techniques. White work needs a contrast of texture and perfectly worked stitches to bring out its full effect. The subtle, monochromatic color scheme of white-on-white can be worked to advantage in pulled work—in which the fabric threads are pulled by the stitching thread (see photograph below), drawn work—in which fabric threads are cut and withdrawn to form open areas (see photograph below left), and hardanger, a form of drawn work (see "Hardanger" in Volume Seven).

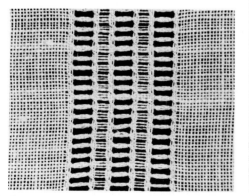

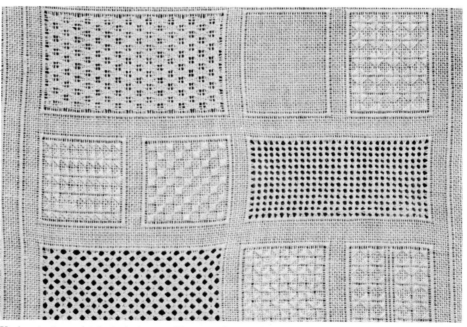

Open-weave areas are achieved by withdrawing fabric threads, as in this drawn-work embroidery.

Various textures, intricate designs, and lacy openings are created by the pulled-thread technique on even-weave linen, as shown in this detail of a white-work sampler.

This flower was done in free-motion embroidery on a straight-stitch sewing machine.

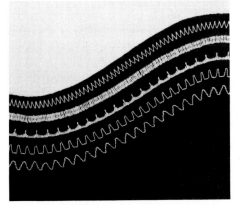

These five decorative stitches can be done on most modern sewing machines.

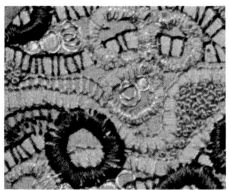

An interesting effect is achieved in this mixed-media embroidery by using rayon and metallic threads to work French knots, satin and blanket stitches. Background fabrics and circular shapes are Indian raw silk and linen.

Machine Embroidery

Anyone who owns or has access to a sewing machine can discover how easy it is to decorate clothing, cushions, tablecloths, and placemats. Shown above right are some of the many decorative stitches obtainable with a zigzag sewing machine or one with zigzag attachments. If you don't have one of these types, don't despair; free embroidery, or free-motion embroidery, can be done on a regular, straight-stitch machine. The photograph above left shows a flower worked on a straight-stitch machine in free embroidery. Simply remove the presser foot, and lower the feed dog teeth (see the manufacturer's operating manual). This allows "free motion," meaning the stitches can go in any direction.

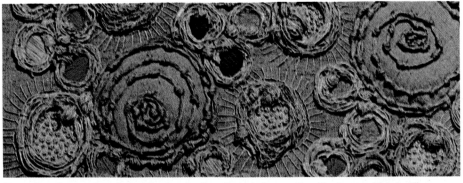

Shown here is a portion of a hanging in mixed-media technique on linen background fabric. The embroidery uses linen and silk threads; the padded circles are appliques cut from the linen fabric.

Silk thread in white and gold combines with beads on a rayon background in this unfinished work. Paper inserted under the circles done in long satin stitches creates a raised effect.

Mixed Media and Creative Stitchery

The mixed media method either uses several different materials in the same piece of embroidery (such as silk and linen yarn, illustrated above), or combines two techniques (applique and embroidery, for example, pages 652 and 653) or both. Creative stitchery uses traditional stitches and techniques in nontraditional ways; for instance, working a delicate technique such as black work in heavy yarn, thus achieving a totally different effect from that of the past. Creative stitchery, therefore, also includes mixed media. Today, many designers draw from the vast heritage of embroidery techniques to cover a surface with the glowing colors and textures of various materials. New and unusual combinations of materials are a natural result of the availability of a wider range of fabrics and threads than were available to our ancestors. Natural and synthetic fabrics and yarns of all weights and thicknesses, beads and buttons, sequins and feathers, are laid one upon another. The stitches secure these various materials or stand on their own as design. Areas are raised and given dimension by padding with paper, fabric, or cotton. Fine gold or silver thread may be combined with coarse unspun yarn. In the mixed media method, apply yarn, fabric, and whatever other materials you choose in the same way that a painter would apply paint.

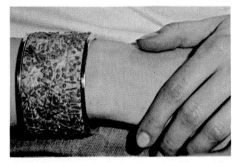

The artist wrapped silk thread embroidery with tiny yellow glass beads around a silver cylinder to make this unusual bracelet.

Before beginning any kind of needlework, be sure that you have the right tools and supplies. Buying materials of the highest quality is of the utmost importance. Knowing the right way to use them will make your work easier and more enjoyable and will give it a professional finish. Read the entry "Crewelwork Sampler" in Volume Five for starting, finishing, and handling yarn lengths; threading the needle; working with a hoop; washing, pressing, and blocking; and mounting the finished piece.

Fabrics

There are many factors that enter into choosing a background fabric: the intended use for the finished product, the embroidery technique, and the kind of yarn or thread you will work with.

For items that will receive a lot of wear, use a sturdy, closely woven fabric such as linen, cotton, denim or a synthetic or a blend. Wall hangings can be worked on loosely woven, delicate, or even gauzy fabrics. Even-weave fabric is used for counted-thread embroidery (see page 646). In general, use lightweight cottons, linens, wools, synthetics, organdy or silk for delicate stitchery; use medium and heavyweight linen, burlap, wool, synthetics and blends for the more substantial stitching. Of course, you can modify these guidelines somewhat if you are experimenting with mixed media or doing creative stitchery. Unless otherwise specified, when cutting the fabric, be sure to leave at least a 2-inch margin on all sides for blocking and mounting (see "Crewelwork Sampler" Craftnotes, Volume Five).

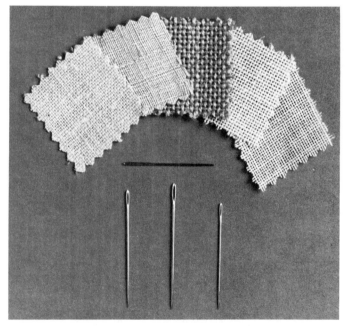

Top left to right are swatches of linen, silk, and coarse, medium, and fine even-weave fabrics; center: tapestry needle No. 22; and bottom left to right: crewel needles No. 3, 1 and 5.

Left top to bottom: crewel yarn, Persian yarn, tapestry yarn, six-strand cotton embroidery floss, pearl cotton No. 3, linen yarn, silk floss. Upper right: pearl cotton No. 5. Lower right: rayon floss.

Yarns and Threads

In general, relate the yarn to the fabric; fine threads and yarns go with lightweight fabrics, heavy ones with heavy fabrics. If the finished article will receive wear and tear (cushions, chair seats, some articles of clothing), use sturdy, tightly twisted yarns such as wool (crewel, tapestry, Persian), some synthetics (such as acrylic yarns), and linen. Six-strand cotton embroidery floss—a basic embroidery thread—matte cotton, and pearl cotton are suitable for embroidering items of clothing such as blouses, shirts, sweaters, and blue jeans; handkerchiefs; household articles such as tablecloths, napkins, and pillows; and wall hangings. Reserve metallic threads, silk or rayon floss, and novelty yarns such as raffia, plastic straw, and bouclé for hangings.

Needles

Needles should be slightly thicker than the thread or yarn being used, to allow the thread to pass through the fabric easily and without fraying. The eye of the needle should be just large enough to receive the thread without forcing it. Crewel needles are of a medium length with a long eye and are used for most embroidery threads. But many embroiderers prefer chenille needles, which are shorter and heavier than crewel needles and have a very long, wide eye. Tapestry needles have a blunt point and a large eye and are useful for counted-thread embroidery (see page 646) and for whipped and woven stitches that are worked on top of the surface of the fabric.

Hoops and Frames

A hoop or frame, although optional, will make most forms of embroidery easier. Beginners are especially urged to use a hoop or frame, as it stretches the fabric taut and prevents puckered, uneven stitching. Hoops consist of two concentric wood or metal rings. To secure fabric in a hoop, lay the cloth on the smaller ring; place the larger ring on top of it and press down.

Hoops come in many styles, from the ones held in the hand to

ATERIALS AND HOW TO USE THEM

those with stands that rest on a table or the floor. To prevent pressure marks when embroidering delicate fabrics, lay a few sheets of tissue paper over the fabric before placing the outer ring over it. Then tear a hole in the paper, exposing only the area of the fabric to be embroidered.

Professionals prefer a frame because it eliminates completely the pressure marks caused by a hoop. Directions for securing the fabric to the frame are included with the purchase, which can be made at well-stocked needlecraft shops. To use a frame, prop it against the edge of a table and rest the bottom edge in your lap. If you are working on a large hanging, you can construct a frame the size of the finished piece from artists' canvas stretcher strips (available in many sizes at art-supply stores). Hammer the strips together to form a frame of the size and shape required, making sure the corners are square. Place the fabric face down on a flat surface with the frame centered over it; staple or thumbtack the fabric to the back of the frame, stretching the fabric evenly. Block and frame it on the same strips when it is finished.

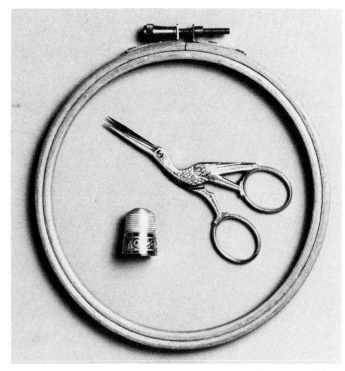

The 5-inch wooden embroidery hoop shown here has a thumb screw to enable the embroiderer to adjust the hoop to the thickness of the fabric. Within the hoop are embroidery scissors and a silver thimble.

Thimbles and Scissors

Some embroiderers find a thimble indispensible, whereas others feel it's a nuisance. A thimble should fit the middle finger of the right hand (if you are right-handed) and be made of metal rather than plastic. Be sure that the surface indentations are deep enough to prevent the end of the needle from slipping when you use the thimble to push the needle through.

Embroidery scissors are small, with narrow, pointed, sharp blades. They are necessary for ripping out mistakes and should be used for this purpose only. Use good fabric shears or household scissors to cut the background fabric.

Transferring the Design

Most designs are transferred directly onto the background fabric. Needlepoint and counted-thread embroideries are exceptions and are usually worked from a chart (see page 646). The first step in transferring is to make a paper pattern the desired size of the design. There are several ways of doing this. If the design is already available in the correct size, simply place a piece of tracing paper over it and trace its outlines. If it is larger or smaller than you need, have it photostatically enlarged or reduced (photostat services are listed in the telephone book) and make the tracing from the photostat. Or, enlarge the design by copying it on a grid as described on page 57, Volume One. The next step is to transfer the tracing paper pattern onto the fabric. There are several ways to do this, depending upon the type of fabric and how often the pattern will be used.

Dressmaker's carbon: This is used for smooth-surfaced medium weight and heavyweight fabrics. Place the carbon paper face down between the tracing and the fabric and then trace the design through with a dull hard lead pencil. Further explanation is given in "Crewelwork Sampler," page 540, Volume Five.

Direct tracing: Use this procedure when the design is small and the fabric is of a light color and weight. Tape the tracing, which has been marked in heavy, dark lines, on an artist's light box or a well-lit window pane, and then tape the fabric on top. The light shining through the pattern and the fabric will enable you to trace the design directly onto the fabric with a soft pencil.

Transfer patterns: These are commercially available and normally can be reused several times. They are good on smooth-surfaced fabrics but do not work successfully on textured fabrics, coarse wools, or velvets. Pin or tape the fabric to your ironing board. Tape the transfer, face down, on the fabric. Set your iron to "low" or "rayon" and use a firm stamping motion to transfer the design. Lift a corner of the transfer to see if the design has transferred satisfactorily. After you have completed the stamping, run the iron lightly over the transfer, and quickly remove it.

Transfer pencil: You can make a transfer pattern of your own by using a transfer pencil, also known as a hot-iron pencil. On the wrong side of your tracing paper pattern, go over the lines of the design with the transfer pencil. Pin or tape the tracing paper face down on the fabric. Use as you would a transfer pattern, above.

Basting stitches: Use this method for soft, fluffy fabrics, such as sweater knits, or very heavy or textured fabrics. Pin the tracing paper pattern to the right side of the fabric and with sewing thread of a contrasting color baste around all the design outlines, using small running stitches. Carefully tear away the paper and work your embroidery stitches right over the basting stitches.

Starting the Yarn

Starting the yarn with a knot is fine for a wall hanging (see "Crewelwork Sampler" in Volume Five); on objects that will be used a lot and washed frequently, do not start off with a knot. Instead, anchor the end of the thread with a few running stitches (tiny straight stitches in a row). Anticipate the direction in which you will be embroidering and make the running stitches in a place where they will be concealed by subsequent stitches.

This plain sweater owes its new personality to the embroidered rose, which was carefully attached using a buttonhole stitch.

Needlecrafts
Embroider a flower applique

In the past, when embroidery included gold, lace, and jewels, much of it was reused when the original article was discarded. In addition, embroiderers often worked elaborate motifs on fine linen, which were then cut out and applied to velvets and brocades, fabrics unsuitable for a direct application of stitches. Today, using the same method, you can decorate lush velvets or stretchy knits, patch blue jeans, liven up tote bags, and personalize blouses and jackets. This way furnishes an excellent introduction to embroidery for the beginner.

The flower motifs on this page are done in basic embroidery stitches. You can practice on a piece of fabric and, when satisfied with the result, cut it out and sew it to whatever you wish to decorate.

Of course, if the background fabric permits, and if you feel sure of yourself, you may embroider the motif directly onto the fabric.

Making the Applique
You will need: tracing paper; dressmaker's carbon paper; straight pins; a pencil; closely woven mediumweight fabric such as cotton or linen; an embroidery needle; and yarn (six-strand cotton embroidery floss or wool yarn such as crewel or Persian yarn). First trace one of the actual-size motifs from the photographs below, or use one of your own. Transfer the motif(s) to the fabric using dressmaker's carbon paper (see the Craftnote on page 651). Place the fabric with the designs on it in a hoop or on a frame, following the directions in the Craftnote. Using your own colors or those shown in the photographs, embroider the motifs using the stitches listed below (see "Crewelwork Sampler" Embroidery Craftnotes: Stitches, pages 542 to 545, Volume Five; the numbers following the names of the stitches refer to their sequential numbers in the Craftnotes): straight stitch (2), backstitch (3), satin stitch (6), lazy daisy (12), coral stitch (28), and French knot (29).

When you have completed a flower to your satisfaction, cut it out carefully, allowing for ¼ inch beyond the outline for the single flower. For the group of flowers (top, left) cut out in a square or oval shape, leaving the background fabric visible. Pin and baste the embroidered applique on the article you wish to decorate. Sew the applique to the article with thread to match the embroidery or the fabric. Using a tiny buttonhole stitch ("Crewelwork Sampler" Embroidery Craftnotes, Figure 27, page 545 in Volume 5), cover the edge of the applique completely.

French knot

Lazy daisy

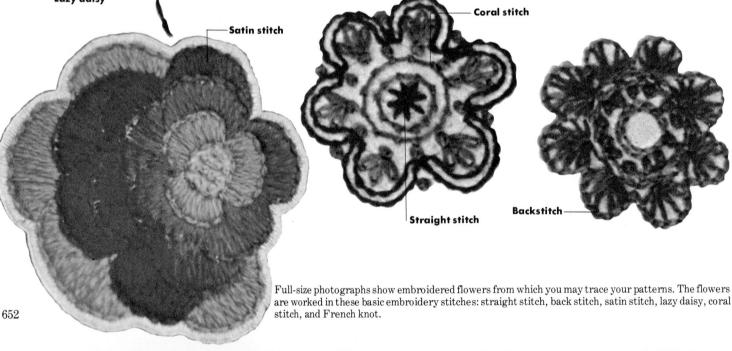

Satin stitch

Coral stitch

Straight stitch

Backstitch

Full-size photographs show embroidered flowers from which you may trace your patterns. The flowers are worked in these basic embroidery stitches: straight stitch, back stitch, satin stitch, lazy daisy, coral stitch, and French knot.

Needlecrafts

Circles within a circle

The large, colorful mixed media piece pictured on page 647 utilizes the two needlecraft techniques of embroidery and applique. Since the finished work was to be displayed as a hanging, I was free to use delicate silk and rayon yarn and fabric. I find these materials particularly appealing because of their luxurious sheen and luminosity. The directions that follow are for a 36-by-36-inch hanging. If you are embroidering something that will require frequent laundering, such as a bedspread or tablecloth, stay with machine-washable materials such as cotton and linen fabrics, and use six-strand cotton embroidery floss or No. 3 pearl cotton. If you wish to adapt the design area to fit a larger or smaller area, refer to the entry "Applique," Volume One.

Materials

As with all embroideries this large, it is best worked on a large frame. I suggest that you buy two pairs of 36-inch-long canvas stretcher strips, on which you can stretch the fabric and see the entire work at all times. When the embroidery is complete, it will already be mounted and ready for framing. You will also need two yards of 45-inch-wide background fabric in blue, one yard of 45-inch-wide red fabric; ¼ yard of 45-inch-wide fabric or 1/3 yard of 36-inch-wide fabric in magenta; scraps of fabrics in other colors (see photograph on page 647) for the small appliques; rayon floss, six-strand cotton embroidery floss, or No. 3 pearl cotton for the embroidery; sewing thread to sew on the appliques; sewing and embroidery needles; thimble; scissors; an electric iron. You may work with the colors shown, or choose your own to match your decor.

Making the Hanging

To begin, stretch a 40-inch square of blue fabric onto the frame (see Craftnotes, page 650). Cut a 32½-inch-diameter circle from red fabric (see Figure B for how to draw large circles). This is the first applique. Turn the edges of the circle under ¼ inch and press with an iron. Pin and baste the applique to the center of the stretched background fabric. Since this applique is so large, baste carefully, making sure it lies absolutely flat. Using matching sewing thread and a sewing needle, sew all around the folded applique edge with tiny overcast stitches. Then, from the remainder of blue fabric, cut a 31½-inch-diameter circle, and from the center of this cut a 29½-inch circle to form a 1-inch-wide ring. Fold and press ¼ inch under all around both outside and inside edges, forming a ½-inch-wide ring. Pin and baste to the center of the first large circle; sew on as before. The next applique is a smaller ring. From the center of the 29½-inch blue circle cut a 27½-inch circle, which will leave you with a 1-inch-wide ring. Apply as for the first ring.

The next step is to apply a series of seven circular shapes (magenta color), and then a ring on top of each of them. Cut seven 5-inch-diameter circles from magenta fabric. Fold the edges under ¼ inch and apply to the large red applique, arranging them at random in the upper half of the circle. For the ring at the center of each of the circles, cut a 3½-inch circle from red fabric, and from the center of this cut a 1-inch circle, to form a 1¼-inch-wide ring. Apply to the circles as directed above. For a special effect, I embroidered a row of backstitches in orange (see "Crewelwork Sampler" Embroidery Craftnotes, Figure 3, page 542, Volume Five), around some of the magenta circles.

Fill in the bottom section and the spaces between the 5-inch circles with circular shapes ranging in size from ½ inch to 1¼ inch in diameter. About half of these are appliques cut from the fabric scraps. The rest are satin stitches (see "Crewelwork Sampler" Embroidery Craftnotes, Figure 6, page 542, Volume Five), worked in four layers of about six stitches each (Figure C). When all the small circular shapes are completed, work orange French knots (see "Crewelwork Sampler," Figures 31A and 31B, page 545, Volume 5) between them.

If necessary, wash and press or block, and mount as directed in "Crewelwork Sampler" Craftnotes, pages 546 to 549, Volume Five. If you want to frame the finished hanging, see the entry on "Framing" in this volume.

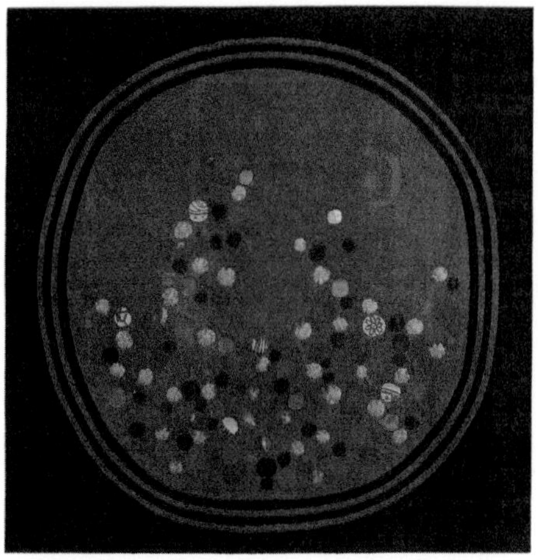

Full view of Solweig Hedin's mixed media wall hanging shown in close-up on page 647.

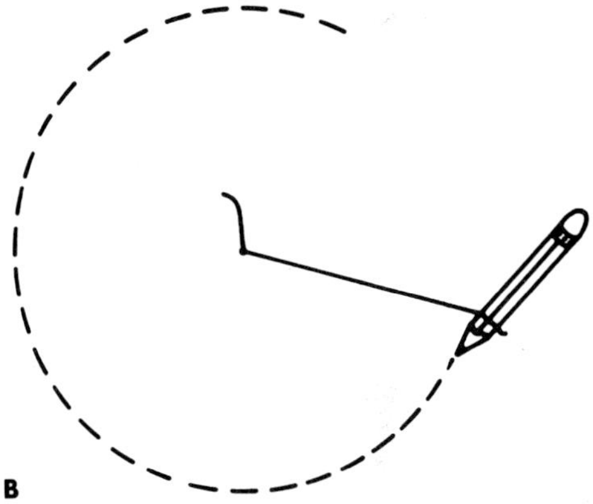

B

Figure B: To draw a large circle, make a compass using string, a ruler, and a pencil. Tie the pencil to one end of a piece of string the same length as the diameter of the desired circle. Measuring from the pencil, mark half the width of the circle on the string and tie a knot at this mark. For instance, for a 20-inch circle, measure and mark off 10 inches. With one hand hold the knot on the fabric where the center of the circle is to be. Holding the pencil in a vertical position in your other hand, pull the string taut and mark the circle.

C

Figure C: Detail showing how overlapping layers of satin stitch form a circle.

Needlecrafts
Black work tissue covers

Black work can be simple or elaborate. Today it need not be limited to black and white, as the tissue covers, below, illustrate. These tissue covers are easy to make, and are practical, colorful gifts.

Materials and Basic Procedures

Fabric: Black work is a counted-thread embroidery technique (see page 646) that must be done on an evenly woven fabric. Even-count fabric is necessary in order to avoid distortion of the fillings. For instance, on fabric with more vertical threads per inch than horizontal threads, the fillings will be elongated. I suggest that you use finely woven hardanger fabric (22 threads per inch), Aida (usually 8 to 11 threads per inch), or Monkscloth (16 threads per inch). These fabrics are available at well-stocked needlework shops. More widely available fabrics that make good substitutes are burlap (usually 13 threads per inch), or coarse linen or wool. Remember that since the fillings are worked by counting threads, a finer fabric will reduce the scale of the fillings, and a coarser fabric will enlarge the scale.

Thread: For black work embroidery in which an airy, lacy effect is desired, use a fine thread. I especially recommend six-strand cotton embroidery floss for the beginner, since it is easy to handle. No. 8 pearl cotton may also be used. For the more experienced needleworker, silk and rayon floss (which also come in six strands) may be used. Rayon and silk are a bit more difficult to work with, but the rich effects obtainable are worth it. Separate the six strands, and use the correct number for each filling as specified in the project directions that follow. The more strands in the needle, the darker the filling will appear.

Marion Scoular, a graduate of London's Royal School of Needlework, is a nationally known lecturer and teacher of hand embroidery. She owns and operates the Robin Hood Wool Shop in Clemson, South Carolina where she teaches, specializing in counted-thread embroidery and canvas work. Author of a correspondence course in black work for the Embroiderers' Guild, Marion travels extensively, lecturing and conducting workshops.

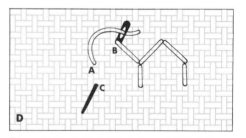

Figure D: Backstitch: Work from right to left, following the filling pattern. Bring needle up at A, insert at B, bring up at C. Form the next stitch by reinserting needle at A.

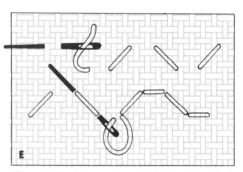

Figure E: Double running or Holbein stitch: Work from right to left. Work a row of running stitches over two fabric threads, under two threads, over two threads, etc., following the chart for the filling you are working (top). When the row is complete, turn work around and return, stitching (also on the right side of the fabric) over the threads that were stitched under previously (bottom). The number of threads covered by one stitch can vary throughout the overall design but will always be the same in one filling.

Covers for pocket pack of tissues, done in the black work embroidery technique.

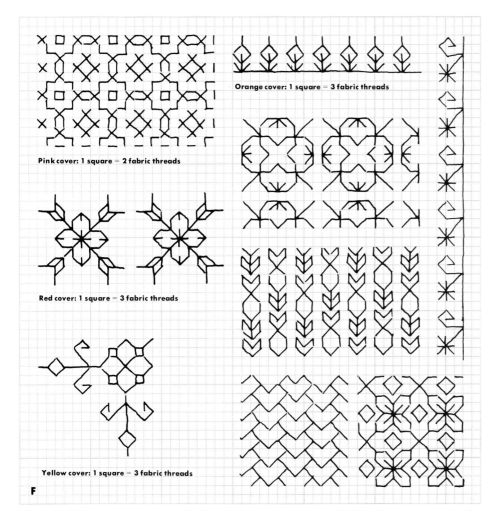

Pink cover: 1 square = 2 fabric threads

Orange cover: 1 square = 3 fabric threads

Red cover: 1 square = 3 fabric threads

Yellow cover: 1 square = 3 fabric threads

F

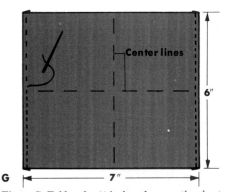

G

Figure G: Fold under ¼ inch and crease the short sides of a 7½-by-6-inch piece of fabric. The piece will now measure 7 by 6 inches. Using one strand of No. 8 pearl cotton or two strands of six-strand cotton embroidery floss, work a row of double running stitches over three fabric threads, two threads in from the fold. Fold fabric in half lengthwise. Unfold, and following the fabric grain, baste along the fold to mark the center. Fold fabric again crosswise, and mark the center with basting stitches.

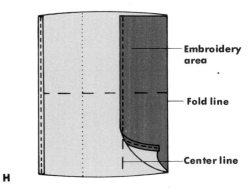

H

Figure H: With wrong sides facing, fold the fabric once more as shown, and match the rows of double running stitches with the second line of basting. The folded edges will overlap slightly. Unfold and baste along crease. Choose a border or motif from Figure F, above left. Embroider the design within the area marked by the double running stitch and last line of basting. Remove basting.

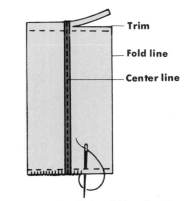

I

Figure I: With right sides facing, fold again as in Figure H. Stitch ends together, taking ½-inch seams. Trim seams to ¼ inch and finish seam edges with the buttonhole stitch. Turn right side out, gently poking out the corners with either blunt-pointed scissors or a crochet hook.

Figure F: Filling stitch patterns for black work tissue covers on page 654. For the patterns used in the tissue covers shown, the number of background fabric threads represented by each square on the blue grid is specified. If you want to use one or more of the other patterns, count each square on the grid as two or three fabric threads, depending upon the type of effect you want to achieve. Bold designs should be worked over three threads; a more delicate result is obtained by counting each square as two threads.

Needles: A blunt-pointed tapestry needle is used for this type of embroidery. See Embroidery Craftnote on needles, page 650.

The stitches: Only a few basic stitches are actually used to create the various filling patterns. Two of these are the backstitch and the cross stitch (see "Crewel-work Sampler" Embroidery Craftnotes: Stitches, page 542, Volume Five). The backstitch (Figure D) and the double running stitch (Figure E) are shown here on even-weave fabric. Most fillings use the backstitch; the cross stitch appears only when there are crosses within the fillings (as for the pink cover pattern, Figure F, and patterns 7, 8 and 12, Figure K). The double running or Holbein stitch is reversible and is used mostly for items where both sides are visible.

Making the Tissue Cover

I worked the tissue covers on even-count fabric with 24 threads per inch, using either two strands of six-strand cotton embroidery floss or its equivalent, one strand of pearl cotton No. 8, in a No. 24 tapestry needle. You may use the colors shown or any combination that pleases you. Start with a piece of fabric 6-by-7½ inches; fold it and secure the folds by making a row of double running stitches. To mark the vertical and horizontal centers, fold the fabric in half in both directions; and baste as shown in Figure G. Choose a filling stitch pattern from Figure F. After marking the boundaries as in Figure H, embroider each of the top sides, centering the design and repeating it from edge to edge. Sew ends together and finish, following Figure I; insert the packet of tissues.

"Barnes Owl" worked by Maggie Barnes in black work technique using contemporary colors. Marion Scoular, who designed the outlines of the owl, chose this piece as an example of good distribution of light, medium, and dark-toned filling patterns.

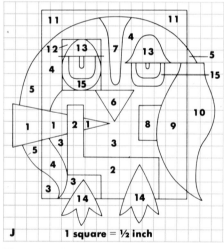

Figure J: Enlarge owl pattern by following the directions on page 57, Volume One. Each area is keyed to the numbers indicating the specific filling patterns shown in Figure K on the page opposite.

Needlecrafts
Black work owl

I originally designed the black work owl and gave only the outline to my students, who then filled in the areas with black work filling stitch patterns of their choice. Maggie Barnes produced the hanging you see here. The project directions that follow allow you to duplicate the owl exactly. If you wish to create an original work, follow the suggestions at the end of the project directions.

Making the Owl
Before beginning, read Materials and Basic Procedures for the tissue covers, page 654. It will give you information on fabric and yarn substitutions, needles, stitches, and working from a chart. The owl was worked on white even count fabric with 22 threads per inch. The finished size is 12 inches square, but cut the fabric 16 inches square to allow a 2-inch margin on each side for blocking and mounting. See "Crewelwork Sampler" entry, Embroidery Craftnotes: Preparation and Techniques, page 540, Volume Five, for starting and finishing yarn, threading the needle, and working with a hoop. Maggie used six-strand cotton embroidery floss in brown and gold, with the strands separated into one or two to work the various fillings and outlines. Use a No. 24 tapestry needle for the filling stitches. For the outlining, which will not always follows the weave of the fabric, use a pointed needle, such as a No. 5 crewel needle.

In the design pattern (Figure J), each square on the blue grid equals ½ inch. To start, enlarge the design (see Craftnotes on Enlarging Patterns, Volume One, page 57). Using the enlarged paper pattern, transfer the outlines of the design to your fabric, with dressmaker's carbon paper (see Craftnotes, page 651).

Place fabric in a hoop or on a frame as directed on page 651. Using the number of strands specified in Figure K, embroider the areas of the design with the various filling stitches. The areas on the pattern (Figure J) are keyed to the numbers identifying the filling stitches in Figure K, page 657. Directly below each filling stitch you will find information indicating the number of strands of floss to use. For instance, the beak is worked in filling pattern 6 with two strands of floss in the needle. The best place to start is the center of each area to be filled. It is easier first to establish one or two complete sections in the center and then branch out, repeating the design until the entire area is filled. Fit the pattern into the corners where outlines converge. When you have completed the fillings, embroider the pupils of the eyes in satin stitch with two strands of brown floss; then outline the areas of the entire design with outline or chain stitch (see "Crewelwork Sampler" Craftnotes: Stitches, pages 542 through 545).

Wash and press the finished embroidery, and then mount it on a 12-inch-square board as directed in "Crewelwork Sampler," pages 546 through 549. To frame the mounted hanging, see "Framing" in this volume.

To Create Original Designs
If you would like to create your own black work owl, follow the directions above, but change the color and number of strands of threads specified, the color of the background fabric, or both. For instance, try a reverse effect, with a light colored thread and dark background.

To vary the design even more, simply transfer the outlines of the owl to the fabric and use other black work fillings shown on page 657.

You can choose a different design from the Master Pattern section, Index Volume. Or, if you really feel daring, make up your own design. Transfer the outlines to the fabric, and use whatever fillings you like. Once you have done black work, you may even decide to invent a few filling stitches of your own. The only rules to remember are to count carefully and to choose fillings that will work well within the outlined shapes, following the suggestions below. The shapes of the design should be large enough for the fillings to show to advantage. Use simpler fillings for small areas, and save the more elaborate ones for large areas. Fillings have different visual effects—their tones vary from dark to light. Close your eyes

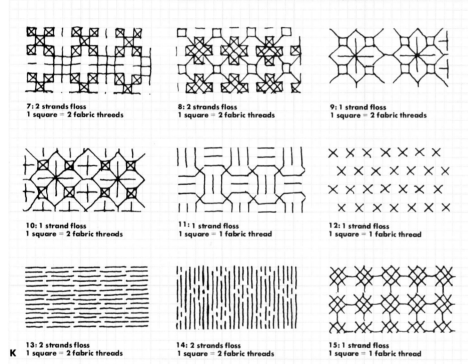

1: 1 strand floss
1 square = 2 fabric threads

2: 1 strand floss
1 square = 2 fabric threads

3: 1 strand floss
1 square = 2 fabric threads

4: 1 strand floss
1 square = 2 fabric threads

5: 1 strand floss
1 square = 2 fabric threads

6: 2 strands floss
1 square = 2 fabric threads

7: 2 strands floss
1 square = 2 fabric threads

8: 2 strands floss
1 square = 2 fabric threads

9: 1 strand floss
1 square = 2 fabric threads

10: 1 strand floss
1 square = 2 fabric threads

11: 1 strand floss
1 square = 1 fabric thread

12: 1 strand floss
1 square = 1 fabric thread

13: 2 strands floss
1 square = 2 fabric threads

14: 2 strands floss
1 square = 2 fabric threads

15: 1 strand floss
1 square = 1 fabric thread

Figure K: Filling stitch patterns for the black work owl shown on page 656. The number of strands of embroidery floss to use for each pattern are given in addition to the number of fabric threads each blue square represents.

slightly when looking at the fillings illustrated above; you will notice how some appear darker than others. A good black work design balances these tones within the design. To help decide on the positions of the filling patterns, try the following method: Place a piece of tracing paper over the design. Using a pencil, color in the areas with light, medium and dark tones, distributing them evenly throughout the design. When the various tones are arranged to your satisfaction, refer to the pencil sketch as a guide in choosing your light, medium and dark fillings. If you want to use a particular filling, but it is not the right tone, varying the number of strands of yarn in your needle will change the apparent tone of the filling. Use only one strand for a light filling, and three, four, or more strands for a darker one. Plan your design carefully, try out the stitches you want to use on another piece of the fabric. Ripping out stitches will make the fabric look worn, and it is easier to erase on paper than to cut out carefully counted stitches.

For related projects and crafts, see "Applique," "Crewelwork Sampler," "Crochet," "Florentine Stitch," "Granny Squares," "Hardanger," "Needlepoint," "Patchwork," "Quilting," and "Sewing."

Figure L: When working black work embroidery, you need not limit yourself to flat design. Tonal effects, as illustrated above, may be obtained by working a filling pattern in part of an area, then simplifying the pattern, gradually lightening it.

657

ENAMELING METAL
Fusing Color in a Kiln

Ellen Green is a professional enamelist and teaches the art in New York City. She is also working with various combinations of clay and enamel in experimental sculptural forms.

Enamel is an enduring, lustrous, colored glaze on a metal base. The enamelist creates the glaze by applying glass, usually as a powder but sometimes in other forms such as lumps or threads or even moist dabs, to a clean metal surface and heating the piece in a kiln. The heat of the kiln melts the glass and fuses it to the metal in a smooth even coat.

Each step required to enamel objects like bowls, dishes, jewelry or tiles is simple, and a great variety of effects can be achieved with little equipment.

The decorative panel shown in the photograph at left was made by cementing enameled steel tiles to a piece of ¾-inch plywood. Although the panel is large each tile was fired individually in a small, inexpensive kiln. Directions for making tiles like these start on page 665.

The shallow dish shown suspended on edge in the photograph opposite is larger than a tile and requires a larger kiln. Its design was created by sifting powdered enamel of different colors through a strainer onto the surface of a pre-formed piece of copper. See page 664 for instructions for making a similar dish.

Earrings, bracelets, pendants and other small articles of jewelry require only a small kiln. Instructions for making a pendant, in which small dabs of enamel melt into a flower-like design, begin on page 661. These instructions also include directions for the three basic operations of all enameling: cleaning the surface of the metal, applying the enamel, and firing the piece in a kiln.

How Enamel is Made

The term "enamel" can be confusing. To a handyman it may refer to a hard, glossy paint used on woodwork and metal. To a dentist, it is the coating on a tooth. But to an artist, true enamel is a thin layer of glass fused to a metal surface. The colors can be vivid or subdued, the design bold or subtle, or as plain as the workaday surface of an enameled kitchen stove or other household appliance.

The basis of enamel is flux, a clear glass compounded of silica with other minerals that keep its melting point fairly low—around 1500 degrees Fahrenheit—and make it lustrous. The flux is colored by the addition of metal oxides while it is molten. Cobalt oxide, for example, turns the flux blue. Iron oxide creates red or brown. Copper oxide makes green. The character of the additive also determines whether the enamel is opaque, translucent or, in a few cases, opalescent.

When the molten glass cools, it is broken into chunks and ground to powder or made into other forms for use by the enamelist.

Start with eight or ten colors of 80-mesh enamel. It comes in a great variety of colors and you can experiment as you go along. If you want to keep using a color, record its number. Manufacturers change the names of colors frequently, but the numbers remain the same. (If you plan to enamel steel tiles, you will need a form of enamel called screening paste. It is sold under the trade name *Versa Color*.) Other materials you will need include an enamel adhesive, a liquid that holds the enamel powder to the surface of the metal; a copper cleaning solution; fine steel wool; waxed paper and heavy glazed paper.

Metals to Enamel

Copper is the metal most widely used for enameling; it is relatively inexpensive, it forms a bond readily with molten glass and it can withstand as many as ten firings in a kiln without deteriorating. You can purchase pre-formed copper shapes such as the ones used here for the pendant and the shallow dish. Craft supply stores carry a great variety of copper articles from small pieces for jewelry to bowls, dishes and boxes, as well as the fittings necessary for mounting jewelry.

The design on the shallow dish hanging in the photograph opposite was created by sifting enamel powder on a pre-formed copper shape. See page 662 for enameling a similar dish.

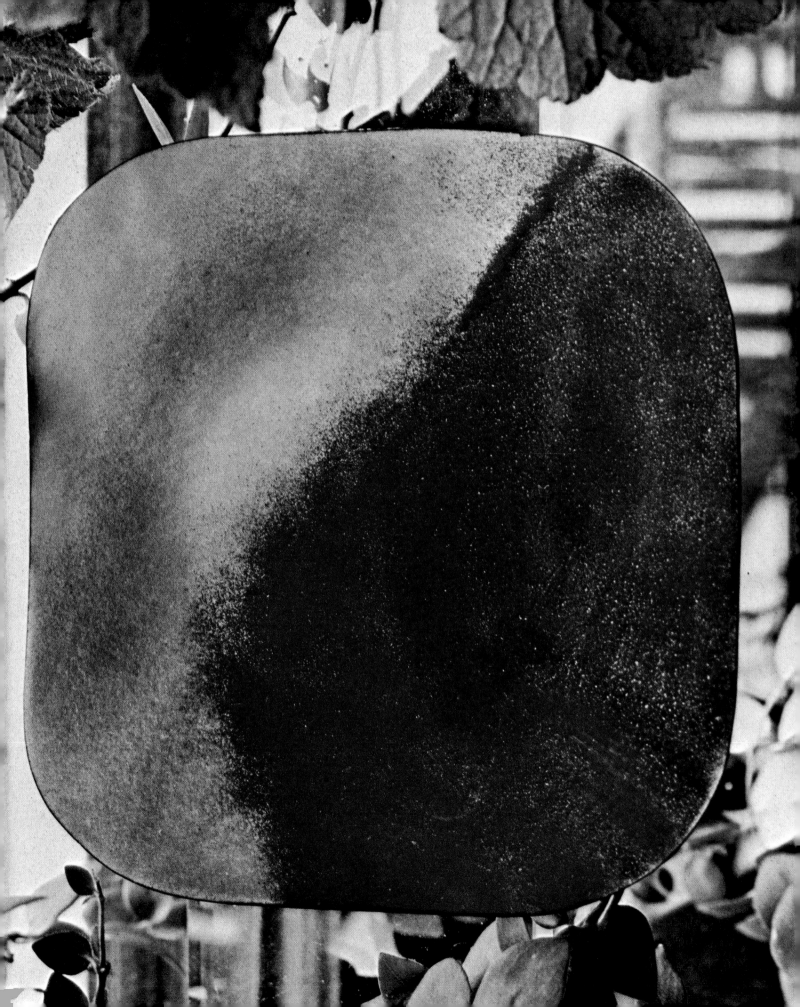

Enamelists also work with steel. Craft stores sell steel with two coats of enamel pre-applied and ready to receive a design. This is called enamel-on steel and it is available in white and a variety of colors. Squares of enamel-on steel are needed for the tile project.

Enameling gold or silver produces striking results, but enamelists rarely attempt it until they are skilled. The cost of these metals makes mistakes expensive.

Enameling Equipment

The enamelist's most important piece of equipment is the kiln. This is the insulated, electrically heated oven where crushed silica-glass particles are fused onto a metal base, resulting in a smooth, brilliant coat. Kilns vary in size and cost. A large one, capable of firing sizeable pieces such as plates, bowls, vases and boxes, is in the same price range as a 10-speed touring bicycle. A smaller kiln, suitable for jewelry and other small, flat pieces, costs about half as much. Pyrometers, which measure high temperatures, and heat controls are optional.

Match your firing equipment to the size of your kiln. This equipment should include at least two asbestos boards—one to put the kiln on and one to hold hot tools and work that has been removed from the kiln to cool—as well as a steel firing mesh called a planche (pictured on opposite page), which serves as a convenient platform for small objects; assorted firing stilts (also pictured opposite); tongs or large tweezers; an enameling spatula or enameling fork; and asbestos gloves. Make sure the gloves are asbestos. Substitutes, such as kitchen mittens or pot holders, are not sufficiently heat-resistant for enameling.

Other equipment you will need: an 80-mesh enameling strainer; round and flat brushes; an atomizer; small paper or plastic cups; a very small spatula for manipulating small quantities of enamel; a replaceable-blade knife; a 10-by-10-inch sheet of window glass; a 4-inch brayer, a kind of roller; a large plastic bowl; a rubber kitchen spatula; a carborundum stone.

Enameling equipment and materials are usually available at craft stores, but it may be cheaper and easier to order by mail from enamel suppliers. Here is a list: AMACO, 4714 West 16th Street, Indianapolis, Ind. 46222; Thomas C. Thompson Co., Highland Park, Ill. 60035; Macto Studio, 10300 Superior Avenue East, Cleveland, Ohio 44106; Seaire, 17909 South Hobart Boulevard, Gardena, Cal. 90248.

CRAFTNOTES: FIRING SAFETY

Enameling is no more dangerous than cooking or carpentry, but like these activities, it demands safe working habits.

Kilns rarely overheat, but they can. The safest practice is to remain in the room while a kiln is turned on. An unattended kiln can be a danger to others—small children, particularly.

Always wear asbestos gloves while firing. The 1500 degrees Fahrenheit temperature of the kiln can heat the spatula or enameling fork in your hand very quickly. Keep the gloves on throughout the firing; the time is short and you will be prepared to remove a piece the instant it is ready.

Arrange your work area so you can move a piece from the kiln to the asbestos board where it will cool without having to lift it over or around any obstruction.

Make sure the cooling board is in a place where you will not be likely to brush inadvertently against a hot piece of enamel while you are at work on something else.

Never leave hot work unattended. It doesn't look hot and someone might attempt to pick it up. A severe burn would result.

Stand, rather than sit, while firing. If a hot piece of work does tumble from the spatula, it will be easier to get out of the way if you are on your feet than if you are seated.

Store flammable liquids in another room. A hot kiln can ignite vapors from paints, lacquers, solvents and similar materials.

Always work in a well ventilated room, but do not place your kiln or cooling board in a direct draft. Sudden changes in temperature can crack an enamel surface before it is cool.

Dabs of enamel created the elaborate pattern of this pendant as they melted in the kiln.

Jewelry, Lapidary and Metalwork
Copper pendant

The pendant shown in the photograph above can be fired in a small kiln. See page 660 for basic enameling equipment and materials for this project. You will also need a 3-inch disk of 18-gauge copper with a small hole drilled near the edge; a neck cord to hang the pendant on, and a jump ring to join the pendant and the cord.

Getting Ready
Turn on your kiln and let it heat. Spread a sheet of waxed paper on your enameling table. Put a planche on the paper and a small enameling stilt on the planche.

Mix a solution of copper cleaner and water in a plastic bowl, stirring with a rubber spatula. Non-metallic materials must be used for this because metal could react with the cleaner and subsequently with the copper. If you do not want to use a commercial preparation, make your own by dissolving 1½ tablespoons of salt in 1 cup of vinegar.

Cleaning the Copper
The copper disk must be absolutely clean. Grease and dirt can create dark spots under the enamel and even prevent the enamel from adhering to the copper. Clean the disk by heating it in the kiln, cooling it and soaking it in the cleaner.

Look in your kiln. If the interior glows cherry red it is hot enough for enameling. If you have a kiln with a pyrometer to measure high temperatures, the instrument should indicate 1500 degrees Fahrenheit. Put on asbestos gloves and place the disk into the kiln with an enameling spatula. Leave it there until it glows red. Then, lift it out with the spatula and put it on the asbestos board until it is cool.

As soon as the disk is cool enough to touch, pick it up with tweezers (photograph 1) and rub each side with fine steel wool. Rinse the disk under running water to remove any cleaning solution or steel wool splinters, then dry it with paper towels, holding the disk through the toweling, so your hands do not touch the copper. Place the disk on the enameling stilt (photograph 2).

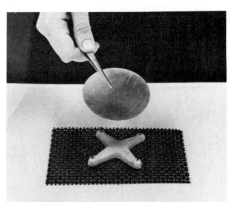

1: Remove the copper disk from the cleaning solution with tweezers. Any oil or grease on the surface—even fingerprints—can flaw the enamel.

2: Place the disk on an enameling stilt until you are ready to spray it with binder. The stilt is on a steel mesh called a planche.

3: Hold the strainer with one hand and tap it with the forefinger of the other hand to sift enamel on the disk. Do edge first, then center.

4: Dry the piece on top of the kiln. If you use a large kiln, hold the piece inside it on a spatula for 3 seconds, then remove it.

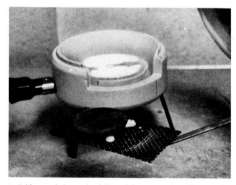

5: Lift work into the kiln with a spatula. This table is heat proof. If you enamel at home put kiln on an asbestos board. Keep another board handy for hot work and tools.

Laying the Foundation

The disk must have an unflawed layer of enamel on each side. The layer on the front acts as a base for the dabs of enamel that form the design. The layer on the back is to prevent the piece from warping. It is called counterenamel. Every flat or nearly flat piece of enamel work is counterenameled so that, when the piece shrinks as it cools, the stresses on the back and front are equal.

Make sure your hands are clean. If you are using a vinegar and salt solution, dip your fingertips in it and dry them on a paper towel. Pick up the disk with your fingertips just touching the edge. Don't let them curl over and touch the surface. Hold the disk vertically and spray one face with enamel binder, an adhesive that holds enamel powder to metal. Hold the atomizer about 18 inches from the disk and cover it with an even coat without drips or runs. Return the disk to the stilt with the sprayed side up.

Sifting Powder on the Disk

Fill an 80-mesh enameling strainer with green 80-mesh enamel. Hold the strainer full of enamel with one hand and tap it gently with the forefinger of the other as you move the strainer over the disk, first around the rim and then over the center (photograph 3). Let the enamel fall from the strainer so it forms a smooth layer on the disk, somewhat thicker around the edge than at the center.

Make sure no copper shows through the powder, but keep the thickness of the layer less than the thickness of the copper. If the enamel is too thin, it will burn off when you fire it. If it is too thick, it will crack when it cools. Spray the dusted surface with binder, holding the atomizer far enough away so the mist falls on the enamel powder without disturbing it.

After you have sprayed the enameled surface with binder, return the disk to the stilt with the bare copper side up and the side with the enamel powder on it down. The binder will prevent the powder from falling off. Sift enamel over the bare surface, just as you did for the reverse side. You do not need to apply binder this time because you will not turn the piece over again before it is fired. After the enamel is applied, if the hole is clogged with powder, clean it with a toothpick.

Don't worry about wasting the enamel that misses the disk. The paper beneath the planche will catch it. When you have finished sifting enamel, gather the fallen powder in the paper and pour it back into its container. If you have applied several colors at once and there is a mixture on the paper, keep it in a separate container. You can use this mixture for counterenameling.

The First Firing

When the enamel powder is moist with binder or with water, it must be dried before it is fired or the moisture will turn to steam when the piece is in the kiln. Steam bubbles trapped in the molten enamel will pit and crack the surface.

If you are using a small kiln, simply pick up the whole stack—planche, stilt and disk—and place it on top of the kiln, where the warmth will evaporate the moisture in 4 or 5 minutes (photograph 4). Then, put on asbestos gloves, place the stack on the enameling spatula and put it in the kiln (photograph 5).

You can also combine drying with firing. Wear asbestos gloves. Slide the blade of the enameling spatula under the planche—the whole stack is always put into the kiln or removed as a unit—and hold the stack in the kiln for 3 seconds. This is long enough to vaporize the moisture, but not long enough to melt the enamel. Hold the work outside the kiln for 5 or 6 seconds to let all the moisture escape, then return it to the kiln and close the door or lid.

When enamel is fired, it first turns dark. Then the surface turns grainy as the particles of enamel melt and coagulate. Finally, after about 3 minutes, the surface appears smooth and glossy. When this occurs the piece is completely fired.

Watch the disk in the kiln and remove it before it reaches the final stage of firing. The surface should still be grainy. It will become smooth in later firings. Use the enameling spatula to transfer it from the kiln to the asbestos cooling board.

As the piece cools, its color will change from a very dark hue to the color of the finished enamel. Watching the color emerge as a piece cools is one of the most exciting parts of enameling.

Correcting Flaws

When the piece is cool inspect it. If there are small cracks, don't worry. These will fuse closed during subsequent firings. If the enamel is burned away, there is little you can do, although you might clean it, dry it, dust it with clear flux and fire it. Sometimes overfiring produces interesting patterns.

The most likely flaws will show around the rim, where the enamel has crept away from the edge, or in the center where tiny specks of copper may be visible through a thin coat of enamel.

Use a camel's hair brush to paint any bare spots at the edge with binder, then counterenamel and enamel the piece again, just as you did the first time. This second coat of enamel is applied to both sides whether there are flaws or not.

Applying the Design

While the work is cooling, prepare moist enamel. You need six or eight small non-metallic cups, one for each color of the design. I cut the tops off disposable plastic drinking cups. The bottom ½ inch or so of each cup does the job nicely.

Place a small amount of enamel in each cup and add enough water to wet the enamel without leaving any free water in it. The consistency of beach sand when it is cohesive enough for building sand castles is what you are looking for. One way to achieve the right consistency is to tilt the cup so the water and enamel are at one side, then tilt the cup in the opposite direction and let the water run out, leaving a damp heap of enamel at one side of the cup. I use tap water, but in some areas, impurities could spoil the enamel. If you're not sure, use distilled water.

  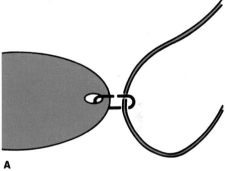

6: Apply more dabs of moist enamel with a spatula, as shown here, after the first application of dabs has been fired, or use a toothpick or the wooden end of a kitchen match.

7: After the final firing of the pendant, rub heat blackened copper from the edge of the disk with a carborundum stone. Keep both stone and pendant wet while you do this.

A

Figure A: A small jump ring links pendant and neck cord. The ring, cord and a large variety of other jewelry fittings for enameled work are available at craft supply stores.

Pick up dabs of moist enamel with a very small spatula, a toothpick or the wooden end of a kitchen match, and cover the disk with dots of different colored enamels, creating a design as you go along.

When the disk is filled with enamel dabs, dry and fire it. This time leave it in the kiln until the surface is smooth and glassy. The dabs may appear as slight lumps, but the overall surface should be smooth. In all subsequent firings leave the piece in the kiln for a complete firing like this one.

Let the piece cool on the asbestos board, apply more dabs of enamel to round out the design (photograph 6). Dry it, fire it and cool it, then sift a light coat of a translucent enamel on the surface. This should be just a dusting. After the piece has been fired and cooled again, the lumps will have leveled off to a flat or nearly flat surface. Some of the edges will be blended while others will have kept their sharpness. Some of the enamel will have broken into flecks of one color within another color. You can create more blends and flecks by dusting the piece lightly with flux and firing it again, or, if you are pleased with the results, you can stop.

After the disk has cooled from the final firing, clean the blackened edge with a carborundum stone. Keep the disk and stone wet in a bowl of water (photograph 7) or under a running tap while you rub the edge down to bare copper.

When the edge is clean, pry open the jump ring with your fingernail, and insert it in the hole in the pendant. Run neck cord through the jump ring and squeeze the jump ring closed (Figure A). The pendant is complete.

Enameled dish $ ⊠ 👫 ⚗

The design on the shallow dish shown in the photograph on page 659 was created with dry enamel powder sifted on the surface so the colors overlapped at the edges.

You will need a pre-formed dish of 18-gauge copper 6 inches square with rounded corners and slightly sloping sides. You will also need a larger kiln than the one used to make the pendant (page 661) and a larger enameling stilt (photograph 8).

Clean the copper dish as you cleaned the pendant disk, spray the bottom side with enamel binder, and place the disk bottom up on the stilt (photograph 8). The stilt should be on a sheet of wax paper that will catch loose enamel, but no planche is necessary. The stilt is on short legs so a firing tool can easily be slid beneath it.

For counterenameling, you can use a mixture of salvaged enamels or you can use the same color you have selected as the background color on the face of the dish.

When you sift, hold the enamel strainer so the forefinger of the same hand is free to tap it. You will need the other hand to tilt the dish. As you sift enamel on each sloping side, raise the stilt beneath it slightly so the dish tilts enough to make the sloping edge horizontal so the enamel falls on a level surface.

Pick the dish up with your fingertips holding the edges, as you did the pendant, and spray the powdered surface with binder again. Turn it over and spray binder on the face of the dish, and place it on the stilt face up. Sift enamel on the face of the dish. As you cover each edge, level it by lifting the stilt on the opposite side.

The next step is to dry and fire the piece. Wear asbestos gloves. Slide an enameling fork or spatula under the stilt. Hold the work in the kiln for 3 seconds (photograph 9), remove it long enough to allow the moisture of the binder to dissipate and return it to the kiln. Fire the piece until the surface is grainy, then place it on an asbestos board. When the dish is cool, paint any bare spots at the edges with binder, then counterenamel and enamel the dish again.

Applying the Design
The colors of this design were sifted on the piece dry rather than applied in moist dabs as they were for the pendant. I used a very dark green, cocoa, brick, and a light red over a yellow background.

Using an 80-mesh strainer, sift the colors on the dish one at a time, lifting the stilt to level the edges as you cover them (photograph 10). Use fairly large masses, bands, curves or other elements, allowing the colors to overlap at the edges. You can also move enamel about on the surface with a brush (photograph 11).

Fire the piece until the surface is smooth and glossy. Let it cool and sift more color as necessary. If you are satisfied with the design, stop. If you want to continue, you can. I worked on the design through two firings, then sifted on a light coating of transparent orange enamel and fired it again. To complete the dish, clean away the blackened copper at its edge with the carborundum stone.

8: Place the dish upside down on the enameling stilt after it has been cleaned and the bottom has been sprayed with binder. This large stilt requires no planche. Simply slide a fork or spatula under and lift.

9: Dry the moisture in the binder by holding the piece in the kiln for 3 seconds. Remove it for 5 to 6 seconds to let the moisture evaporate, then return it to the kiln for firing.

10: Level a sloping edge by reaching under the piece with your fingers and raising the stilt to tilt the piece. It is easier to cover a level surface with powder than a sloping one.

11: You can use a brush to manipulate enamel powder on the surface. Here the powder is swept into a sharp edge. Other implements, a toothpick, for example, create different effects.

Jewelry, Lapidary and Metalwork
Enameling steel tiles $ ● ☗ ♨

An enameled steel tile can serve as a decorative piece by itself or as a part of a large panel, like the one shown in the photograph on page 658.

I made the single tile pictured below to demonstrate the technique, using a 4-inch square that had been given a base coat and a primary coat of enamel at the factory. Steel already coated in this way is available from craft stores in several sizes and colors. It is called enamel-on steel. Instructions for making this tile, using stencils to create the design, begin on the next page.

Enamel-on steel is more convenient than copper because it comes with two coats already applied; it requires no counterenameling or base coat. In addition, it is more resistant to weathering and airborne pollutants than copper.

Enamel-on steel can be treated like copper and coated with ordinary powder enamel. I used screening paste on the tile, however, because it is convenient and more weather- and chemical-resistant than powder enamel.

Commercially prepared screening paste (*Versa Color*) comes in tubes, like artist colors. Unlike powder enamels, screening pastes can be mixed to form new colors. In addition, after a coating of screening paste has dried 24 hours, more screening paste can be applied over it. This means that you can complete a whole design, then fire the piece just once to complete it. Screening-paste colors are less brilliant than powder enamels, but you may not consider this a drawback.

Kay Whitcomb's enamels are in collections throughout the world. She alternates periods of work in her studio in La Jolla, California, with teaching and lecture engagements.

The disk and Roman numerals of the enameled steel tile were formed by rolling screening paste through stencils. Large letter stamps were used to apply the word OCLOCK, but it also can be done with the stencil in Figure D on page 666.

Kay Whitcomb made this large, decorative panel with a small, inexpensive kiln. Enamel designs were fired on 4-by-4-inch tiles one at a time. These steel tiles were then arranged on exterior-grade plywood and cemented in place.

Once you have made some small tiles, you may want to purchase a large panel of enamel-on steel, apply screening paste colors and return the piece to the factory for firing in an industrial-size kiln. Large sheets, as well as panels formed of tiles, can be used as bed headboards, table tops and wall surfaces.

Stenciling a Tile

To make an enameled steel tile, you will need, besides the basic enameling equipment listed on page 665, a 4-inch square of white enamel-on steel; screening paste; a 4-inch brayer; a 10-by-10-inch sheet of window glass; three sheets of heavy glazed paper for stencils; and a replaceable-blade knife.

Draw the pattern for the stencil of the disk and trace the Roman numeral XII (Figures B and C) directly on sheets of heavy glazed paper and cut out the design with a replaceable-blade knife or a single-edge razor blade. Trace the word OCLOCK (Figure D) directly and cut out the stencil.

Wash the enamel-on tile with soap and water to remove any oil or grease and place it on your work table. Squeeze a blob of red screening paste about as big as the tip of your thumb onto the sheet of glass and roll the brayer back and forth over it until the roller of the brayer has an even coat of paste. This method can also be used to mix colors. Just roll two blobs together and the two colors will blend to form a new color just as if you were mixing paint.

Rolling on the Paste

Place the stencil of the disk on the tile, hold it steady with your fingers at one edge and roll the paste-filled brayer over it (photograph 12). Wipe the roller and glass clean with a cloth. Wait 24 hours for the screening paste to set.

When the red screening paste has dried on the tile, squeeze a small dab of blue paste on the glass—about the size of your little finger nail—and roll the brayer back and forth over it a few times. Do not coat the brayer evenly. Just get a thin coat around the central portion of the roller. Roll the lightly coated brayer over the tile to form a large, irregular patch of blue on the face of the tile. It should be light enough so the red and white already on the tile show through the blue in places. Clean the brayer and the glass sheet and allow the blue screening paste on the tile 24 hours to set.

Adding the Numeral

Next, fill the brayer with red screening paste, place the stencil of the Roman numeral XII on the tile in the center of the disk and roll on red screening paste. Remove the stencil and wipe the roller and the glass clean.

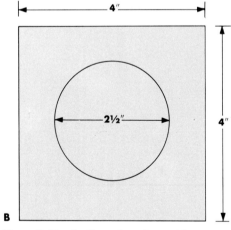

Figure B: Use the dimensions above to draw a disk on heavy glazed paper for a stencil.

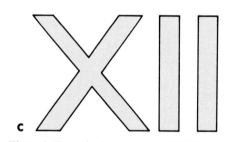

Figure C: Trace the Roman numeral XII directly on heavy glazed paper. It needs no enlarging.

Figure D: Trace this design directly on heavy glazed paper. It needs no enlarging.

Without waiting for the tile to dry, use a bluntly pointed piece of wood, the end of a brush handle, or a sharpened dowel, to scratch away the screening paste to form the dot in the center of the disk (photograph 14). Scratch down to the white enamel surface of the tile. If necessary to bring out the numerals, scratch along their outline, but do this gently enough to remove only the soft red screening paste, leaving the hardened blue screening paste beneath it undisturbed. Also scrape away screening paste to form the blue areas within the numerals.

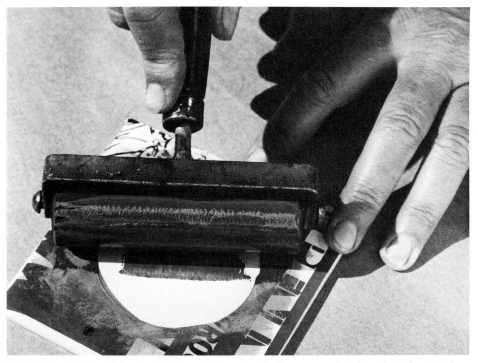

12: With the disk stencil placed on the tile, roll the paste-filled brayer over it to form the disk on the tile. The Roman numeral, XII and the word OCLOCK are formed in the same way.

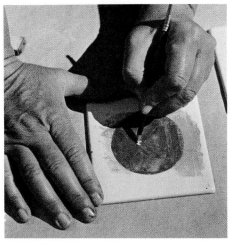

13: Use the end of a brush handle or sharpen a dowel or stick to a dull point to scratch away one layer of color to let another color beneath it show through, as in center dot.

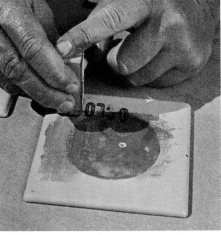

14: You can use letter stamps, available in stationery stores, to apply OCLOCK to the tile if you do not want to use the stencil in Figure D. Use the glass sheet as a stamp pad.

After the tile has dried for 24 hours, stencil on the word OCLOCK in blue screening paste. If you choose, you can purchase large rubber stamp letters and print the word, spreading a coat of paste on the glass and using it like a stamp pad (photograph 14).

Allow the tile to dry for 24 hours, then bring your kiln up to 1500 degrees Fahrenheit. Small kilns have no pyrometer to indicate temperature. They are ready when the interior glows cherry red. Place a firing stilt on a planche. Place the tile on the firing stilt and lift the whole stack—planche, stilt and tile—into the kiln with an enameling spatula or fork and fire it until the surface is smooth and glossy. Because steel conducts heat less rapidly than copper, firing should take 5 minutes, rather than the 3 minutes needed to fire enameled copper.

For related projects, see "Pottery," "Silvercraft," "Stenciling," "Tiles."

FLAGS AND BANNERS
Personal Pageantry

Flags and banners have long been used as visual symbols to identify and to decorate. They come in all sizes and shapes – from small triangular boat pennants, to rectangular wall hangings, to large and elaborate street banners. But their effect is always the same – flags and banners add a zestful visual flourish to the messages they convey.

Early banners and flags were made of silk, velvet, linen or cotton, with appliqued and embroidered emblems. Today's flags and banners are usually made of cotton bunting or nylon. These fabrics are strong, weather resistant and supple enough to float freely in the breeze. If the flag or pennant is not too large, it may be made of felt. Felt is, by the way, an ideal material for small children to use. They can cut the pieces for their own personal pennant with blunt-nosed scissors, then attach them to a larger felt background piece with white glue.

Sebastian Suma is president and chief designer of the Arista Flag Company, New York City. In his studio, he designs banners and flags for use in parades, in meeting halls, and for advertising. He also makes decorative banners from various artists' paintings and sketches.

A professional flag- and banner-maker created this felt banner to show a variety of designs and lettering styles that volunteer fire companiés might use in designing their own banners.

Felt is also a good material to use for a wall hanging, since it is heavy enough to hang flat and needs no weather resistance indoors. The decorative wall hanging opposite was made from scraps of colored felt sewed to a large felt rectangle. Instructions for making it start on page 674.

Club Banners and Boat Pennants

If you want to hang a banner to identify a group you belong to, you can make the felt club banner (page 670) or try a more elaborate design, using the same basic techniques. The sample volunteer fire department banner shown above may increase your store of ideas for lettering and decorating.

The boat pennant on page 672, with its anchor and club initials, is an identifying flag. Unlike the club banner, it has a design on each side, and it is made of nylon so it will withstand high winds and heavy weather when flown outdoors. It is fitted with tie tapes that can be knotted to a flagstaff or hoisting rope.

Flag or Banner?

The words "flag" and "banner" are sometimes used interchangeably, but among those who make them professionally, there is a clear distinction. A flag, such as the boat pennant, is designed to stream in the wind. It is mounted at the side and sags limply until a breeze lifts it and stretches it out horizontally. A banner is intended to hang flat and straight down, like the decorative hanging, opposite, and the club banner on page 670. These two are mounted by inserting a crossbar into a sleeve running across the top edge of the banner.

A blend of abstract leaves and flowers make an eye-catching felt wall hanging. It is hung, as a banner, from a broomstick run through the top hem. Instructions for making it begin on page 674.

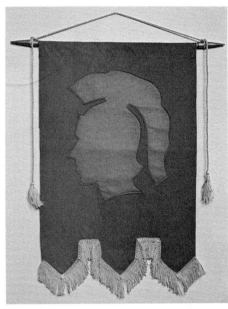

This red and blue club banner is trimmed with fringe and gold tasseled pole rope. You can duplicate it by following the instructions here, or you can use this method and your own design.

← Pole sleeve turnover

A   1 square = 1 inch

Figure A: Pattern is for a felt club banner that can be made with the sewing technique described in the text or by cutting out the silhouette and gluing it to the background piece.

Needlecrafts
Club banner

$ ☒ 👥 ⚗

Red and blue felt were used to make the club banner at left, but you can use heavy cotton, linen or synthetic fabric. The banner measures 16½ by 26 inches. To make it you need 1 yard of red and ½ yard of blue 50-weight felt; ¾ yard of gold fringe trim; pattern paper (brown wrapping paper will do); dressmaker's pattern wheel; No. 240 sandpaper; felt blackboard eraser; 1 can of light dressmaker's stamping powder; straight pins; a weight (an iron is suitable, or a large can of food); 8- or 9-inch dressmaker's shears; small scissors; ¼-inch dowel 18 inches long; two pole caps to slip on the ends of the dowel; ½ yard of braided tasseled rope. You can sew the banner by machine or by hand. Use No. 50 mercerized cotton thread or medium cotton-covered polyester thread. Except for the sandpaper and the weight, these materials are available in fabric stores.

Preparing the Pattern
Enlarge the pattern in Figure A on pattern paper (both soldier and outline of banner). For instructions on enlarging patterns, see the Craftnotes on page 57, Volume One. Spread a thick towel or blanket on your work table and place the pattern on it. Roll the dressmaker's tracing wheel over the lines (photograph 1), pressing firmly and steadying the pattern with your other hand.

As you roll, the points of the wheel will perforate the lines. Turn the pattern over. The rim of each perforation will be slightly raised. Sand the perforations until they are wide open, and brush the pattern clean. Check by holding the pattern up to the light.

Transferring the Design
Spread the red felt on a work table (the side that is up will be the back of the banner). Put the pattern on the felt so what you see on the table is a mirror image of the front of the banner. Hold the pattern in place with a weight.

Fill the blackboard eraser with stamping powder and stamp it on the paper over the perforations (photograph 2). Work carefully, making sure that you have covered all the perforations with stamping powder.

With the weight still in place, raise the pattern at each corner in turn and look at the felt. You should see the pattern duplicated in lines of dots formed when the powder fell through the perforations. If there are blanks, lower the pattern and stamp it again with the powder-filled eraser.

If the soldier silhouette stamped on the back of the banner faces right, it will face left on the front. If you use lettering, it must appear backward on the back of the banner if it is to read correctly on the front.

A simple test: if the design stamped on the back of a banner looks correct in a mirror, it will look correct on the front of the banner.

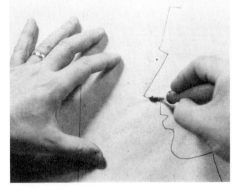

1: Roll a pattern wheel along lines of pattern with enough pressure so the wheel's teeth perforate the paper. Spread pattern on thick towel to protect work surface.

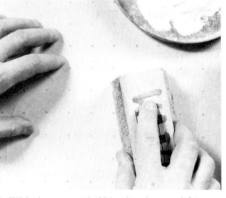

2: With the pattern held in place by a weight, stamp a powdered blackboard eraser over the perforations. The powder will go through the holes and mark the design on the felt.

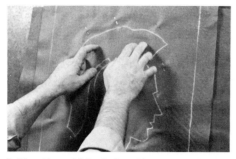

3: Place the red felt, design-side up, over the blue felt, so that all portions of the design are backed by the blue felt. Pin, then baste the red felt to the blue outside the design.

4: Sew the double thickness of felt along the silhouette outline on the red felt. The blue is under it. Sew slowly, guiding the felt carefully so you can follow the design accurately.

5: Using a pair of small scissors, cut off excess blue felt ⅛-inch outside the stitching. As you cut, remove small pieces of felt to make the cutting easier and neater.

Sewing on the Design

Place the blue felt on the table and lay the red felt over it so the silhouette design on the red felt is completely backed by blue felt (photograph 3). Pin, then baste the red and blue felt together. Baste outside the silhouette design to avoid puckering the felt when you sew. Sew along the outline of the silhouette (photograph 4). Remove the work from the sewing machine and turn it over, right side up. Remove the basting and trim off the excess blue felt ⅛ inch outside the stitching with small scissors (photograph 5). Finally, turn the banner over and cut it out, using shears and following the stamped line.

6: Pin fringe trimming to the bottom of the banner. Cut and fit a separate piece of fringe for each straight section of the bottom.

7: On the wrong side of the banner, turn down and pin the top 1½ inches to make a pole sleeve. Sew ⅛ inch from the turnover edge.

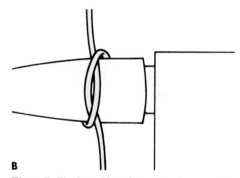

B

Figure B: Tie the gold cord to each pole cap with this simple knot.

Baste and sew the fringe trimming to the bottom of the banner (photograph 6). Cut, fit and sew a separate piece of fringe for each of the straight edges of the streamers and the notches between them. Next, turn down 1½ inches at the top on the wrong side of the banner (photograph 7) and sew the turned-down edge to the banner. Sew close to the edge to form a sleeve.

Insert the dowel in the sleeve and attach a pole cap to each end. Pole caps are sold in notions stores or they can be improvised from wood furniture knobs or beads. For a finishing touch, add the braided rope with tasseled ends, as shown in the color photograph opposite. Tie the rope to each end of the pole with a half hitch (Figure B), leaving enough slack in the rope to use it for hanging banner.

Assembling the Banner with Glue

This club banner, or any other felt banner, can be glued rather than sewn. Use white glue. Enlarge and perforate the pattern as for sewing. Stamp the whole design, both banner outline and Roman soldier silhouette, on the red felt, and the silhouette alone on the blue felt. Cut the banner out of the red felt and the soldier silhouette out of the blue felt. Using the stamped outline of the soldier on the red felt as a guide for positioning, glue the blue silhouette to the red banner. Glue on the fringe and glue down the turnover for the pole sleeve. Be sure the glue dries for 24 hours before inserting the pole through the sleeve. If you do not, the glue may adhere to the pole, making it impossible to remove without damaging the banner.

671

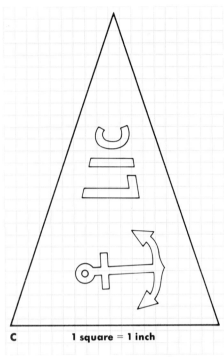

Figure C: Pattern for boat pennant. Stamp pennant outline on white nylon, anchor on yellow nylon, letters on red nylon.

C   1 square = 1 inch

Make this nylon pennant following the pattern in Figure C, or design your own. Images like the anchor and the letters can be traced from newspapers, magazines or posters and enlarged.

Needlecrafts
Nylon boat pennant $ ▨ ♠ ⚗

The boat pennant in the color photograph above is a single-reverse flag; each side shows the design; one side is the mirror image of the other. Nylon is used because it is sturdy and weatherproof. You don't have to limit yourself to the anchor and lettering shown here. If you cannot draw well, trace your design from a newspaper, magazine or any other source and enlarge it. Alphabet letters in many sizes and styles are sold by art supply stores and some stationers.

To make this flag you will need the same equipment as for the club banner (page 670), but you will need dark stamping powder instead of light. In addition, you should have 1 yard of white nylon; ⅓ yard each of red and yellow nylon; 2 yards of ¼-inch-wide white bias tape; ½ yard of 1-inch-wide white bias tape.

Making the Design
Enlarge the pattern (Figure C), using the method given on page 57, Volume One. You can also use this method to enlarge any letters or designs from other sources that you wish to use on a flag or banner. After the pattern is enlarged, lay it on a spread blanket or thick towel and perforate it with the pattern wheel as for the club banner (page 670).

Stamping powder will not adhere to nylon, so a stamping paste is necessary. To make it, mix a spoonful of benzine into dark stamping powder a little at a time, until it becomes a thin paste just slightly thicker than heavy cream. You can also make a homemade stamping paste by mixing water and food coloring into a cup of cornstarch to make a dark paste. Add water slowly in small amounts. The tint is important. Make the paste dark enough to show clearly on red nylon. To use either paste, rub it through the holes in the pattern with a wad of felt scrap or other clean cloth (photograph 8).

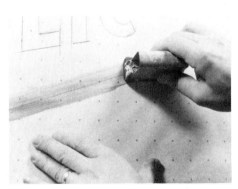

8: Rub stamping paste through the pattern perforations with a wad of scrap felt. The tool shown here, made in a professional banner shop, has layers of felt held by a bent sheet-metal handle, but a wad held in the hand will do as well.

Spread the white nylon on your work table and place the pattern over it. Hold the pattern and nylon in place with one or more weights. An iron will do, or some heavy food cans, or anything of similar size and weight.

Rub the stamping paste through the perforations forming the triangular outline of the pennant. The pattern should be right side up, rather than wrong side up as in the club banner. Use the same method to transfer the anchor design to the yellow nylon and the letters to the red nylon.

Assembling the Parts

Cut out the triangular pennant from the white nylon. Next, cut a rectangle around the anchor silhouette on the yellow nylon. Do not follow the outline of the anchor The rectangular cut you make should leave space around the anchor silhouette. Do the same for the letters, cutting around them as a group. There should be at least two inches of clear nylon around the anchor and the group of letters. Cut out matching blanks of yellow and red nylon.

9: Pin the marked red and yellow rectangles to one side of the pennant, and blank rectangles of red and yellow in matching position to the opposite side. Baste each set of three layers together, remove the pins and sew along the lines of the pattern with a zigzag stitch.

Place the white triangular pennant flat on your work table and pin the anchor and the letter rectangles to it so the anchor and letters are in position. Turn the pennant over and pin the blank rectangles in matching positions: yellow opposite yellow and red opposite red, with the white pennant sandwiched between them (photograph 9). Place pins outside the design and letter group to help keep the material from puckering when you baste the material together.

With all the pins in place, baste the anchor and its matching blank in place. Do the same for the group of letters. Remove the pins and sew the pennant.

Sewing the Pennant

Sewing nylon can be tricky. If you are sewing by hand, use lingerie gauge cotton-covered polyester thread. If you are sewing by machine, use a new ball-point needle with either cotton-covered polyester or plain polyester thread.

Sew along the lines of the pattern for the anchor and letters with a zigzag stitch to prevent fraying. Tie off the threads and trim the excess fabric on each side of the pennant ⅛-inch outside the stitching of the anchor and each letter. Turn down and sew ¼-inch at the top and bottom of the pennant; then sew 1-inch bias tape along the side (Figure D). Use ¼-inch bias tape for the tie strings. Cut the tie strings 18 inches long, fold each at the center and sew the folded end to the side of the pennant as shown in Figure E.

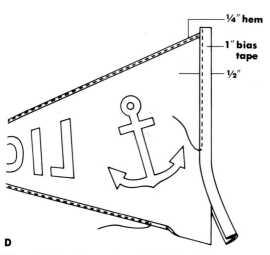

Figure D: Turn down and sew ¼-inch hem at top and bottom of the pennant. Then sew bias tape along the side after the design is completed.

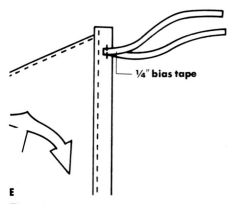

Figure E: Cut two 18-inch lengths of ¼-inch bias tape for tie tapes. Fold each in half and sew to the side of the pennant as shown.

673

Lisa Peck worked with Canada's leading artists in making graphic arts banners for the Vatican Pavilion at Montreal's Expo '70. Since then she has been making and selling her own creations, including the banner shown on page 668.

Graphic Arts
Decorative banner $ ● ♢ ⚲

The first and most challenging step in making a decorative banner like the one on page 668 is sketching a design. This is also the most fun. As in painting, printmaking or sculpture, banner design is personal; there are no rules about subject matter, materials or techniques.

The banner shown in the photograph was made of scraps of felt sewn on a 36-by-52½-inch piece of red background felt and stitched in embroidery floss of contrasting color. To make it you need 1 1/3 yards of red felt for background and 1/3 yard each of purple, pink, white, orange and green felt; chalk; pattern paper; dressmaker's shears; small scissors; needle; embroidery floss; a 40-inch broomstick; and screw eyes for hanging. (Additional interest can be achieved by adding other textural elements. I have used all kinds of odds and ends, buttons, sequins, bits of chain and found objects in banners I have made.)

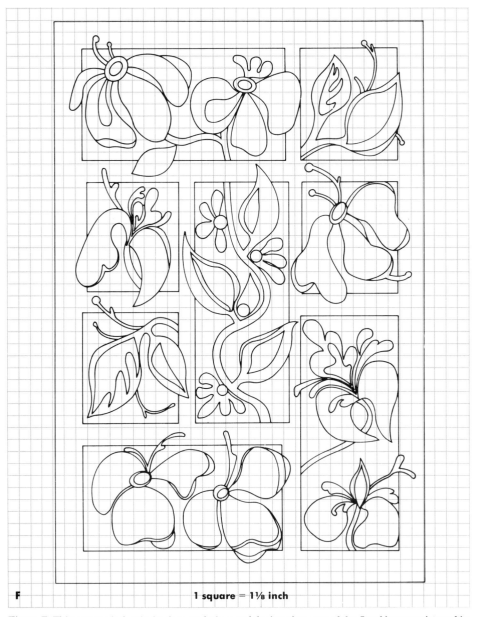

F   **1 square = 1⅛ inch**

Figure F: This pattern is for the background piece and design elements of the floral banner pictured in color on page 668. Cut pieces of felt to match the colors in the photograph.

Start by cutting out the background piece and the border pieces. Each border piece is 6 inches wide. The two side pieces are each 54½ inches long and the top and bottom pieces each are 38 inches long.

Next, enlarge the pattern (Figure F) as explained on page 57, Volume One. Cut out the large rectangles from the pattern. When a floral part spills out of its rectangle, cut around it and then back to the straight edge of the rectangle. To transfer the rectangles to felt, mark the corners of each rectangle on the felt with chalk, then join the corners with straight lines. Cut the rectangles out of felt and baste them to the background according to the pattern (photograph 10).

After the felt rectangles are basted to the background, cut out the floral parts for one rectangle from the pattern and trace them on felt of appropriate colors (photograph 11). Cut out the felt floral parts and assemble them in position on the banner. If the fit is correct, baste the pieces in place. If it is poor, correct it first by trimming or by making the part again. Follow this procedure for each rectangular section of the overall banner design.

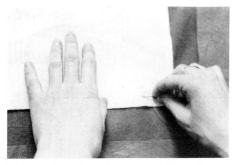

10: Baste the rectangular pieces of felt to the background, using the pattern as a guide.

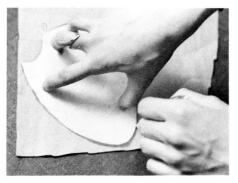

11: Trace the shape of each floral part on felt with a piece of chalk and cut it out. The floral designs are cut from the pattern after the rectangles have been basted on the background.

The rectangular and floral design elements are sewn to the background with embroidery floss after they have been basted in position. Use a whipstitch to attach the floral parts and a blanket stitch for the background rectangles.

When all the elements of the design are basted to the background, sew them in place with embroidery floss of contrasting color (see color photograph above). Follow Figures G and H to attach the border pieces. Whipstitch bottom corners closed and embroider entire inside edge of the border on the front of the banner with a blanket stitch. (To do these stitches, see "Crewelwork Sampler," Volume Five.) Leave top corners unsewn so top border forms a pole sleeve, and snip away any excess felt. Insert a 40-inch broomstick.

For related topics, see "Batik," "Embroidery," "Heraldic Designs," "Pageants and Parades" and "Sewing."

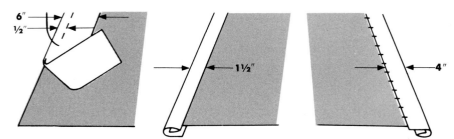

Figure G: Sew border strip to the face of the banner (left), fold it back under banner (center), then turn banner over and hem free edge of border to back of banner (right).

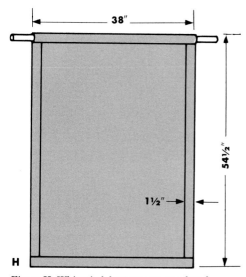

Figure H: Whipstitch bottom corners closed. Leave top corners open so border forms a sleeve.

675

FLORENTINE STITCH
Three-Dimensional Color and Pattern

Phoebe Fox, a free-lance designer, is a graduate of New York University, where she studied fine arts. A former staff member of McCall's Needlework & Crafts, Mrs. Fox has also produced craft articles for American Home *magazine and created designs for foreign and domestic publications and craft supply companies. She presently resides in Brooklyn Heights, where she divides her time among such crafts as crochet, macrame, knitting, and needlepoint.*

The Florentine stitch, also known as Hungarian point and Bargello, is a particular needlepoint technique with many variations that are easy to learn. The design is worked with yarn on needlepoint canvas, a stiff cotton or linen fabric consisting of threads woven with regular spaces between them for the needle and yarn to pass through. Unlike the short diagonal stitches in regular needlepoint, Florentine stitches are long and usually vertical. The stitches are worked across the canvas threads in rows, in various colors, to form striking, repetitive geometric patterns, as illustrated in the color photograph opposite.

The projects that follow are presented in ascending order of difficulty, progressing from very simple designs to the intermediate, and on to the more advanced. Each succeeding project builds upon the knowledge and experience acquired with the project or projects preceding it. You can use the colors I did, or substitute your own choices. If you've worked with needlepoint before, you may have enough yarn on hand left over from previous projects to complete the first three projects, since their yarn requirements are small. Choose your colors carefully, since an illusion of depth and shading is accomplished by working the rows of stitches in several shades of one or more colors, with the shades gradually progressing from light to dark, or dark to light. All the designs, except the zigzag, illustrate this effect. When working with Florentine stitchery, I find it very exciting to see my designs develop from preliminary sketches and charts into patterns with depth and texture. In planning original designs (see page 687 for suggestions), there is a challenge in selecting yarns, colors, and canvas, but once such decisions are made, the work progresses fairly rapidly to completion.

Materials

The Florentine stitch is worked on either of two basic types of canvas: mono (single thread), or penelope (double thread). I prefer mono canvas for the Florentine stitch because the single threads facilitate counting. Although other canvas sizes (canvases with more or fewer threads per inch) are available (see page 687), I work all my designs on No. 14 canvas with approximately 14 threads per inch. I prefer to work on this canvas with Persian or tapestry yarn because I find the relationship of yarn to canvas the most comfortable. Working on a smaller size canvas (with more threads per inch) is very delicate and becomes tedious. On a larger size canvas (with fewer threads per inch), the stitches become too long (on No. 5 canvas a single stitch worked over five threads will be 1 inch long), and are therefore prone to being caught and pulled. With the larger size canvases, several strands of yarn are used to cover the canvas, and great care must be taken to avoid excess twisting which causes canvas show-through.

All the designs that follow were worked in wool yarn. I used either three strands of Persian yarn or one strand of tapestry yarn, which is thinner. Use a tapestry needle, which has a blunt point, rather than a sharp-pointed needle which might penetrate the actual threads of the canvas, rather than slipping easily in and out of the openings between the threads. A No. 20 tapestry needle is the correct size for the yarn and canvas on which the following projects were worked. For other types of yarn and other canvases, see page 687.

In addition to the yarn, canvas, and needle, you need large household scissors for cutting the canvas and fabric; small, sharp-pointed embroidery scissors for ripping out stitches to correct mistakes; a ruler; masking tape; and a waterproof marking pen. The amounts of canvas and yarn and any additional materials needed to complete each project are listed within the project directions.

This Florentine stitch pillow illustrates the striking optical illusion of depth achieved by the careful choice of color and pattern. The overall design combines three distinct patterns: A pomegranate pattern at the center, framed by rows of Gobelin stitches, and an outside border of a textured chevron pattern in long and short stitches.

The Basic Stitch

The Florentine Stitch is basically a vertical stitch usually worked over two to six canvas threads. Each stitch is worked on the canvas by referring to a chart in the form of a grid, as in Figure A, at left. The simplest pattern or arrangement of these upright stitches is one that places them side by side in a straight row, as in photograph 1. In this most basic form, it is called a Gobelin stitch. If these vertical stitches are worked with each succeeding stitch one canvas thread above the last, the effect is that of steps going up. If the procedure is reversed and each succeeding stitch is worked one canvas thread below the last, the effect is that of steps going down. If you repeat the entire procedure, using the same number of stitches, the total effect is that of a simple zigzag pattern with uniform peaks, as in Figure A and photograph 2. The pattern is formed by working a 4-1 step. The first number designates the number of canvas threads over which the stitch is worked (the length of the stitch); the second number indicates the step or number of canvas threads up or down each succeeding stitch shifts.

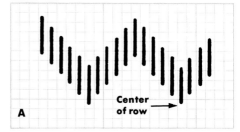

Figure A: Chart for a simple zigzag pattern shows length of stitch (number of canvas threads over which yarn is worked; four in this case), and "step" (the number of canvas threads a stitch moves up or down from the previous stitch; in this case one). You can follow this chart to achieve the pattern shown in photographs 2 through 6.

1: Basic upright Gobelin stitch, worked here over four canvas threads. This stitch is worked over two canvas threads in the box cover on page 683 and in the pillow on page 677.

2: Simple zigzag pattern in a 4-1 step. A 4-1 step means each stitch is worked over four canvas threads, and each succeeding stitch is worked one thread above or below the last.

The horizontal and vertical grid lines on the chart represent the horizontal and vertical threads of the canvas. To make a stitch, first count the number of horizontal grid lines over which the stitch is drawn on the chart; then work the stitch over the same number of horizontal threads on the canvas. The next stitch is stepped up or down one horizontal thread, depending on the stitch it follows. All Florentine patterns are formed by stitches worked in such steps repeated in various sequences. The design is determined by the length of the stitch, the number of canvas threads in the step, and the number of stitches in each step.

To begin: In working a specific Florentine design, first prepare the canvas. Determine the desired size of the finished project (this is given in the project directions). Add about two inches on each side of the four sides to allow for blocking, and then cut the canvas. Fold strips of masking tape over the raw edges to keep the canvas threads from raveling and catching the yarn. Now with a waterproof felt marker, outline the exact dimensions of the finished piece, forming a rectangle or square, centered on the canvas. Mark the center of the top of the marked outline. This top center is the starting point where the first row, which usually establishes the pattern, is started. Cut yarn into 16-to-20-inch lengths. Thread the needle, following directions in Embroidery Craftnotes, in the "Crewelwork Sampler" entry, page 540. To work the first row of a zigzag pattern, for example, refer to the chart for the pattern (in this case, Figure A). Begin at the center point marked on the canvas, working this row from the center (marked on the chart) to the far left, ending at the marked line (as indicated in photograph 3). Start the first stitch with the first length of yarn, leaving a yarn end of about one inch at the underside of the canvas. Hold the yarn end in place under the canvas and work subsequent stitches over it to secure it. Always bring the needle up at the bottom of the stitch and insert it down through the canvas at the top of the stitch. This is especially important when working subsequent rows, in order to avoid splitting the yarn of the previous row. At the end of a row, work the yarn into the underside of the stitches previously made. (Use this same method when yarn runs out before a row is complete, and to begin subsequent new strands.) Return to the center point and work the right half of the row as a mirror image of the left half

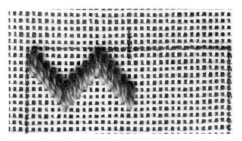

3: Using this zigzag pattern as an example, start at the center of the top row and work from right to left to complete the left half of this row.

4: With left half of first row completed, start back at the center and work from left to right to complete the perfectly centered first row.

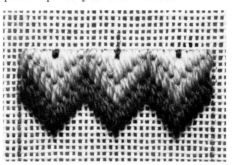

5: The entire second row can be worked from right to left. The top of the second-row stitch, a shade darker, is worked in the same hole as the bottom of the first-row stitch directly above it.

6: To achieve a straight edge along the top of this zigzag design, use compensating stitches (worked here in a still lighter yarn) to fill in small areas as needed. Use same method to fill in at the bottom.

(photograph 4). Work the second and subsequent rows from right to left (or left to right if you are left-handed), making one continuous row. It is not necessary to start these at the center, since the pattern has been centered by the first row. The top of each stitch in the second row (and subsequent rows) is worked in the same hole as the bottom of the stitch directly above it (photograph 5).

Working repeats: Each Florentine stitch design is composed of a single pattern repeated several times. The zigzag, the scallop, and the flame design are one-row repeats, which means the overall design is formed by repeating the same row in different colors. For these designs, only the first row is shown on the chart. The circles, the diamonds, and the pomegranate designs all belong to another category, and the overall design is formed by enclosing shapes within outline rows. Each enclosed shape, plus the portion of the outline rows surrounding it, is called a repeat pattern. The charts for these designs show one repeat pattern rather than the entire design. They also include the first few stitches of the next repeat pattern in order to show how the repeats fit together.

Compensating stitches are used to maintain a straight edge at the top and bottom edges of a design. These are stitches of shorter lengths used to fill in areas where needed (photograph 6).

As you work, the yarn has a slight tendency to twist. To untwist yarn, hold the canvas up in the air, allowing the needle and yarn to swing freely; the yarn will automatically unwind. To correct mistakes in stitching, use the sharp points of an embroidery scissors to cut the stitches. Cut the stitches on the surface of the canvas, being careful to avoid cutting the canvas threads. Then pull out the tiny yarn ends. Unless the mistake involves only a few stitches, never undo stitches and reuse the yarn, because it will be too worn and thin.

Blocking: After the design is completely stitched, the canvas will be slightly distorted. This is because the stitching process exerts pressure on the canvas threads, pulling them out of shape. To avoid this as much as possible, don't pull the stitches tightly. However, since some distortion is inevitable, the piece will need blocking (see Embroidery Craftnotes in the "Crewelwork Sampler" entry, page 546). Blocking shapes the finished needlepoint, and requires the following materials: A soft wood board larger than the needlepoint, aluminum foil, rust-proof thumbtacks or pushpins, a sponge, and a roll of paper towels.

Eyeglass case of rainbow colors worked in a simple zigzag design. It has a layer of felt inside to help cushion the glasses.

Eyeglass case

Stitch detail of a simple zigzag design.

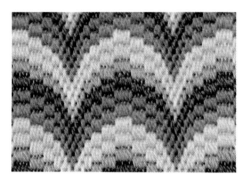

Stitch detail of a simple scallop design.

This is a basic project, within the capabilities of the beginner. There is a choice of the two simple designs shown above: a zigzag worked in an array of rainbow colors, or a scallop for which I used cool tones, suggesting waves.

To complete an eyeglass case using either the zigzag or the simple scallop design, you need tapestry yarn in the colors and amounts listed under the chart for each design; a 5½-by-5½-inch piece of felt; white glue; a 7⅛-by-7⅛-inch piece of fabric for the lining (such as medium or lightweight cotton) to match one of the yarn colors; sewing thread to match the lining; and a sewing needle. The eyeglass case was worked with the canvas selvedge positioned at the side. Make sure the selvedge is in this position to insure that your project works out to be the same size as mine, because No. 14 canvas does not have exactly 14 threads per inch in both directions.

Prepare a 10-by-10-inch piece of canvas as directed on page 678, marking a 6⅛-by-6⅛-inch square in the center. Following the general directions on pages 678 and 679 and the chart (Figure B for the zigzag pattern or Figure C for the scallop design), work the first row of the design, starting at the center point shown in Figure B or C. Work from the center to the marked line at the left, then from the center to the marked line at the right. Once this first row is established, work the remaining rows all the way across, from the right marked line to the left marked line. Work these remaining rows following the sequence in which they are listed under the chart. Both designs are one-row repeats, meaning the design is actually formed by repeating the same row in different colors. When the marked line at the bottom is reached, work compensating stitches to fill in the areas at the top and bottom, again following the color sequence.

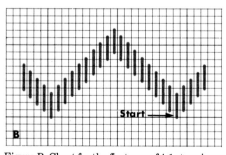

Figure B: Chart for the first row of 4-1 step zigzag design used for the eyeglass case shown above. When beginning this row, start at the center (marked by arrow). To make the eyeglass case in this design requires tapestry yarn in the following colors and amounts:

■ red: 8 yards (first row)   green: 7 yards
orange: 8 yards   blue: 7 yards
yellow: 7 yards   purple: 8 yards

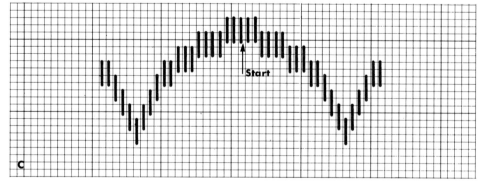

Figure C: Chart for the first row of a 4-2 step scallop design, an alternate design to use for making an eyeglass case. When beginning this row, start at the center (marked by arrow). To work this design, you need tapestry yarn in the following colors and amounts:

■ dark purple: 9 yards (first row)
medium purple: 8 yards
light purple: 8 yards
light blue: 8 yards
medium blue-green: 8 yards
dark blue-green: 9 yards

Block the canvas as directed in "Crewelwork Sampler" Embroidery Craftnotes page 546, Volume Five. When needlepoint is dry, trim the canvas margins to ½ inch on each side. Apply a line of glue all around the 5½-by-5½-inch square of felt, close to the edges. Center the felt on the back side of the needlepoint, glue side down; press together. When dry, fold canvas margins back, over the edges of the felt, trimming excess canvas at corners to make flat folds. Sew margins to felt using large basting stitches. Take the 7⅛ inch by 7⅛ inch square of lining fabric and fold its edges under ½ inch on all sides; then press with an iron. With wrong side facing the felt, pin lining to needlepoint, matching folded edges carefully. Sew the lining to the needlepoint, catching every canvas thread with a tiny stitch. Fold the lined needlepoint in half with the lining inside. Sew together along sides and bottom, again using tiny stitches. (Note: If you wish to center the design exactly, after stitching the sides together, reposition the side seam to lie along the center of the back and then stitch the bottom seam closed while in this position.)

Needlecrafts
Pocket for tote bag

¢ ◫ 𝐀 🐁

The two designs shown for this project, the patterns for which are on the next page, are slightly more advanced than those for the eyeglass case. The flame design, shown below, right, requires careful counting, but is again a one-row repeat where the first row establishes the pattern and all the subsequent rows are worked in the same pattern as the first. The enclosed circles design (directly below and above, right) introduces a new concept. Here, a variation of the simple scalloped or curved line is worked upside down below another exactly like it. The result is an enclosed shape of a circle, outlined by the curved rows. Work these outline rows first (using brown yarn), and then fill in the concentric rows within the circles, diamonds, and half-diamond shapes.

This Florentine stitch pocket adds a touch of color to a plain tote bag—and it's just the right size for tucking in a shopping list, loose change or keys.

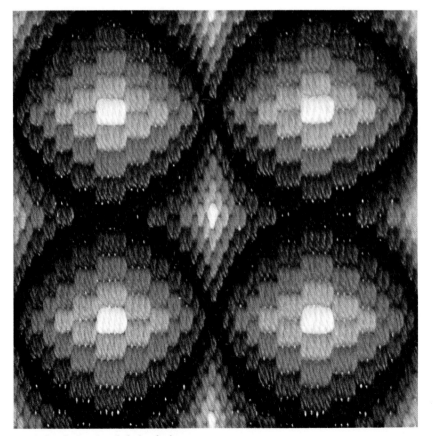

Stitch detail of enclosed circles design.

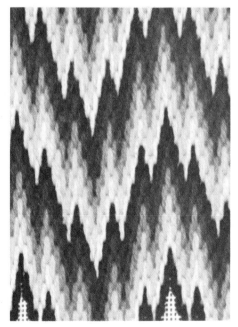

Stitch detail of the flame stitch.

To make a Tote Bag pocket, using either one of the designs shown on the previous page, you need: tapestry or Persian yarn in the colors and amounts listed in Figures D or E below; fabric for lining, such as medium-weight cotton to match one of the yarn colors; thread to match the lining; a sewing needle.

With the canvas positioned so the selvedge is at the side (see Eyeglass Case directions, page 680, for explanation), prepare a 9-by-9-inch piece of canvas as directed on page 678, marking a 4¾-by-5-inch rectangle in the center of the canvas. Following the directions on pages 678 and 679 and the chart for the design (Figure D for the flame or Figure E for the enclosed circles), establish the first row. For the flame pattern, work subsequent rows in the sequence in which the colors are listed under Figure D. For the enclosed circles pattern, work remaining outline rows and the stitches within the enclosed shapes following Figure E and the color key below it. When the line marking the bottom of the design is reached, fill in top and bottom edges where necessary with compensating stitches.

Block the finished needlepoint by following the directions in Embroidery Craftnotes, in the "Crewelwork Sampler" entry, page 546. When dry, trim the canvas margins to ½ inch, and fold the ½ inch margins under to wrong side. (Trim corners if they seem too bulky.) Using large basting stitches, secure margins to back of needlepoint. Cut a 5¾-by-6-inch piece from the lining fabric; fold all edges under ½ inch and press with iron. With wrong sides facing, sew lining all around to needlepoint, catching every canvas thread with a small stitch. Now pin to a plain tote bag, a blazer, or jeans. Sew on pocket, making tiny stitches around sides and bottom.

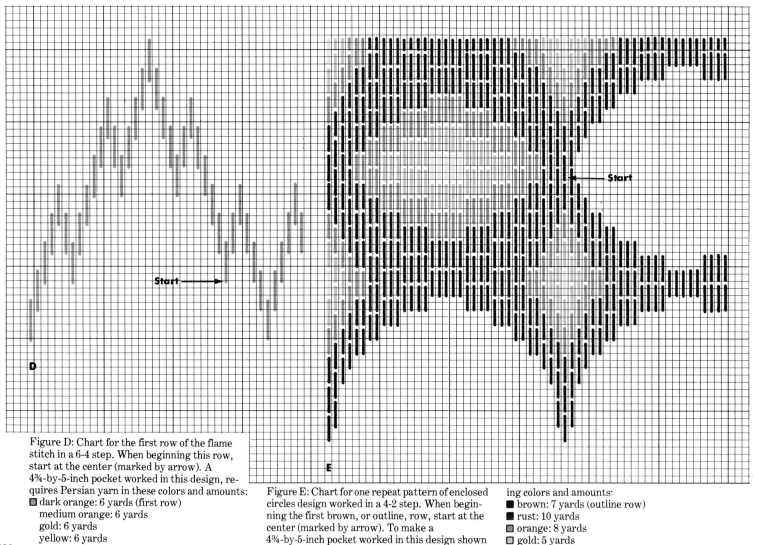

Figure D: Chart for the first row of the flame stitch in a 6-4 step. When beginning this row, start at the center (marked by arrow). A 4¾-by-5-inch pocket worked in this design, requires Persian yarn in these colors and amounts:
☐ dark orange: 6 yards (first row)
medium orange: 6 yards
gold: 6 yards
yellow: 6 yards
light yellow: 6 yards

Figure E: Chart for one repeat pattern of enclosed circles design worked in a 4-2 step. When beginning the first brown, or outline, row, start at the center (marked by arrow). To make a 4¾-by-5-inch pocket worked in this design shown on page 681, you need tapestry yarn in the following colors and amounts:
■ brown: 7 yards (outline row)
■ rust: 10 yards
▨ orange: 8 yards
▨ gold: 5 yards
☐ light yellow: 1 yard

682

Stitch detail of enclosed diamonds design shows how shades of color can be used to create depth.

A Florentine stitch cover made for an ordinary plastic photo cube transforms the cube into an attractive container for small items.

Needlecrafts
Plastic box cover   ¢ ⊠ 🚶 🎯

A clear plastic photo cube (the kind with a foam block inside to hold photographs in place) is transformed into a unique container for candy, jewelry or cosmetics with the addition of an attractive needlepoint cover. Like the enclosed circles design on page 681, this diamond design is a series of enclosed shapes. The first row is established as previously described, then another row is worked upside down directly below the first row. The diamonds that result are then filled in with increasingly darker shades of green, giving the illusion of depth.

To make the cover for a clear plastic photo cube, 3⅞-by-3⅞-inches square, you will need: tapestry yarn in the colors and amounts listed under Figure F; printed or solid color fabric for the lining, such as light-weight cotton, to coordinate with the yarn colors; white glue; poster board; sewing thread to match the lining; braided or twisted cord trim in dark green; a sewing needle; and straight pins.

Prepare an 8-by-8-inch piece of canvas as directed on page 678. With the selvedge at the top, mark a 3⅝-by-3⅝-inch square at the center of the canvas. The box cover design is 54 threads wide and 56 threads high; and for this design to fit a perfectly square box, the selvedge is positioned at the top (see Eyeglass Case directions, page 680, for explanation). Following the directions on pages 678 and 679 and the chart for the design (Figure F), establish the outline rows (light green) beginning with the first row. Follow the color key below Figure F to fill in the diamonds and compensating stitches. The last step is to work the border; this is the Gobelin stitch introduced on page 678. Here it is worked over two threads all around the design, forming a solid border. Note that there is one diagonal stitch at each corner of the border.

Block the finished needlepoint by following the directions in Embroidery Craft-

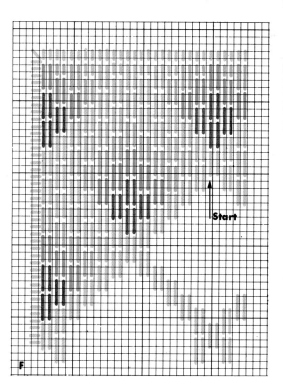

Figure F: Chart for one repeat pattern of enclosed diamond design is worked in a 4-2 step with two stitches in each step. When beginning the first light green, or outline, row, start at the center (marked by arrow). Border is worked over two threads. To complete this design for the box cover, including the border, you need tapestry yarn in the following colors and amounts:
☐ light green: 7 yards (outline row)
☐ chartreuse: 4 yards
☐ medium green: 4 yards
☐ dark green: 3 yards
■ orange: 3 yards

683

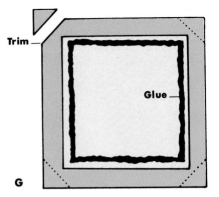

G

Figure G: To make the stopper part of the cover for the photo cube, place a piece of fabric, face down, on a flat surface. Center three pieces of poster board on top of the fabric; if desired, glue the pieces together to form a single three-layered board. Trim fabric corners as shown. Run a line of glue around the four sides of the top board, near the edges, and fold the fabric edges over. Let glue dry.

Detail of pillow, showing pomegranate design at center.

notes, in the "Crewelwork Sampler" entry, page 546. While the needlepoint is drying, prepare the cover for the photo cube. For this you need two components — a top piece that rests on the outside edge of the cube, and attached to this piece, a stopper that fits into the opening of the cube. For the stopper, cut three pieces of poster board 3½-by-3½-inches square or ⅛ inch smaller than the inside measurements of the opening. Check the inside dimensions of the cube opening carefully to make sure the stopper will fit. Glue the three pieces of poster board together so all sides are flush. Then cut a 4½-by-4½-inch square of fabric, fold its edges back over the poster board stopper and glue to the boards as shown in Figure G. For the top piece, cut two 3⅞-by-3⅞-inch pieces of poster board, and glue them together. Then cover the boards with a 5-by-5-inch square of fabric; and glue fabric to them as directed for the stopper. When the needlepoint is dry, trim the canvas margins to ½ inch. Fold back trimmed margins to the underside, snipping off margin corners to reduce bulk. Using large basting stitches, tack down margins to back of needlepoint. Place needlepoint on the top piece, with the wrong sides facing each other and with the edges matching. Sew needlepoint to top-piece fabric, catching all canvas threads and edge of fabric. Center wrong side of stopper on underside of top piece, and glue them together. Glue green trim around needlepoint edge, holding it in place with straight pins until dry.

Needlecrafts

Pillow

The pillow design shown on page 677, combines three designs, and is a more difficult project requiring advanced needlepoint skill. I chose two of my favorite colors—purple and orange—and used four shades of each, graduating from very dark to very light. By arranging the shades from light to dark and back to light again, a sense of depth was achieved.

To make the 15½-by-14½-inch pillow, you need: Persian yarn in the colors and amounts listed with Figure H; a 16½-by-15½-inch piece of fabric for the backing, color coordinated with the pillow yarn; 2 yards of velvet cording to match the backing fabric; sewing thread to match backing fabric; a sewing needle; a 15-inch square of foam or kapok-filled, knife-edged pillow form.

Making the Pillow

The three designs of the pillow are worked in the following order: First the center pomegranate design; then the inner border of Gobelin stitches; then the outer border in the short and long stitch chevron design.

With canvas positioned so the selvedge is at the side (see Eyeglass Case directions, page 680, for explanation), prepare a 19½-by-18½-inch piece of canvas as directed on page 678. Mark a 5⅞-inch wide by 6⅛-inch high rectangle in the center of the canvas. Work the pomegranate design in this area, following the directions on pages 678 and 679 and the chart (Figure H opposite). The pomegranate design consists of outline rows in peach color worked so that several pomegranate-like shapes are enclosed within them. Establish the first row (peach); then work the next row of peach, which is the first row upside down. The next two rows of peach are worked as you did the first two. When these peach outline rows are complete, fill in the enclosed areas and work compensating stitches at the top and bottom, following the color key under the chart (Figure H).

Next, work the inner border of eight rows of Gobelin stitches around the pomegranates, following the color key and the chart. Beginning at the upper right corner, work each row completely around the four sides, working the diagonal stitch at each corner. The chart shows the upper right-hand corner only; work all corners the same.

The last section is the long-and-short chevron design around the Gobelin stitch rows. The placement of one long stitch (over four threads) next to three short ones (over two threads) gives this pattern a textured appearance. Because the design has already been centered on the canvas, it is not necessary to start the first row of this section at the center. Start with orange at the upper right corner as indicated on the chart and work the entire first row across the canvas, ending at the upper

Start chevron design

Start pomegranate design

Figure H: Chart for Florentine stitch pillow showing upper right-hand corner of the design. Begin pomegranate design (center portion), Gobelin stitch border, and long and short chevron design as indicated in chart or text. To complete the pillow, you need Persian yarn in the following colors and amounts:

☐ peach: 38 yards   ■ violet: 35 yards
☐ apricot: 39 yards   ■ magenta: 34 yards
☐ orange: 38 yards   ■ rose: 34 yards
■ rust: 37 yards   ☐ pink: 33 yards

H

685

This detail of the upper right-hand corner of the pillow shows part of the pomegranate design, the upright Gobelin stitch inner border, and the long and short stitch chevron design in which the outer border is worked. You can see the diagonal stitches used to work the Gobelin stitch corners, and how the chevron pattern rows meet to form a mitered corner.

left corner. Turn the canvas clockwise so the next side is positioned at top, and establish the first row in orange on that side. Repeat on the two remaining sides. Following the chart and the color key below it, fill in the remaining rows, working the rows one at a time all around the four sides. Fill in the compensating stitches at the top and bottom of each side to complete the pillow. When working, note that one long stitch always falls directly above or below three short stitches.

Block the finished needlepoint as directed in Embroidery Craftnotes, in the "Crewelwork Sampler" entry, page 546. When the needlepoint is dry, trim its canvas margins to ½ inch. With right sides facing, pin and baste the needlepoint to the backing fabric with the edges of both pieces even. Sew together around three sides, stitching exactly along the edge of the needlepoint stitches; use a sewing machine or make small stitches by hand (Figure I). Turn right side out and insert the pillow form. Fold raw edges of needlepoint canvas and fabric ½ inch to the inside; sew together with tiny stitches. Sew the velvet cording all around the perimeter of the pillow using tiny stitches, as in Figure J.

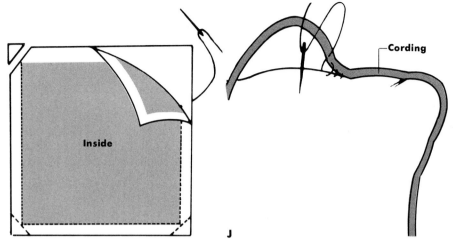

Figure I: Right sides facing, stitch needlepoint to pillow backing by sewing along three sides. Trim corners, and turn right side out.

Figure J: After inserting the pillow form and sewing up the fourth side, sew the cording all around the edges, using small stitches.

7: These Florentine stitches on No. 5 penelope canvas have been worked with two strands of wool rug yarn. Four strands of tapestry yarn or nine strands of Persian yarn also covers No. 5 canvas well. For yarn this thick, use a No. 13 tapestry needle. For a dimensional effect, the double threads of the canvas are separated and the areas between the heavy upright stitches filled in with smaller, plain needlepoint stitches using one strand of tapestry yarn.

Experimenting with Other Yarns and Canvas

As explained earlier, I prefer to stitch on No. 14 needlepoint canvas with either one strand of tapestry yarn or three strands of Persian yarn. There is, however, a wide variety of canvas sizes and yarn types available. To experiment with other yarns and canvas, keep these points in mind:

Canvas: Canvas is sold by the yard or fraction of a yard, and is available in widths from 18 to 60 inches. Canvas sizes (the number of threads to an inch) range from the very large No. 3 or 5 (used mainly for rugs) to the very small No. 40 (a fine gauze-like fabric used for items which require a delicate effect, such as handbags or jewel boxes). Mono (or single thread) canvas provides uniform, easily counted spaces. There are, however, advantages to penelope (or double thread) canvas; it is stronger than mono canvas, and the double threads can be separated to add extra stitches when combining Florentine stitches with needlepoint stitches. See photographs 7 through 9 for some frequently used canvas sizes, yarns and needle combinations.

Yarn: Use smooth-surfaced yarns, since the yarn is pulled in and out of the canvas many times as the design is stitched. Above all, relate the thickness of the yarn to the size of the canvas mesh. The canvas should be completely covered by the stitches. If the yarn is too thick, it pulls the canvas out of shape and makes it hard to pull the yarn through the openings; if the yarn is too thin, the canvas shows through between the stitches. Avoid knitting worsted yarn for Florentine stitches since worsted tends to stretch and fray as you work with it. Crewel yarn can be used very successfully. Like Persian yarn, several strands of crewel yarn are used simultaneously for a large canvas; and for a smaller canvas single strands are used. Cotton, silk, or rayon embroidery floss and metallic threads are best confined to small areas for highlights, since they do not wear as well as wool.

Needles: Tapestry needles come in several sizes, identified by numbers from 24 to 13; the higher the number, the smaller the needle. Needles must correlate with both the yarn and canvas, as indicated in photographs 7 through 9. The eye of the needle should be slightly wider than the yarn is thick, but slender enough to slide through the canvas openings easily.

Yarn estimating: To estimate the amounts of yarn needed for a project, work one entire repeat motif of the design in scraps of yarn of the same type and weight you intend to use; keep track of the amounts of each color used. Then with the design centered on the canvas, determine the number of times the motif will be repeated in the design. Multiply the number of times the motif is repeated by the amounts of yarn used to work the one motif.

For related projects and crafts, see "Applique," "Crewelwork Sampler," "Embroidery," "Granny Squares," "Hardanger," "Needlepoint," "Patchwork," "Quilting," and "Sewing."

8: On this No. 10 canvas, two types of yarn were used. The top row was worked in two strands of tapestry yarn; for the bottom row, five strands of Persian yarn were used. A No. 18 tapestry needle is the proper size for yarn of this thickness.

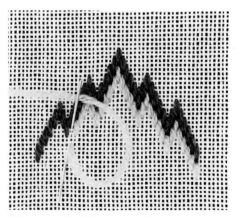

9: Two strands of Persian yarn (crewel yarn can be substituted) have been worked on No. 18 canvas here. A No. 20 tapestry needle was used.

687

FLOWERS (ARTIFICIAL)
Beauty for all Seasons

Marilyn Nierenberg has taught a variety of arts and crafts both as the Recreational Therapy Director of Bellevue Hospital in Manhattan and as a public school teacher.

Artificial flowers can reflect the colors of spring throughout the year. Since no upkeep is required, they are easy to live with, and they make ideal get-well gifts, party displays, or decorations for your home.

Designs for artificial flowers can be adapted from nature or they can be your own inventions. One of the projects in this entry describes how crepe paper can be stretched and curled to resemble roses and tulips; another shows how sparkling metallic mums and daisies are made from discarded aluminum pie pans; another is a gay bouquet from fabric matching your upholstery. The wide variety of materials you can use to fashion colorful, handsome flowers seems endless.

First, you need to know how to transfer a pattern. To design the pencil posy below, or any of the blossoms in this section, simply trace the parts of the pattern shown full size. As you outline the shapes, be sure to make a separate cardboard template for each part; dotted lines indicate cutting lines. To avoid destroying your book, place a sheet of carbon paper on top of a piece of thin cardboard and place them both beneath the pattern. Transfer each shape onto the cardboard by tracing over the pattern with a stylus (you can use the point of a dried-up ball point pen). Then, cut out the pattern.

Toys and Games
Pencil posy

This beginning project, the pencil posy, is an easy one for you and your child to assemble in a matter of minutes. You'll need cardboard and scissors; and each posy will require at least two pieces of colored felt fabric 3-by-5 inches; a pencil with an eraser; and a bead threaded on a straight pin about ½ inch long.

Trace the patterns in Figure A on cardboard and cut out; then place the smallest and largest cardboard patterns on one scrap of felt and trace the outline onto the felt with a ball-point pen. Trace the middle circle onto felt of a contrasting color. Cut along dotted lines of the smallest circle to create petals.

To assemble the posy, stack the three felt pieces, aligning centers, with the smallest piece on top and the largest on the bottom. Run the pin with the bead on it through the felt and into the eraser.

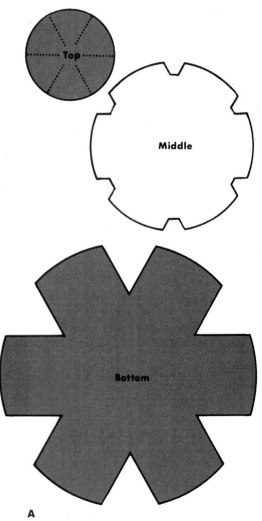

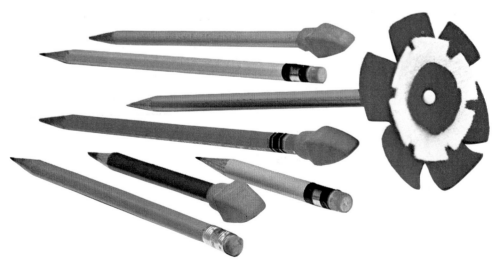

A

Figure A: For a pencil posy, top and bottom patterns are cut from one color of felt, the middle pattern from a contrasting color.

Want a neat, quick project to make with your child? Eraser-tipped pencils and crayons can be dressed up with colorful posies of soft felt fabric made from patterns shown at left.

To form this attractive tissue paper bouquet, also shown on the cover, see Figures B through E, right.

Paper Folding and Cutting
Tissue paper flowers

¢ ⊠ 👤 🗲

The translucency of tissue paper can give flowers a luminous quality, yet the paper has sufficient body to be folded for making large flowers. Craft or hardware stores stock the following materials that you will need: a selection of colorful tissue paper sheets 10-by-15 inches; one dozen No. 16 stem wires 20 inches long; green floral tape for concealing the wire; a block of foamed plastic cut to the diameter of your vase; and a pair of scissors.

To make one of the medium-sized flowers shown above, you will need six multi-colored sheets of 10-by-15-inch tissue paper. Stack the sheets evenly, then fold all six layers together in accordion pleats (as in Figure B). Each pleat should measure approximately 1½ inches wide. Pinch the center of the strip lengthwise at the 5-inch midpoint and wrap one end of a No. 16 stem wire twice around the middle to hold the pleated paper in place. The shape should then roughly resemble a bow tie as in Figure C.

To make scalloped petals, cut a semi-circle at each end of the bow tie as shown on the left side in Figure C. Pointed petals are made by cutting triangles at both sides of the bow tie, as on the right side in Figure C. Or try designing your own petal cuts to shape the flower. After cutting petal shapes, cup both sides of the bow (see Figure D), and carefully fluff out the petals. Holding the floral tape in one hand, wind the tape around the wire stem in a spiral, working from just below the center of the bow tie to the end of the wire (Figure E). Use a delicate touch to separate the layers of tissue paper and make the flower blossom. Place a plastic foam disk in the bottom of an empty coffee can or tall vase suitable for the size of the flowers. If you use a coffee can, cover it with contact paper, jute, or felt. After you have made enough flowers for your design, arrange them by poking their wire stems into the foam. Alternate the heights of the flowers by cutting the wire stems.

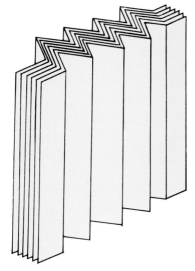

B
Figure B: The first step is to fold six stacked sheets of tissue into even accordion pleats.

C
Figure C: Shape ends of petals by making either semi-circular cuts (left) or pointed cuts (right) on both ends of the tissue paper "bow."

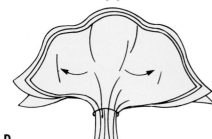

D
Figure D: With fingertips, stretch folds outward to shape tissue paper into a bowl.

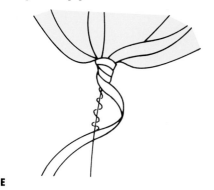

E
Figure E: Use a spiral motion to wrap the entire stem with self-sticking, green floral tape, working from bow to end of wire.

Paper Cutting and Folding
Foil flowers

The stiff, self-supporting sheet aluminum used in foil pans and pie plates can be cut and shaped into intricate flower-like parts. By following these patterns and instructions, you can transform foil into dazzling floral arrangements. Three 8-inch-diameter aluminum pans will yield the twelve flowers shown in the bouquet on the opposite page. Copper foil can also be used to add color, and it is available at hardware or craft shops. One 12-foot roll of 16-gauge aluminum wire for stems; a sheet of broiler foil 12-by-20 inches to cover stem wires; epoxy cement; and long-nosed pliers are also needed to complete the project.

Both the daisies and mums are made in essentially the same way, using three circles of aluminum. Figure F gives a full-sized pattern for the circle that forms the top layer of either flower. Figures G and H are patterns for the second and third layers of the daisy. Figures I and J are patterns for the second and third layers of the mum. Figure K shows how the sections of each flower will be assembled later on a wire stem. Trace patterns onto tracing tissue and transfer them to thin cardboard with carbon paper. Cut out cardboard templates of top layer (Figure F) and petals (Figures G, H, I and J). Lay each pattern on the flat aluminum. With a pencil, outline patterns and cut out aluminum shapes along traced lines. To make the 16 segments shown in Figure F, place the cardboard circle over the aluminum circle and cut through both along the dotted lines. Punch a small hole in the center of each aluminum shape with a scissor point. Cut a 10-inch length of wire to make a supporting stem for each flower.

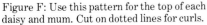
Top

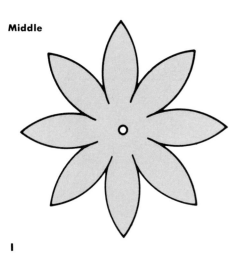

F

Figure F: Use this pattern for the top of each daisy and mum. Cut on dotted lines for curls.

Middle

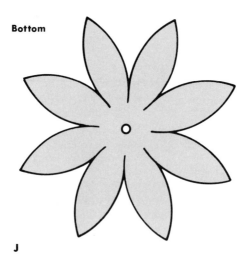

G

Figure G: Use this pattern for the middle layer of petals on a daisy.

Bottom

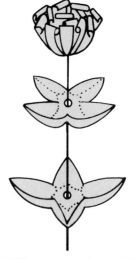

H

Figure H: Make the bottom layer of petals for a daisy from this pattern.

Middle

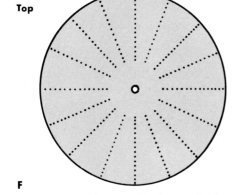

I

Figure I: Use this pattern for the middle layer of petals for a mum.

Bottom

J

Figure J: Use this pattern to make the bottom layer of petals for a mum.

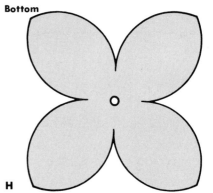

K

Figure K: Middle and bottom layers of daisy or mum slide under top layer and are glued in place.

Shaping and Assembling the Daisy

Curl each segment of the top layer of the daisy upward and inward, using round-nose pliers as in photograph 1. To shape the petals of the middle and bottom layers, grip the centerline of each petal and bend upward. Pinch both halves of each petal inward with your fingers until they almost touch (photograph 2).

Make a small loop at the end of a stem wire by bending it around a pencil. Twist the ends together firmly. Slide the loop off the pencil and bend it at a right angle to the stem. Coat the underside of the loop with epoxy cement. Push the stem through the daisy top (Figure K, opposite) and pull it downward until the cemented surface of the loop is pressed against center of the foil. Ease the curled petals aside with your fingers to allow the loop to pass. Let the epoxy set. Then coat center portions of the top side of the second layer with epoxy and slide it up on the stem until it touches the underside of the top layer. Repeat this procedure with bottom layer, adjusting it on the wire before gluing so that all petals show.

Shaping and Assembling the Mum

Make the top layer of the mum as you did the top layer of the daisy, by curling the petals upward. Alternate upward and downward curls for the middle layer (Figure I). Curve all the segments of the bottom layer (Figure J) downward.

Assemble and cement the mum as you did the daisy, sliding first the top layer onto the stem, then the middle layer, and finally the bottom layer, with epoxy applied where all layers will touch.

Making and Attaching the Leaves

Long curling leaves can be cut from the crinkled sides of the foil pans (photograph 3). Make each leaf about 1 inch wide at its widest point, and about 3 inches long, but with an additional ¼-by-1-inch-long strip at its base. This strip will be bound to the stem after the stem has been wrapped. To wrap the stem cut a strip of aluminum broiler foil ¾ inch wide and 20 inches long. Begin wrapping the stem directly below the bottom layer of petals. No glue is required since the foil conforms to the shape of the wire. Press the foil firmly in place as you twirl the stem. Attach the leaves by twisting the 1-inch strip at their base around the middle of the stem and wrap broiler foil around the juncture of strip and stem to cover. For your floral arrangement, snip the stems to various lengths and stick them into the plastic foam base or clay mound fitted into a suitably sized vase, or tin can covered with contact paper. Cover the plastic foam base with white pebbles or seashells.

1: Curl the petals in the top layer of each flower tightly with pliers. A curled top layer is shown at left. Curl the middle and the bottom mum layers as indicated in text.

2: Bend the center of each daisy petal upward with pliers; push the petals inward with fingertips. Complete petal is shown at right.

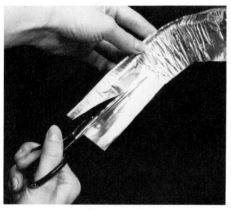

3: Cut long, curling leaves from the crinkled edges of pie pans. The text gives dimensions.

This cocktail table centerpiece started out as four aluminum foil pans left from a meal of TV dinners.

Carl Caronia is proprietor of Caronia and Corless Flowers, Inc., in New York City. Following a family tradition, Carl designs his prize-winning artificial arrangements primarily for stage productions and interior decorators, employing unusual combinations of materials from paper to silk.

Designs and Decorations
Feather flowers

With a bit of ingenuity you can transform household feather dusters into centerpieces of sunflowers, tulips, hibiscus, wild roses or even flowers of your imagination. Feather dusters are available in dime stores or supermarkets, and come in a wide range of colors.

The sunflower shown at left below was made from the individual feathers of a yellow and orange duster. To make the center of the sunflower you need: a round circle 4 or 5 inches in diameter, cut from shirt cardboard; package of split peas, rice, or any small hard beans; white glue; spray can of stain or clear varnish; pipe cleaner; and a desk stapler. Thirty feathers from the duster will each be attached to the stem with a No. 23 floral wire. Self-sticking green floral tape will be wound around an 18-inch garden stake to make the stem. Six leaves for the sunflower stem can be made from crepe paper or green feathers, or you can use artificial leaves from a discarded arrangement. Tendrils can be made by covering a No. 23 wire with brown floral tape and curling the ends around a pencil.

Fold a pipe cleaner in half and bend 1 inch of each tip outward to form a T shape. Staple these tips to the back of the cardboard disk (Figure L). Glue beans on to cover the surface of the disk. When the glue is dry, spray the beans with varnish. Slant the disk at a 45-degree angle. Wrap the loop end of the pipe cleaner around the garden stake and spiral-wrap green floral tape around both.

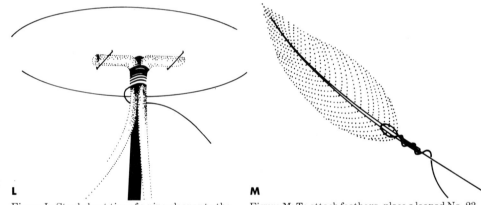

L

Figure L: Staple bent tips of a pipe cleaner to the bottom side of cardboard circle. Wrap a No. 23 wire around the stake tip and pipe cleaner. Twist remaining pipe cleaner around the stake.

M

Figure M: To attach feathers, place a looped No. 23 wire on top of each quill. Twist one end of the wire around quill and loop three times. Wrap wire ends together with brown floral tape.

Split peas and colorful feathers from a household duster were used to make this sunflower. A design like this can be used as a shower gift, a party centerpiece or to decorate a kitchen sill.

Cut the feathers loose at their bases from the duster handle with scissors, beginning with the outer row and gradually working inward. Bend a No. 23 floral wire in half and place it on top of the base of a quill. Wind one end of the wire tautly around the quill three times (Figure M). Keep winding the remaining portion of this end of the wire around the other end of the wire. Cover each quill and its stem wire with green floral tape.

Space ten orange feathers evenly around the center disk so that the end of each one extends about 1 inch beyond the edge of the disk. Bind the wires of these feathers to the garden stake stem with green floral tape. Next mount No. 23 wires on each quill of 20 yellow feathers of about the same size, and round the feather tips with manicure scissors. Arrange ten yellow feathers around the disk, with about 2 inches of the yellow feathers showing beyond the first row of orange feathers. Tape the stems of this second row to the stick stem. Then tape a final row of ten yellow feathers to the stem under the second row. Cover the entire stem with green tape, attaching artificial green leaves or tendrils at intervals, as in the photograph at the left. Feathers attached to wires can be shaped to fill in gaps along edge.

To complete the centerpiece, cover a coffee can with contact paper. Fill the can with cut blocks of foamed plastic to support the sunflower stem and cover the top with artificial moss secured with hairpins.

Orange tulips, two-tone hibiscus and yarn-centered wild roses were made from feather dusters.

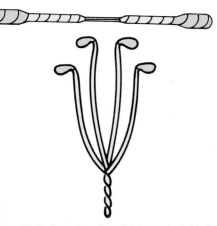

N

Figure N: To form the tulip or hibiscus pistil, bind two No. 23 wires together with four turns of brown tape, thickly covering ¾ inch at each end. Wrap remaining wires with one turn of green tape, leaving 1 inch in the middle bare, as top illustration shows. Wrap another pair of wires in the same way. Bend both pairs of wires in half at the center and twist the uncovered joints together. Bend each brown tip at a right angle and the pistil is complete, as shown.

Tulips and Hibiscus

For the orange tulips and two-tone hibiscus pictured above, you will need: red, yellow, and orange feather dusters; a roll of green floral tape; two dozen No. 23 floral wires; one dozen No. 16 stem wires; and an assortment of artificial leaves from a florist shop or dime store.

To make the pistil at the center of each flower, place two No. 23 wires together and wrap ¾ of an inch in from each end with four turns of brown tape (Figure N). Where the brown tapes stop, start wrapping with one turn of green tape toward the center of the wires, but leave 1 inch uncovered in the middle. Repeat the process with another pair of No. 23 wires. Then, fold both taped pairs in half, and twist the uncovered sections of wire together several times. Bend the brown tip of each pistil outward at a 90-degree angle. Place the twisted joint of the pistils beside a No. 16 stem wire and tape the two together with green tape.

To complete the feather tulip, cut seven orange feathers and attach them to No. 23 wires, as shown in Figure M, opposite. Cut each feather of the tulip to a point with scissors (see orange tulips in photograph above). Space the orange feathers evenly about the pistil, and secure them to the stem, using green tape. Wrap the entire stem with green floral tape. Then bind the wire bases of three slender artificial leaves spaced along the stem with green floral tape.

To make the hibiscus, proceed as you would for the tulip; however, instead of orange feathers, use the tips of five red feathers, 2 inches long, in the first row, and five yellow feathers, 4 inches long, spaced evenly underneath.

Wild Rose

Three-ply, yellow ochre colored wool yarn is needed to make the centers of the roses in the photograph above. Wind the wool about four fingers twelve times. Gather the wool together by wrapping a No. 23 wire around the midpoint of the wool and twisting the wire on itself several times. With scissors, cut all the wool loops apart to form fringe (Figure O). Place twisted wire ends alongside a No. 16 stem wire and tape the two together. Attach No. 23 wires to five red feathers (see Figure M, opposite). Space each feather petal around the trimmed, fringed center. Join feathers to the stem with green floral tape, then continue to wrap the entire stem. Position leaves along the stem and bind them in with green tape.

O

Figure O: To form a fringed center for the wild rose, secure a dozen loops of yarn in the center with a No. 23 wire; then cut through the loops.

Both roses are formed around cotton-ball centers covered with red crepe paper as described in the text. Large rose has six small, seven large petals; small rose has two small, two large petals.

Crepe paper flowers

The elasticity of crepe paper makes this material ideal for stretching and sculpting into more natural floral formations. The rose (left) and tulip (opposite) were made with red, yellow and green crepe paper, white glue with a brush, No. 23 floral wire, No. 16 stem wire or No. 18 garden stakes, white and green floral tape, cotton balls and scissors. The patterns shown (Figures P, Q and R below, and T and U on page 696) are actual size, so simply trace them onto cardboard as explained on page 688. Then cut out the cardboard, trace around it on the crepe paper and cut out the paper. Crepe paper has a grain, so be sure to use the paper so that its grain runs along the length of the petals and leaves.

Rose

To make the center for a rose, cover a cotton ball with a piece of red crepe paper, close the opening with a No. 23 wire and attach it to a No. 16 stem wire with green floral tape. For the large rose shown in the color photograph left, cut six small petals and seven large petals from red crepe paper following the patterns in Figure P. For the small rose shown, cut two small and two large petals. Place your thumbs in the middle of each petal and cup it by stretching the crepe paper outward (photograph 4), then bend the tips of each petal backward by rolling the paper (photograph 5) much as you would curl a ribbon. The curved petals will stand away from the center like those of a fresh rose. Use a brush to apply white glue 1 inch from the base area of each small petal. Hold the bud on the wire upside down and begin to glue on small petals first; then do the larger petals. Be sure to space the petals evenly about the center. Avoid getting glue on the outside of the flower. When all petals have been attached, accordion-fold a 3-by-20-inch piece of green crepe paper, as in Figure B, page 689, for the calyx (cup-like leaves at the base

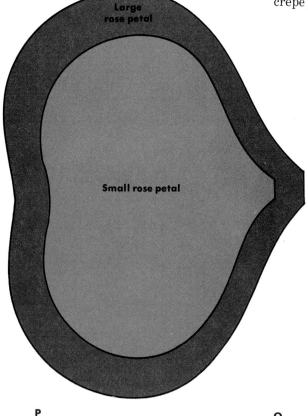

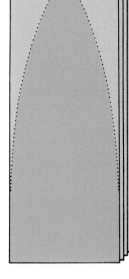

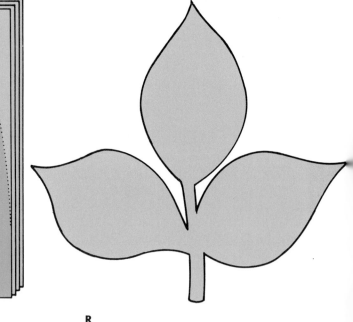

P

Figure P: Rose petals are made by tracing these shapes. For the small petal pattern follow the inside curved line, for the large petal pattern follow the outside curved line.

Q

Figure Q: Cut this curved shape from the accordion-folded crepe paper to make calyx to cup each flower. Cut only along dotted lines, leaving base area of folded paper joined together.

R

Figure R: Cut four of these rose leaves for the stem of each rose. Then, glue a wire between each pair of leaves so you can attach them to the stem and position them easily.

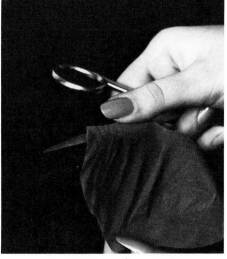

4: Cup each rose petal by stretching the crepe paper with your thumbs in an outward motion.

5: Use a scissor blade or the side of a pencil to curl the edges of the rose petals outward.

With supporting wire loops in each petal (see Figure S), and wire sandwiched into each leaf, you can mold this crepe paper tulip with ease.

of each flower). Each pleat should be about 1 inch wide. To make the calyx, cut along the curved dotted lines shown in Figure Q (opposite) leaving about ¾ inch of the folded paper still joined at the base of the calyx. Unfold the stack of crepe paper, and spread white glue ½ inch from the joined base of the paper. Wrap the calyx around the bottom of the large outer flower petals.

Next, cut two pairs of leaves from green crepe paper (Figure R). Glue each pair with a wire sandwiched vertically between. Allow 2 inches of wire to protrude.

In a spiral motion, wrap the entire stem with green floral tape. Start taping at the base of the calyx and work downward. Attach the leaves to the stem at intervals by wrapping each wire joint in with tape. Freshen the completed rose petals and leaves by shaping them with the edge of a scissor or your fingertips. One or two romantic roses will look attractive in a crystal bud vase. A grouping of roses designed in contrasting colors can be secured in a foam block that has been placed in the bottom of a tall container. Inexpensive arrangements like this can be used on numerous occasions.

Tulip

Actual-size patterns for tulip leaves and petals shown above, right, are given in Figures T and U on page 696. These patterns can also be used to make fabric flowers, using the methods described on page 696. Make pistils in the same way as for the feather tulip (Figure N, page 693). Bind the twisted wire of the pistil base to a No. 18 garden stake with spiral-wrapped green floral tape. Cover four individual No. 23 wires with white floral tape so the wire will not show through the yellow crepe paper petals. Bend each wire in half and form an oval loop (Figure S), and twist wire tips together to close.

Cut eight tulip petal patterns from yellow crepe paper (Figure U, page 696). Sandwich each wire loop (Figure S) between a pair of petals and glue in place. Space the four completed petals evenly about the pistil. Join the petal wires and pistil wires to the garden stick with floral tape. Glue one side of a 1-by-20-inch piece of green crepe paper and spiral wrap it around the entire stem. The wire inside each petal will allow you to bend it upward. Curl petal tips with the side of a pencil.

Cut four slender leaf patterns (Figure T, page 696). Sandwich a wire 9 inches long between each of the two pairs so it runs down the center of the leaves but stops about 1½ inches from the leaf tip. Attach one leaf to the stem 5 inches down from the petals by wrapping and gluing a piece of green crepe paper around the wire joint. Place the second leaf 2 inches below the juncture of the first leaf and stem. Cover the second leaf joint and the remainder of the stem with crepe paper. Bend the leaves so that they branch and curl as in the color photograph above, right. Fix your tulip into a block of foamed plastic that has been placed within a clay pot. Cover the foam with moss as you did for the sunflower.

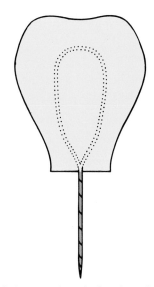

S

Figure S: A supporting wire loop is sandwiched between two tulip petals. Bend a No. 23 wire wrapped with white tape to make the oval loop. Twist the ends of the wire together; then glue on the petals with the loop between.

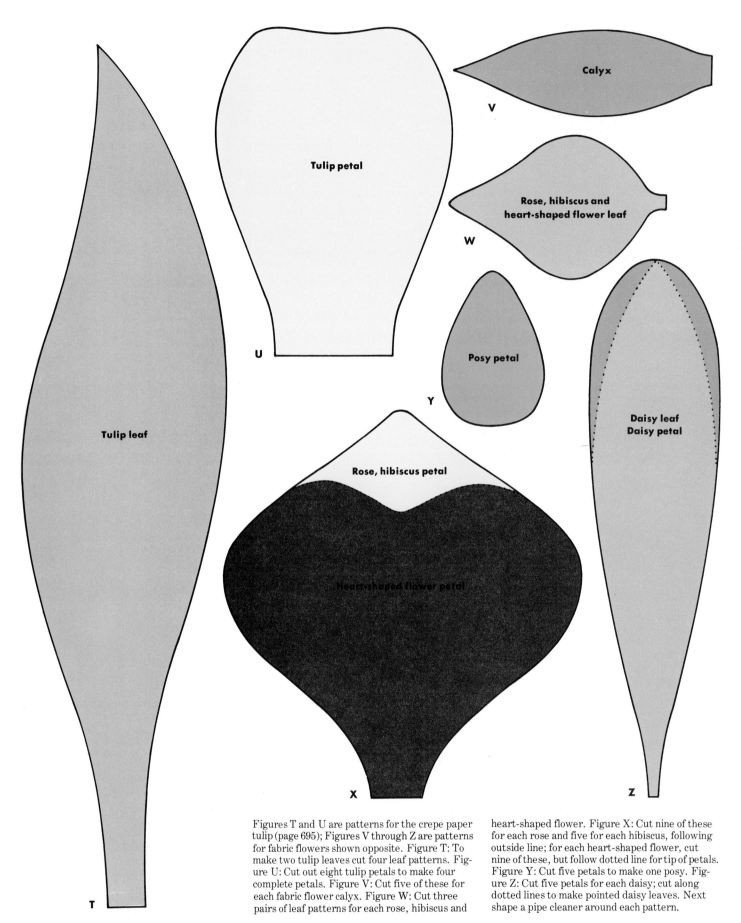

Calyx

V

Tulip petal

Rose, hibiscus and heart-shaped flower leaf

W

U

Posy petal

Y

**Daisy leaf
Daisy petal**

Tulip leaf

Rose, hibiscus petal

Heart-shaped flower petal

X

Z

T

Figures T and U are patterns for the crepe paper tulip (page 695); Figures V through Z are patterns for fabric flowers shown opposite. Figure T: To make two tulip leaves cut four leaf patterns. Figure U: Cut out eight tulip petals to make four complete petals. Figure V: Cut five of these for each fabric flower calyx. Figure W: Cut three pairs of leaf patterns for each rose, hibiscus and heart-shaped flower. Figure X: Cut nine of these for each rose and five for each hibiscus, following outside line; for each heart-shaped flower, cut nine of these, but follow dotted line for tip of petals. Figure Y: Cut five petals to make one posy. Figure Z: Cut five petals for each daisy; cut along dotted lines to make pointed daisy leaves. Next shape a pipe cleaner around each pattern.

This basketful of gingham flowers shows the petal shapes you can use to make imaginative roses, daisies, hibiscus or simple posies.

Designs and Decorations
Fabric flowers

¢ ⊠ 🚶 🧑

Scraps of leftover fabrics are ideal for making cloth flowers. You can coordinate flower colors with draperies or bedspreads for a special effect. Or you can create a patchwork design by using a variety of fabrics in one flower.

To make eight of these flowers of gingham (as pictured above) or other fabric, you will need ½ yard of material; 1½-inch-wide cloth ribbon; five dozen chenille or extra-thick pipe cleaners; three dozen No. 23 wires; one dozen No. 16 stem wires; green floral tape; white glue with brush; four feet of yellow ochre-colored wool yarn; and scissors. Select a container which will harmonize with the arrangement. Place a foam block cut to size within the vase to support flower stems.

The center of a rose is a foamed plastic sphere about 1 inch in diameter, covered with 4-inch-square fabric (photograph 6). The posy's center is a small wad of cotton, covered with 2-inch-square fabric. To secure the material, wrap a No. 23 wire around the base twice. Make a daisy center of yarn as you did the wild rose center (Figure O, page 693). A hibiscus center is made with three pipe cleaners. Using your thumb and forefinger, wind each end of each pipe cleaner on itself four times. Fold the pipe cleaner in half to create two pistils with curled ends. Fold the second pipe cleaner at one-quarter its length and the third at one-third its length to vary the length of the pistils. Attach completed pistils to a No. 16 stem wire with green floral tape.

Transfer petal, calyx and leaf patterns onto cardboard (Figures V to Z, opposite). Each cardboard pattern acts as an edge or template against which you can fit and shape a pipe cleaner. Bend a pipe cleaner in half; align the bend with the apex of each petal or leaf and shape the pipe cleaner around each edge of the template (Figure AA). Twist the pipe cleaner closed twice at the base of the pattern and clip any remaining pipe cleaner strands. Lay the ironed cotton fabric on a flat surface. Brush glue onto one side of the pipe cleaner and place it directly upon the material. When the glue dries, cut the petal or leaf from the fabric, following the pipe cleaner outline. Attach a No. 23 wire to each petal and leaf (see Figure M, page 692). For each flower cut five separate calyx patterns from cloth ribbon. Space petals evenly around either the plastic sphere center or the pistils (depending on the flower), and wrap in place with floral tape. Then glue calyx pieces around the base of the petals. The wire within the pipe cleaner will allow you to shape each petal and leaf. Complete wrapping the stem and attaching leaves with floral tape.

For related projects and crafts see "Dried Flowers," "Origami," "Papier Mache," and "Shells."

6: To make the center of a rose, hibiscus, or a flower with heart-shaped petals, push a No. 16 wire through a 1-inch foamed plastic sphere and cover it with a piece of fabric. Wrap a No. 23 wire below the sphere to secure the cloth to the wire stem.

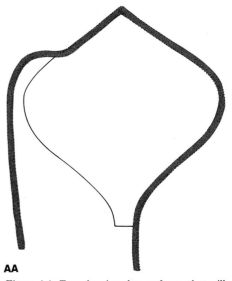

AA

Figure AA: To make pipe-cleaner frame that will hold fabric taut, bend cleaner in half; then, with bend at apex of flower or leaf, shape cleaner around perimeter of each petal and leaf cardboard pattern. Twist pipe cleaner closed at petal base.

697

FOAM FORMS
Expandable Enjoyment

Manny Turano is an award-winning architect. He was the chief architect responsible for designing the spectacular Pan American Airlines terminal at New York's Kennedy Airport. As innovator in the use of materials, he was one of the first to see the possibilities in creating assemblages from foam packing pieces. His foam relief sculptures adorn commercial buildings.

Of the many modern expanded plastic materials, polystyrene foam is the one most readily available to home craftsmen. Used in making drinking cups, egg cartons, ceiling tiles and packing insulation, it can easily be reworked into many useful, interesting or amusing things for the home. The material retards the passage of heat and sound and is surprisingly sturdy for its light weight. It adapts well to craft projects because it can be easily cut or shaped with a knife, and then painted or sprayed to the color desired.

The projects that follow show how to make functional and decorative objects from plastic foam. One is a modernistic assemblage, made of foam packing pieces, that can serve as a wall sculpture or free-standing structure. Another (page 701) is a mysterious-looking lamp, made of foam cups, that demonstrates the translucent quality of thin sections of plastic foam. Still others (page 702) show you how foam cups can be transformed into holiday decorations.

A Foam Mixture That Hardens
Two additional projects (pages 704 and 706) introduce you to a lightweight expanded mixture that, when it hardens, resembles rock rather than a soft plastic. As the projects show, you can carve the material into a primitive-looking sculpture, or mold and incise it to simulate a form of prehistoric cave art. The projects you can make with this mixture, molds, and sand impressions are limitless.

This 40-by-40-inch wall hanging is made of salvaged foam packing pieces. Artfully arranged, these painted pieces were glued to a canvas frame to make an eye-catching structure.

Assemblage of foam pieces ¢ ⌧ 🏃 🎨

The next time you unpack a new television set, phonograph or camera, don't discard the molded plastic foam pieces you find in the carton. These packing pieces are designed to protect the merchandise from damage during shipment, but they can also be used as decorative objects. The pieces come in an endless variety of sizes and curious, irregular shapes; arranged and mounted, they can be made into an abstract sculpture like the one shown on the opposite page. The actual assembly of a sculpture is disarmingly easy; the artistic merits of the finished work will depend on your talent and imagination.

Before starting a sculpture, you will need a good number (at least 20) of the packing pieces from which to choose. If you alert your friends, they can help you assemble a collection of assorted shapes and sizes.

To make a wall sculpture, such as the ones shown on these pages, you will need, in addition to the foam pieces, which come in a great many sizes, something on which to mount them. Artist's canvas, already stretched on a frame, is available in an assortment of sizes at an art-supply store, but scrap lumber will do if you cut it to the measurements of your canvas. The canvas-covered wood frame can be hung as is, or it can be edged with 2-inch-wide strips of ¼-inch plywood, as in photograph 1, to give the mount greater depth when placed on a wall. This trim is essential on mural-size constructions made by joining several 40-by-40-inch modules, but is optional on smaller assemblages.

Materials and tools required include: 1- or 2-inch nylon paint brush; and a quart of black or white flat latex or acrylic paint. In experimenting with various kinds of paint, I found that latex metal primer adheres well to polystyrene foam. Last minute touch ups can be made after all pieces have been glued to the mount.

With the nylon paint brush, apply primer to the front and edge surfaces of the canvas mount. Only one coat is needed, and it will dry in about 30 minutes. Clean up any spills quickly with a damp rag. This paint can be removed with water when wet, but is almost impossible to remove once it has dried. Clean the brush with warm water and scouring powder.

1: To provide a mount for a 40-by-40-inch assemblage that will stand out from the wall, nail 2-inch-wide strips of wood around the canvas-covered frame you purchase or make.

2: Paint all surfaces (except the back) of any packing pieces you wish to use. The latex metal primer paint used here goes on easily, dries quickly, and will cover foam with one coat.

When the painted mount has dried, select your foam pieces and arrange them, flat side down, on the canvas. Take a great deal of time to select, reject, and rearrange the pieces until you are satisfied with the composition. Arrangements can be symmetrical or asymmetrical, have boxes glued within boxes, have pieces that extend beyond edges, even have bits of the background peeking through.

With the 2-inch brush, paint all of the pieces you have selected for the sculpture (photograph 2). Don't paint the backs of pieces that will be glued to the canvas. Allow paint to dry for one hour. Where pieces can be paired off so that they can be attached to the mount more readily as a pair, glue corresponding edges together before mounting. When you are ready for mounting, spread glue over the back of each piece and press in place on the canvas. Let glue dry for about one hour. To hang, attach two screw eyes to the back of the mount and run wire through loops.

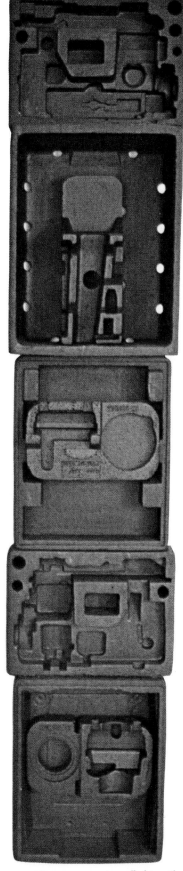

Five separate canvases were nailed together to make the frame for this wall assemblage.

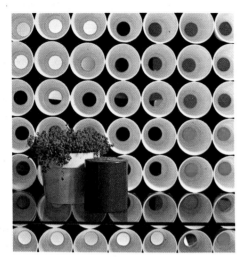

A wall hanging made with foam cups is decorative and, if large enough, it may even help to absorb some noise. The foil at the cup bottoms, reflecting light and color, adds sparkle to a room.

Glass and Plastics
Foam cup constructions ¢ ☒ ♦ 🔥

Of the many objects made from molded foam, insulated drinking cups are probably most often a part of our everyday lives. We use them for coffee and other drinks—hot or cold—at parties and socials. But it might not occur to us that they can be made into decorative objects with scissors and glue. I have used them to make lamps, wall panels, whimsical holiday decorations, and gift-package trims. Directions for all of these follow, but they are only a small indication of the many things you can fashion with this throwaway item.

Wall Hanging
Foam-cup wall panels can be small, decorative hangings such as the one shown in color, left, or they can cover most of a wall. To make a foam-cup hanging, you need a panel of heavy cardboard, fiberboard, or ¼-inch plywood on which to glue the cups. Use a panel of any size, or hang a number of panels to decorate an entire wall. Sixteen 9-ounce cups will cover 1 square foot of paneling. If you want to paint the board or cups, use an acrylic or latex spray paint; other finishes might erode the plastic foam. You also need a yard of silver or gold foil (with or without adhesive backing), scissors, adhesive tape, pencils, and white glue.

Paint the mounting panel and set it aside to dry. If you prefer colored cups, spray-paint them inside and out; set them aside to dry. With scissors, cut a foil disk to fit into the bottom of each cup. Make a cardboard pattern so you can cut several disks at once.

To make a tool for picking up a foil disk and placing it on the bottom of a cup, drape a 2-inch length of adhesive tape, sticky side out, over the eraser end of a pencil. To hold the tape in place, twist ends so their sticky sides face in, and press them firmly against the pencil.

3: Use a pencil with adhesive tape covering the eraser, sticky side out, to pick up foil disk and position it in the bottom of each cup.

4: Glue cups to the mounting panel in straight rows. A small amount of glue at the center of each cup's bottom is enough to hold it.

Place foil disks shiny side up on your work surface. Pick each one up by lightly touching it with the adhesive end of the pencil. Apply a drop of glue on the center of a disk (or remove the protective backing to expose the adhesive surface). Then center the disk at the bottom of a cup. Use the eraser end of another pencil to press the disk in place. Repeat until all cups have foil bottoms.

Place your mounting panel flat on the floor or a table. To attach the cups to it, put glue on the bottom of each cup and press it gently onto the board. Place cups in neat, straight rows. Continue until the board is covered. Don't move the board until the glue has dried (at least 30 minutes). In the photograph, silver foil disks reflect the pink and blue colors of the room.

Globe Lamp

The globe lamp shown below is one of my favorite projects because it is easy to make and inexpensive. It glows with a soft, diffused light, and its design is handsome. The simple form of this glowing lamp made of white foam cups will harmonize with the decor of almost any room in your house. The angled side of a foam cup gives the lamp its spherical shape; if you place one cup against another, side to side, and keep adding cups, it is impossible not to arrive at a sphere.

You need about 125 nine-ounce cups to make a sphere that will measure about 22 inches in diameter. You also need eleven 48-inch rolls of white foam tape that is double-sided (self-sticking on both sides), and a narrow lamp fixture that measures, with the light bulb in place, no more than 10 inches tall. Since it will be hidden inside the sphere, you can use a discarded lamp in good working condition, or buy an inexpensive one at a variety store. You will need a line switch on the electric cord rather than the usual switch below the light bulb, so you can turn the lamp on and off without removing it from the foam sphere. Use a bulb no larger than 25 watts; heat from a brighter bulb might melt the cups. This is not a study lamp; it furnishes soft illumination.

To start the sphere, press a 1-inch length of double-sided tape on a cup's outer side just beneath the rim, and another just above the cup's bottom edge. Press a second cup firmly against the first at the tape points. Add a third cup by placing tape at rim and bottom, as before, but this time on the two sides where the third cup would meet the first two (photograph 5). Continue in this manner—always making sure the tops and bottoms of the cups are aligned—until a sphere is formed. Provide a 6-inch opening for the lamp by leaving out the last two or three cups; then, set the globe over the lamp base, Figure A. Place the base so the 25-watt bulb will not touch or be close to any cups.

5: To build up a sphere, you simply keep adding cups, attaching each one to the adjacent cups. Make sure bottoms and rims of cups being joined align, and press each cup firmly in place.

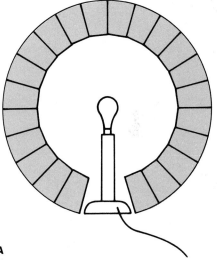

A

Figure A: After foam-cup sphere has been assembled, it is placed over lamp fixture.

This lightweight foam-cup construction becomes a contemporary lamp when set over a lamp base. The globe lamp emits a soft atmospheric glow that is not intended for reading.

Seasonal decorations for gift packages and Christmas-tree ornaments can be made from plastic foam cups. The pieces are cut from foam and glued in place, with sparkle and color added.

Designs and Decorations
Gift and Christmas trims

The thin material of plastic foam cups can be cut almost as easily as construction paper; its lightness and stiffness make it ideally suited for three-dimensional decorations and trims. Several simple foam decorations are shown in color, left, or you can let your imagination take over with designs of your own.

Materials you will need are: A supply of 9-ounce cups (a package of 50 will give you a good start); replaceable-blade knife; pinking shears and scissors; two or three sheets each of tracing and carbon paper; green and blue acrylic spray paint; white glue; red and green sequins; a package of yellow pipe cleaners; some yellow rickrack; one sheet of yellow construction paper; three 12-inch lengths of ribbon in any colors; a 6-by-20-inch piece of red felt; an 8-inch wooden dowel; short lengths of red and gold decorative cord; 6- or 8-inch foam tree form; and a small Christmas ball. Gift wrap and ribbon in solids or prints will complement the decorations.

For all of the items in the photograph—with the exception of the basket-weave cup tree ornament—cut off the bottom and the rim of each cup used with the replaceable-blade knife. Then cut straight up the side with scissors, and open up the cup by gently pressing the foam on a flat surface with your fingers. Don't try to flatten it completely or the foam will break.

Actual-size patterns for the decorations pictured are on these two pages. Trace onto tracing paper and transfer them to the foam with carbon paper. Then cut them out with scissors, and they will be ready to be glued together. Note that some patterns have been superimposed on others.

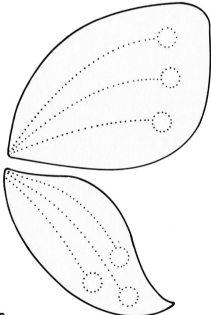

B

Figure B: Trace over these butterfly wing patterns and transfer to foam with carbon paper. Turn pattern over for facing pair of wings. (Dotted circles and lines indicate where rickrack lines and round dots will be added later; do not cut them out.) Cut outlines of wings with scissors and glue edges together where they would meet to form a complete set of wings. Align two yellow pipe cleaners and bend them to form butterfly body and antenna (see photograph above). Glue body to butterfly where wings meet, and add a sequin to form the head of the body. Glue lines of yellow rickrack and small circles, cut from a separate piece of foam, to locations shown by dotted lines.

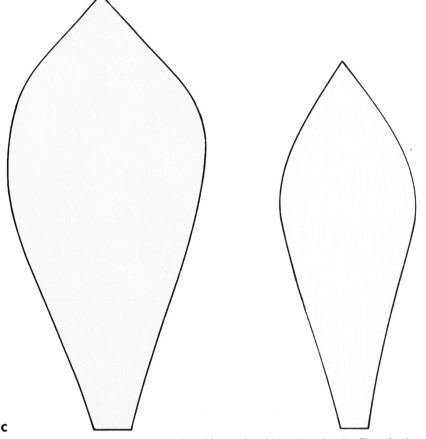

C

Figure C: These two patterns make petals and leaves for white poinsettia trim. Transfer the patterns and cut out six large and six small petals. Lightly score veins in them, using the point of a closed pair of scissors. Paint two or three of the larger petals green. When these have dried, glue all of the petals to each other (green petals at the bottom), spacing them to make the shape shown in the color photograph. Glue five or six red sequins at the center of each flower.

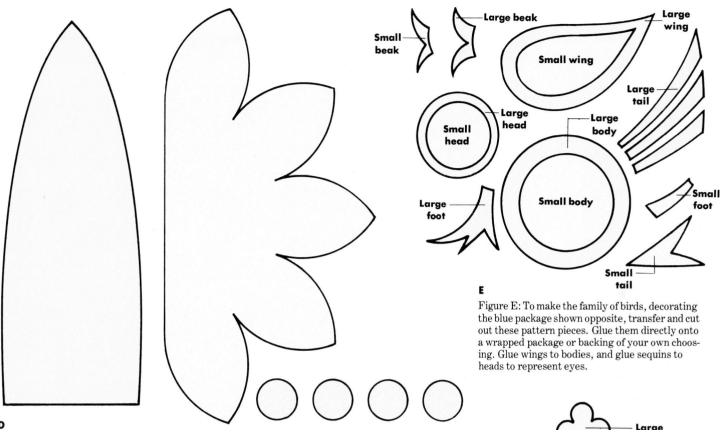

E

Figure E: To make the family of birds, decorating the blue package shown opposite, transfer and cut out these pattern pieces. Glue them directly onto a wrapped package or backing of your own choosing. Glue wings to bodies, and glue sequins to heads to represent eyes.

D

Figure D: Above, left to right, are patterns for the water lily's petal, calyx, and four circular pistil tips (see color photograph opposite). Trace and transfer patterns to foam with carbon paper; turn half calyx pattern over to get second half of pattern. Cut out 10 petals, calyx and four circles. Glue ten ¼-by-3½-inch strips of yellow construction paper with tapered ends down the center of each petal. Use green acrylic paint to cover calyx. When the paint is dry glue five upright petals around the center of the calyx and five more around the first circle. Run the ends of four 3½-inch lengths of yellow pipe cleaners through the center of the flower base and bend tips on a right angle to secure. Fit four foam circles over pipe cleaner tips.

G

Figure G: These small (inside line) and large (outside line) leaf patterns are used to make the small white tree and to decorate the sides of the blue tree ornament-both shown in the color photograph opposite. For the small tree, trace and cut out about 30 large and 30 small leaves. Glue them to a 6- or 8-inch foam tree form, starting at the bottom, alternating and overlapping rows of small and large leaves as you work up the tree. Glue sequins to branch tips and a small Christmas ball at the top. To make the blue and white ornament, glue mouths of two cups together. Paint them and let dry. Trace and cut four large leaf patterns for each cup. Glue a large leaf each quarter turn.

F

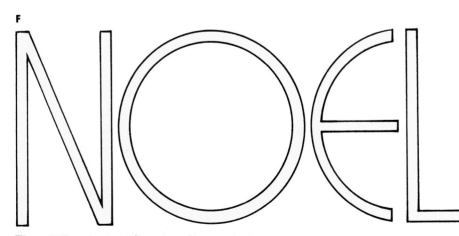

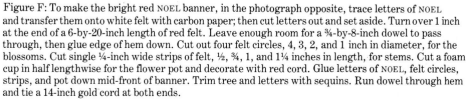

Figure F: To make the bright red NOEL banner, in the photograph opposite, trace letters of NOEL and transfer them onto white felt with carbon paper; then cut letters out and set aside. Turn over 1 inch at the end of a 6-by-20-inch length of red felt. Leave enough room for a ¾-by-8-inch dowel to pass through, then glue edge of hem down. Cut out four felt circles, 4, 3, 2, and 1 inch in diameter, for the blossoms. Cut single ¼-inch wide strips of felt, ½, ¾, 1, and 1¼ inches in length, for stems. Cut a foam cup in half lengthwise for the flower pot and decorate with red cord. Glue letters of NOEL, felt circles, strips, and pot down mid-front of banner. Trim tree and letters with sequins. Run dowel through hem and tie a 14-inch gold cord at both ends.

703

Carving and Molding
Synthetic stone giraffe

¢ 🕐 👫 🏠

The material used for this project and the one following it is a lightweight, carvable, moldable substance that looks like rock. The ingredients are available at hardware stores that carry gardening supplies. It is an inexpensive craft material, weatherproof enough to be displayed outdoors or in. It can even be painted if your imagination calls for colored rock. This is the same kind of material often used to simulate rock formations on stage sets and in outdoor, full-scale reconstructions such as those the late Walt Disney inspired.

You can carve a sculpture similar to the giraffe shown below by enlarging and tracing the pattern in Figure H onto a block of synthetic rock made from the recipe given on the opposite page. You probably have all the tools you need for the project around the house.

Dr. Robert Peters of U.C.L.A. began working with the synthetic rock formula described in this project as another application of his wood carving skill. Some of his carvings from wood and artificial stone have been exhibited in art galleries and pictured in magazines.

This primitive-looking giraffe was carved from an expanded synthetic rock made from a simple recipe of ingredients available in hardware and garden supply stores. Use pattern on grid, right.

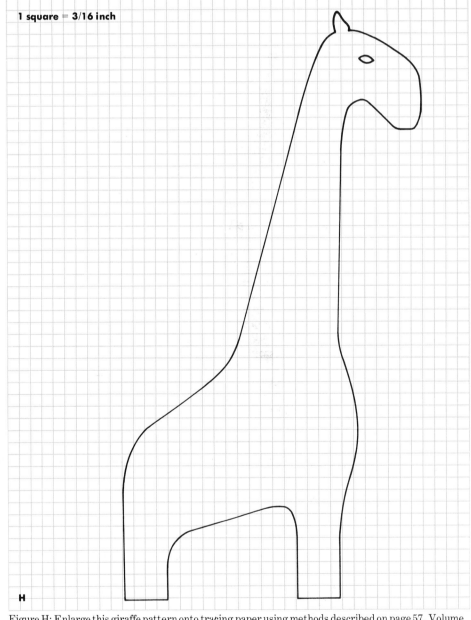

1 square = 3/16 inch

H

Figure H: Enlarge this giraffe pattern onto tracing paper using methods described on page 57, Volume One. Then transfer the pattern through carbon paper to each side of a block of synthetic rock, making sure that the patterns on both sides face the same way.

Tools: A cup measure; piece of scrap wood to use as a scraper and pulverizer (a piece of 2-by-4, about 4 inches long, does nicely); plastic bucket or large mixing bowl; large, strong mixing spoon; paring or pocket knife; pencil or ball-point pen; tracing paper and carbon paper; ½-gallon milk carton cut in half lengthwise; cardboard box about shoe-box size; medium-fine sandpaper.

Materials: At least 3 pounds of agricultural vermiculite. This is a very absorbent silicate mineral derived from mica, used primarily as an artificial soil for starting plant seeds and cuttings. Gardening supply centers and some hardware stores generally sell it in 1-pound bags. You will also need 2 cups of plaster of paris; 3 cups of patching cement—the kind sold by hardware stores for patching sidewalks, driveways, patios and other cement repair jobs; a small bottle of white glue; and a spray can of clear acrylic or polyurethane. The basic recipe for this expanded synthetic rock is: two parts ground vermiculite; two parts plaster of paris; one part patching cement; and enough water added to that mixture to make a thick, creamy syrup. For this giraffe project, mix in plastic bucket or mixing bowl 6 cups of the ground vermiculite, 6 cups plaster of paris and 3 cups patching cement. Add water slowly while stirring with the mixing spoon until the mixture is creamy enough to pour into the wax-coated milk carton you have cut in half lengthwise (photograph 6). Allow two days for the mixture to harden. If you do not use a waxed milk carton as a form, line a box with waxed paper to keep the hardened mixture from sticking to the sides of the container. It is important to clean all tools immediately after using, otherwise the mixture will harden, making it difficult to remove. Rinse your utensils and bowls out-of-doors; the mixture may clog drain pipes.

6: This shows the consistency of the synthetic rock mixture when it is ready to pour into the half milk-carton form to harden.

Carving the Giraffe

Tear the milk carton away from the hardened block. Enlarge the giraffe pattern (Figure H) onto transparent tracing paper. Place carbon paper between the tracing and one side of the block and re-trace the pattern. Trace the same pattern onto the other side of the block. The head of the giraffe should face the same way on both sides of the block and the feet should touch the bottom of the block.

7: Carve the hardened rock by taking many shallow, successive cuts as you work your way in toward the pattern outlines. Use knife point to make eye indentations.

Cut into the block, following the pattern, with the pointed blade of a stiff-bladed paring or pocket knife. Make shallow cuts, gradually working in deeper and deeper from both sides until the cuts meet and the giraffe form is freed from the block. Shape the rough-cut form by carving (photograph 7). Then use medium-fine sandpaper to smooth the contours. Don't expect to get fine details. This medium produces a rough-hewn look. To repair any broken pieces apply white glue to both surfaces, wait until it is tacky, press the pieces together and wipe away any excess glue. Fill holes with a mixture of plaster of paris and patching cement in equal parts moistened with water. After any repairs have set, spray with clear polyurethane or acrylic to help weatherproof and protect the surface. If you choose to paint the artificial stone surface, do so before spraying with acrylic.

Carving and Molding
A fish impression

You can also cast the expanded, synthetic rock mixture into abstract shapes in sand, then carve impressions into them to simulate prehistoric pictures of fish carved in real rock. Use the tools, materials and ingredients on the following page to make the fish carving shown below in color. (Pattern of fish skeleton on opposite page is general guide; use as much or as little detail as you like in your carving.) The preceding two pages give details about the expanded rock mixture ingredients and where to get them.

Tools and materials: Shallow, round bowl or pan 10 inches in diameter filled with sand; cup measure; mixing bowl; mixing spoon; pencil; small paint brush; ½-inch nail; scrap of wood; drill with a 1/16-inch bit; saw; wire coat hanger; wire-cutting pliers; tracing and carbon papers; medium-fine sandpaper; white glue; and a spray can of clear acrylic or polyurethane. Ingredients: ¾ cup vermiculite; ¾ cup plaster of paris; ¼ cup plus 2 tablespoons patching cement; 2 tablespoons of paprika.

This fanciful fish is carved with a nail point into a light-weight synthetic stone made from inexpensive modern materials available in hardware and garden supply stores. The rock has been tinted with a mixture of paprika and water, as if it had been stained with iron oxide.

Casting the Rock

Fill a shallow, round bowl or pan with sand. Dampen the sand with water and press it flat with your hands. Then round out an oval depression in the center of the sand roughly 6 inches long by 3 inches wide. The depression should be about 1½ inches at the center or deepest point, and slope gently upward from that point.

Combine the expanded-rock ingredients in a bowl, as described in the instructions for the giraffe project, on page 705. Spoon the creamy mixture into the sand depression until it is filled (photograph 8), being careful not to mix it with the sand on the depression walls. After two hours, remove the molded shape from the sand. Brush off sand particles with a paintbrush, and pare off rough edges or bumps with a sharp knife. Set the rock aside for two days to harden.

Making the Fish Impression

Transfer as much of the actual-size pattern (Figure I) as you want onto the flat side of the rock by tracing the pattern through carbon paper. Cut the outlines for the fish into the rock by drawing a sharp nail several times along the lines until the strongest lines of the pattern are about ⅛ inch deep (photograph 9).

8: Make an oval depression in the sand about 6 inches long and 3 inches wide. Spoon the mixture into it without disturbing the sand.

9: After having traced the fish directly on the fully hardened mixture, use a sharp nail to carve out the outline and details.

10: To give the finished piece a reddish cast, dampen it and rub paprika into it with your fingers. Then spray with acrylic for protection.

Carvings can be made in stones of almost any color. If you want to give the carving a reddish tint, as if the rock had been stained by iron oxide, first dampen the incised surface with water; then sprinkle some paprika over the surface and rub it into the impression and the pores and crevices of the rock with your fingers (photograph 10). After applying the paprika and while the surface of the rock is still damp, spray it with six coats of clear acrylic or polyurethane. Allow 15 minutes drying time between coats or follow the directions on the label. This heavy application of acrylic or polyurethane will protect the paprika finish and give a slightly milky cast to the rock surface, contributing to an aged appearance. Let the final coat of spray dry for at least 24 hours before handling to avoid embedding fingerprints.

Mounting Stand

Cut a 7-inch length from a piece of 1½-by-2-inch scrap wood. (The dimensions don't really matter if it is wide enough to be stable and thick enough to seat the wire firmly.) Sand the rough surfaces. Drill a ½-inch-deep hole in the center of one of the 2-by-7-inch surfaces with a hand or power drill fitted with a 1/16-inch bit. Drill the same size hole ½ inch deep into the center of the bottom surface of the synthetic rock. Glue 2-by-7-inch piece of felt to block bottom to protect display table.

Cut a 2-inch piece of straight coat-hanger wire, and apply white glue to both ends. Insert one end into the hole in the rock and the other into the hole in the wood block. Bend the wire if necessary to make the rock balance. Let the glue set overnight before handling the finished display.

For related crafts and projects, see the entries "Carving," "Casting," "Christmas Celebrations," "Dioramas," and "Sculpture."

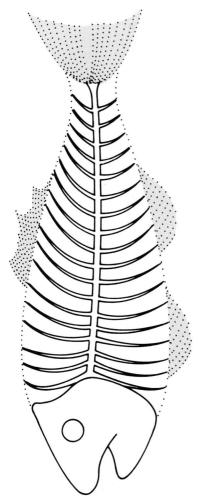

I

Figure I: A fish skeleton reproduced actual-size for the project on these pages.

FOLK ART
Designs That Celebrate Nature

Barbara Auran-Wrenn designs craft kits, and lectures and writes on contemporary crafts. As an indication of her wide-ranging interests, Barbara describes for this entry the decoration of native objects by Pennsylvania Germans and the painting of Senufo wall hangings by African tribesmen.

The folk artist, wherever he lives, adopts the animals, flowers, and other natural objects around him as the inspiration for his decorative motifs. His imagination may create strange looking animals, people or plants you have never seen. Still, you can appreciate the way these figures, worked into vivid designs, often became powerful symbols of faith or superstition.

The projects on the following pages provide examples of diverse, but in some ways parallel, folk art in different lands. You can decorate documents and furniture with unicorns, distelfinks (thistlebirds or finches), tulips and other motifs that fascinated German immigrants who settled in Pennsylvania in the eighteenth and early nineteenth centuries. The motifs they used are shown here and on pages 710 and 711. Or you can paint your own *kohorgo* wall hanging by imprinting imaginative animals on coarsely woven cloth (page 714); this is an art form practiced by Senufo tribesmen from Africa's Ivory Coast today. You can also make the mobile weather vane silhouette featuring sprightly reindeer described on page 716. Laplanders used similar designs on weather vanes, barns, and other buildings. Finally, you can create your own folk art, adapting some of the familiar motifs shown on pages 712 and 713.

Paint and Color
Making a fraktur trauschein ¢ ▨ ♀ ⬚

During the eighteenth and nineteenth centuries, Germans emigrating to Pennsylvania (commonly called the Pennsylvania Dutch, after the word *Deutsch* meaning German) to escape religious persecution brought with them a highly developed folk art. One example of it was *fraktur Schriften* (meaning broken writing, so called because of the sharp, angular lettering used). This was a blend of folk designs with Germanic script, as shown at left. *Fraktur Schriften*, or *Fraktur* as it was more commonly called, was adapted from the quill-lettered script and brush-painted designs of medieval German illuminated church manuscripts. By the middle of the eighteenth century, *fraktur*-style decorations were being applied to personal documents, furniture, glass, pottery, linens and even buildings.

A favorite candidate for *fraktur* art was the marriage certificate or *Trauschein* (from *Trauung* meaning marriage and *Schein*, meaning certificate). These certificates were often decorated with an expanded heart flanked by the wedding couple as shown opposite. To make such a *Trauschein*, trace the patterns shown opposite, or develop your own design, using motifs shown on pages 712 and 713. You won't need the goose quill pen, plant pigment inks and rag paper used by the original *fraktur* folk artists. But you will need 8½-by-10-inch sheets of tracing paper and carbon paper; a piece of 12½-by-15-inch mat illustration board; a ruler; pencil; gum eraser; stylus; black ink; masking tape; No. 1 and No. 3 sable brushes; paper towels; and tempera paints for your design. I used yellow ochre, olive, rust, sky blue, orange, black and white. Local art supply stores stock the matboard, brushes, stylus and paint.

Lightly tape the tracing paper over the illustration opposite, so it won't shift as you draw. Copy the outline of the heart, the figures, tulip, and arch. Then lightly mark horizontal guidelines for the written inscription. Lift the tracing paper off. With a ruler and pencil rule a border two inches in from the top and sides of the illustration board and three inches in from the bottom. Lay the carbon paper within the border of the illustration board and center the tracing over it; tape both down. With a dull hard pencil or stylus, impress the pattern onto the surface of the board. Using the illustration opposite as your color guide, paint the designs. With a stylus dipped in black ink or a black ball-point pen, write in script the couple's names, and the date. Use gum eraser to remove pencil marks and the certificate is complete.

German colonists in the U.S. often commissioned artists to design birth certificates or *Taufscheine* (from *Taufe* meaning baptism, and *Schein*, meaning certificate) for their newborn. This *Taufschein* was lettered and painted in *Fraktur*, a style named after the sharp, angular lettering used. (The German word *fraktur* means to break or fracture.) Inscribed on the certificate are the child's name, birthdate and a brief family history.

Barbara Gordon
Paul Carpenter
~married~
May 1
·Anno 1974·

Figure A: The bride and groom, expanded heart and tulip shown here were popular *Trauschein* motifs. Other motifs commonly found were trumpeting angels, shooting stars, and doves.

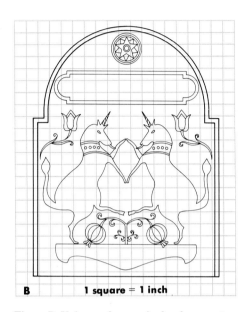

B   1 square = 1 inch

Figure B: Unicorns shown paired and rampant were a favorite dower chest motif. Occasionally they were shown singly, with a lion or horse opposite them. Unicorns were supposed to be drawings of rhinoceroses artists had heard about but never seen.

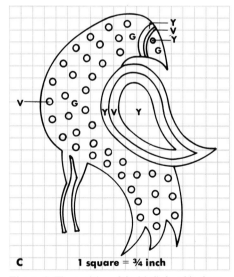

C   1 square = ¾ inch

Figure C: The position of the bird's head is characteristic of the distelfink or goldfinch design used by the Pennsylvania Germans on their wares. Other popular bird motifs included doves, eagles, pelicans (as symbols of maternal devotion), and paired robins (as lovebirds). Color key to paint enlarged distelfink is Y, chrome yellow, V, vermillion and G, olive green.

710

D

Figure D: Tulips and unicorns (the traditional guardians of maidenhood) were popular motifs on dower chests. The owner's first name was often lettered free-hand in a blank bar below a hex sign. Hex signs were geometric designs intended to attract good luck (in this case, make the sun shine), or to ward off such trouble as demons and lightning.

Furniture Refinishing
Decorating a hope chest

A *fraktur* marriage certificate, or *Trauschein*, as used by the Pennsylvania Germans, was traditionally pasted inside the lid of a dower chest. This was a hope chest designed to serve both romantic and practical functions. When a young girl reached marriageable age, she stored linens and laces inside the chest. After marriage, in a couple's sparsely furnished dwelling, the chest doubled as a seat by day and a child's bed at night. It also served as a trunk when goods had to be transported. The bride's father or the decorator who designed her marriage certificate applied appropriate motifs to the chest. These symmetrical designs were scratched into the wood's surface with a metal stylus or painted freehand. Some typical designs for such a chest are shown on these two pages. The front of the chest opposite consists of three evenly spaced arched panels. Sometimes additional single panels were applied to each end of the chest. On more elaborate chests the front middle panel bore the bride's first name as on the unicorn panel opposite, and sometimes the date and year of presentation. Inscriptions were often bordered by tulips, hearts, and unicorns (the traditional guardians of maidenhood).

Undecorated dower chests can sometimes be found at country sales or in antique shops. Furniture stores stock unfinished storage chests which approximate the 22-by-28-by-48-inch size of the chest in the color photograph below. To paint the background and feet of such a chest, you will need one quart of primer and about two quarts of oil base paint. Raw umber paint was used for the background color of the chest below, but barn red, dark green and dark blue are also traditional colors. You will need to mix a pint of white and ½ tube of raw umber paint to paint the background of each panel ivory. Limit yourself to five colors for ornamentation so your design doesn't become too busy. Oil-base yellow ochre, Prussian blue, vermilion, chrome yellow, and olive green are suggested colors. To thin paint and clean brushes you will need 12 ounces of turpentine. Other essentials are: a 2-inch nylon paint brush; a No. 4 sable brush for designs; masking tape; ruler; compass; 3 sheets of 14-by-20-inch carbon transfer paper (dressmaker type); 3 sheets of 14-by-20-inch tracing paper; plenty of rags and newspapers. Place the chest in a large, well-ventilated space that can enable you to work on several sections of the chest simultaneously and decrease drying time of painted surfaces.

Spread newspapers over your work area. If you are working with raw wood, seal the surface of the wooden chest with a coat of primer. (To restore the surface of an old chest, see Furniture Refinishing on page 726 of this volume.) To use the unicorn/tulip design (Figure B) for your center panel and the small tulip design (Figure E) for your side panels, trace the designs on tracing paper and enlarge them as indicated following instructions on page 57, Volume One. Lay the chest on its back and tape the enlarged tracing of each panel with a piece of carbon underneath it to the chest front. Leave 2½-inch spaces at the sides and between each panel. The midpoint of the top rounded arches on each panel should be located four inches below the chest lid. Trace only the outlines of each panel. Remove tracing. Cover background of chest outside the panel areas with two coats of raw umber paint and fill in each panel with two coats of ivory. Allow two days for the paint to dry between coats.

Retape tracings on top of carbon transfer papers to chest so that panel outlines match. Then transfer outlines for designs within panels. Use illustrations (Figure D and Figure F) for color guides as you paint in the design details.

To decorate the ends of the chest, enlarge the distelfink design (Figure C) by tracing it on a grid according to instructions on page 57, Volume One. Transfer the design to the ends of the chest as you did the front panels. Center each design five inches from either edge of the chest, with the top of the bird's head four inches below the top lid. To paint the bird, use vermilion, olive green and chrome yellow oil-base paint, as indicated in Figure C.

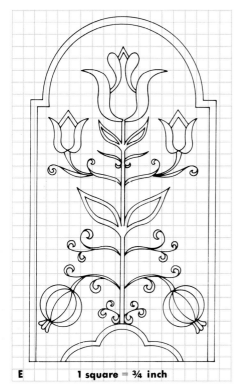

Figure E: Tulips symbolized the Trinity. This design, enlarged to scale shown, can be used for two smaller panels flanking a unicorn center panel on your dower chest.

Tulips growing out of slender urns were painted on each arched panel to decorate this antique eighteenth century Pennsylvania German dower chest. Vines and leaves tie together the design. You can decorate a similar chest using the unicorn panel (opposite) and the tulip panel (right).

Figure F: Follow this color scheme to paint tulip panels after tracing design on chest.

711

Native Decorations

In many lands magic and fertility cults developed which were accompanied by folk decorations. Today, most of these cults have disappeared, but we can still enjoy the expression of these early myths through native designs.

G

Figure G: The tulip is a familiar folk art motif throughout Central Europe and in America. When used in groups of three, it was originally thought to represent the Holy Trinity.

I

Figure I: Roumanian folk artists gave the round sun human facial qualities. It symbolized life, energy and a good harvest, and was a widely used decoration on linens and clothing.

J

Figure J: Roumanians painted delightful blossoms with graceful leaves on their wares. Peasants would design plants and flowers in hope that the sun would induce a plentiful harvest.

H

Figure H: Flowers like this were commonly embroidered on Ukranian linens. Flowers were associated with curative powers, the promotion of good health, and the encouragement of sunshine.

K

Figure K: The silhouette of this rooster was cut from paper and decorated with colored paper shapes. Poles associated the rooster with fertility and hung these bird designs in their homes.

Figure L: This water buffalo design is a tribal motif taken from an appliqued umbrella. African kings gave umbrellas decorated with such motifs to brave warriors.

Figure O: This bird, which was sewn on a towel, has a golden crown that suggests power. It is a Ukranian motif believed to attract good fortune and repel evil forces.

Figure N: This version of a folk art heart is believed to have originated in Russia. Folk artists from many lands use heart motifs as a symbol of fertility, good crops and love.

Figure M: Spotted reindeer detail was hand-painted on a Roumanian plate. The designs that accompany the reindeer on the dish recount the story of a famous hunt.

Figure P: This is a Kurbits, a large flower drawn by Swedish folk artists as a symbol of the flower thought to have protected Jonah from the sun as he wandered through the desert.

Paint and Color

Senufo wall hanging

$ ● 👥 🎨

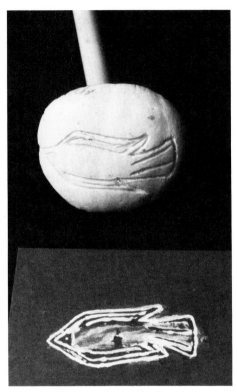

African craftsmen make stamps like this one carved from dried gourds to reproduce designs. Bamboo handles allow the artist to roll the stamp in dye and apply the design onto cloth.

Senufo is the name for the designs members of the Senufo tribe on Africa's Ivory Coast apply to wall hangings and ceremonial garments. For their motifs, they use stylized birds, chameleons, fish, and masked dancers, and figures of mythological origin, as in the illustration opposite. Senufo wall hangings are prized today for their lively, dramatic graphics.

The original Senufo cloth was made from long, narrow strips of coarsely woven cotton (called *korhogo*). The strips were sewn together and tacked to a board with nails. Figures were temporarily sketched with a dull knife dipped in a yellow-green dye extracted from boiled swamp leaves. Once the design was complete, a permanent black dye made from strained mud was applied over the sketch outlines with a metal or wood knife. To reproduce designs quickly stamps were often carved from dried gourds to print designs much as we carve linoleum blocks today. Designs were cut into the skin of the gourd; then the stamp was rolled in the dye and pressed onto the fabric to make a print, as in photograph at left.

To make a Senufo wall hanging you will need a 32-by-50-inch piece of white burlap, a work table or a piece of ¼-inch plywood at least 30-by-48-inches on which to tack the stretched burlap; two sheets of carbon and tracing paper 32-by-50-inches to transfer designs (you may have to tape two 16-by-25-inch sheets of each paper together to get a large enough piece). I used a black waterproof marker to fill in the Senufo (photograph below), but you can use any colors. Other essentials are: two 1-inch steel nails; two ¾-inch wooden dowels 48 and 50 inches in length; 40 thumbtacks or pushpins; a needle and white thread. Press burlap to remove all wrinkles. Use thumbtacks spaced 4 inches apart to fasten burlap to wood along the top edge. Pulling burlap taut as you go, fasten sides down with tacks spaced 4 inches apart. (Don't pull so hard that cloth fibers are separated.) Tack along bottom, stretching and smoothing fabric as you go.

Trace the patterns from the grid shown opposite onto tracing paper and enlarge them, following instructions on page 57 of Volume One. Place the carbon paper face down on the burlap, then lay enlarged pattern over the carbon and tape the pattern lightly to the burlap to hold in place. Using a pencil, transfer the enlarged patterns onto the burlap working from top left to right, then bottom left to right. Check underneath the carbon to make sure pattern is transferring to the cloth. Fill in patterns with waterproof marking pen using broad strokes, as in photograph below. Allow ink to dry for several hours. Conceal raw edges by basting a 1-inch closed hem on both sides of the Senufo. Next, turn over and sew hems along the top and bottom of the cloth but leave 1 inch open in each hem. Push the 48-inch dowel through the bottom hem and the 50-inch dowel through the top hem. Display the Senufo by resting the top dowel on two nails spaced 47½ inches apart.

Use waterproof felt marking pens to fill in figure outlines on burlap. Do stripes next, then fill in the heavy black areas as above. Allow the ink to dry for several hours.

Q   1 square = ¾"

Figure Q: Senufo pattern includes: large and small four-footed chameleons (top right and bottom left); Comoe River fish (lower right); mythological figure and masked dancer (with palm leaf between them, upper left); and guinea hen with beak pointing to small soul bird in flight. Enlarge to scale and center tracing on burlap so you have about a 1-inch hem on all sides.

George Cohen was born in St. John, New Brunswick on the Bay of Fundy. He moved to New York City in 1925 and worked as a fabric and furniture designer. Now retired, he has begun a new career as a sculptor. He works mainly with wood scraps that he collects, assembles, carves and paints. His designs add a touch of humor and sophistication to old-world folk art themes.

Carving and Molding
Reindeer weathervane

The folk sculpture pictured below is an adaptation of a Lapland reindeer design. It can be hung indoors as a wall plaque, or mounted outdoors as a weather vane, as Laplanders mounted theirs atop barns, churches, houses and ships. The decorative weather vanes had to be clearly silhouetted against the sky, so they could be read quickly from a distance. Carved motifs included animals, heraldic designs, biblical figures or trade symbols reflecting the special interests of local craftsmen.

To make the reindeer decoration shown below, you will need a 4-by-36-inch and a 10-by-36-inch piece of 1-inch-thick pine, poplar or maple; a 6-inch length of ⅜-inch doweling; a set square; a calibrated T-square; 4 sheets of medium-fine sandpaper; a vise, two 3-inch C-clamps; cheesecloths; 4 ounces of white glue; two 1½-inch nails; two ½-inch-long screw eyes; a hand jigsaw or sabre saw with a woodcutting blade; a drill with ⅜-inch and ½-inch diameter bit at least 6 inches long. From art supply stores, you will need: 1 pint each of barn red and slate blue acrylic paint, and 2-ounce tubes of yellow ochre, black, and white acrylic; a No. 2 sable brush, a 1-inch bristle brush; 4-by-36- and 10-by-36-inch sheets of tracing paper (you may have to tape several smaller sheets together); 8-by-10-inch sheets of carbon paper; 4 ounces rubber cement and a rubber cement pickup; 3 feet of picture wire.

If you want the reindeer to be a weather vane, you will need: a ½-by-48-inch rustproof metal rod and a sturdy wooden or metal base with a center hole ½ inch in diameter to balance and support the entire structure (hardware or naval supply stores and mail order catalogs for farm equipment carry a selection of manufactured weather vane bases); and 2 pieces of ½-inch-by-6-inch scrap metal for the metal strips to make the bent tail decorations in the photograph shown below.

Clamp the two 36-inch-long boards so their ends are flush. Measure 18 inches in from one end and use the T-square to mark a vertical centerline through both boards. Then, following the instructions on page 57 of Volume One, enlarge the patterns in Figure U, opposite, and transfer them onto tracing paper. Coat one side of the 4-by-36-inch and the 10-by-36-inch pieces of wood and the backs of the base and reindeer tracings with rubber cement. Allow the cement to dry thoroughly. Then, using the centerline marked on the boards as a guide, gently press the 4-by-36-inch tracing for the base and the 10-by-36-inch tracing for the reindeer over the corresponding pieces of wood.

Clamp pieces of wood in a vise and cut along pattern outlines with a jigsaw or sabre saw with a wood-cutting blade. When both patterns have been cut out and rough edges sanded, line up the centerlines and peg marks you had previously

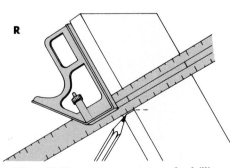

Figure R: Use a set square to transfer drilling marks (dashed lines on pattern, figure U) to the bottoms of the legs and the top of the base.

The carved sculpture above was adapted from a Lapland folk motif. Cut-out areas enhance the profile of the simple design, which can be hung on a wall or mounted as a weather vane.

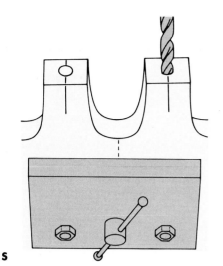

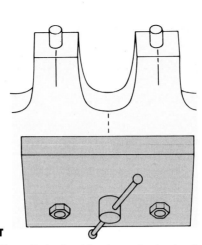

S

Figure S: Drill ⅜-inch-diameter holes ¾-inch deep for the four pegs to be placed in each fore and hind leg of the reindeer decoration. Drill four corresponding holes in the base.

T

Figure T: Apply white glue to the tip of each peg and insert into fore and hind legs of the reindeer decoration. These pegs will fit into holes on the base when you are ready to assemble.

marked on both. Lift off tracing and use rubber cement pickup to remove excess cement. Adjust tracings over cut wood pieces to center circle atop triangle and zigzag designs on reindeer front. Lay carbon paper beneath designs on tracings and use a pencil to transfer designs onto wood surface. Then transfer drilling marks for the location of dowel holes from the side to the edge of each board as in Figure R. Divide thickness of board in half and mark center for drilling.

Drill four ⅜-inch-diameter holes to a depth of ¾ inch at the marked centers in the reindeer legs and base (Figure S). If you are making a weather vane or plan to add curved metal tails as shown in the color photograph opposite, drill a ½-inch-diameter hole through the center of the reindeer and the base. Smooth all rough edges with medium-fine sandpaper.

Cut the ⅜-inch dowel into four 1½-inch lengths. Cover one end of each peg with white glue, then insert one in each of the four legs (Figure T). After cleaning areas to be painted with rubber cement pickup, coat the front and edges of the reindeer with barn red acrylic paint thinned to creamy consistency with water. For an antique finish, streak the painted surface by dragging a cheesecloth across it while the paint is still wet, following the same direction as the wood grain. Allow paint to dry for one hour, then repeat the process on the reverse side. Next coat one side of the base and edges with thinned slate blue paint and streak the surface with a cheesecloth. When the paint has dried, repeat the procedure on the back. Dip a corner of a cheesecloth into thinned black paint and speckle the front and back of the reindeer and base by dabbing cloth against the wood; allow 30 minutes drying time. With undiluted black, yellow ochre, and white acrylics, fill in the details on the reindeer and base with a No. 2 sable brush. Use the color photograph opposite as your painting guide. Apply white glue to the protruding pegs in the reindeer legs and push them into the corresponding holes in the base. Wipe off excess glue. Shape the ½-inch strips of scrap metal to make the curved tail decorations shown in the color photograph. Push them into the top of the hole drilled through the center rump that both reindeer share. To complete the weather vane insert a ½-by-48-inch metal rod through the bottom hole of the base and reindeer. Place the rod within a wooden or metal weather vane base that has a corresponding ½-inch hole long enough to balance the weight of the weather vane. Secure the stand in an unsheltered spot on your deck, roof, or in your garden where the weather vane will be visible from a distance and can revolve freely.

To use the reindeer design as a wall plaque, simply twist two small screw eyes into the middle of the back of the reindeer, spacing them about 13 inches apart. Run a 15-inch length of picture wire through the screw eyes and twist 2 inches of each end of wire around itself, snug at the eye, to secure. Suspend the sculpture from two nails spaced 12 inches apart.

For related entries see: "Antiquing Furniture," "Block Printing," "Calligraphy," "Colonial Crafts," "Furniture Refinishing," "Framing," and "Heraldry."

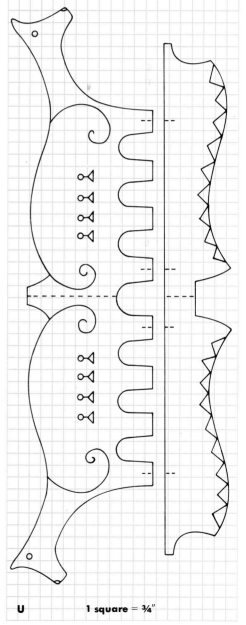

U   **1 square = ¾"**

Figure U: When enlarging and tracing the patterns for the reindeer and its base, be sure that you transfer all design lines and dotted guidelines for the pegs that hold the two parts together.

FRAMING
Completing the Picture

An early use of framing to complement paintings developed in Italy in the thirteenth century. The actual painting surface was hollowed out of a wood panel and the edges of the panel were left at the original level to form the frame. During the Renaissance, the idea of frames as added embellishments came into being. The early Renaissance frame was a small raised edge on each side of a flat panel, but many frames of the later Renaissance used more elaborate moldings that were large, richly carved and gilded. A common finish in Renaissance times was gold leaf on gesso, a plaster mixture applied to seal the wood. In Colonial America, the settlers made beveled moldings from native woods, such as maple and pine. Today many frames have returned to the unadorned simplicity of the early Renaissance.

Harmony of picture and frame is governed by scale and proportion—the balance achieved by the picture and the frame. There are no hard and fast rules but there are several helpful guidelines. The width and depth of the molding determines the visual weight of the frame; it should not seem so heavy that it overburdens the picture. The shape of the molding is also important: a molding with rounded edges works well with a picture having rounded shapes; an angular molding blends with pictures having many straight lines or geometric shapes. The finish should also be compatible with the picture: a burnished wood frame matches warm colors, an antiqued frame goes well with an old print, a narrow black frame sets off a modern print, etching or photograph. Do not use such bright colors that the frame competes with the picture for attention.

A mat, a border cut from heavy paperboard to separate the picture from the frame, creates a visual space that helps isolate the picture; it is particularly useful for artwork that will hang on a wall that is patterned or brightly colored. A mat also makes the finished size larger and more important, if that is the effect you want. Matboard is available in a variety of colors and textures so it can easily harmonize with any artwork or frame.

Sometimes artwork is mounted on a stiff board of paper or foam at least ¼ inch thick; this kind of mounting will support needlework or keep a photograph smooth and flat. Glass is used as a protective covering for a work that might be damaged by dust. Nonreflective glass is available at a glazier; it is more expensive but worth the money if the picture is going to be in direct sunlight or strong indoor light. Glass is not usually used with a textured work such as an oil painting or heavy needlework where the glass could not lie flat against the surface of the artwork. Frames follow furniture styles to some extent, so the decor of the room should be considered. But the primary function of a frame is to enhance the display of the picture it surrounds.

Beth Wigren is a commercial artist and interior decorator who has made a specialty of creative picture framing. She studied art at Rhode Island School of Design and examples of her work have been pictured in books and national magazines.

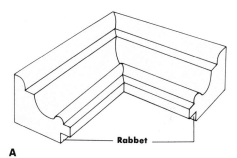

Figure A: Traditional picture frame molding is constructed with a rabbet, the notch that holds the picture and glass.

Furniture and Finishes
Basic wood molding $ ▯ ☂ ⚒

The basic wood frame consists of four pieces of molding joined at the corners with 45-degree mitered joints. This molding has a rabbet—a notch along the inside edge of the back to receive the picture and glass (Figure A). You can buy picture-frame molding sold by the foot at frame shops and lumberyards. You can also make frames from standard trim moldings—the kind used around windows and doors or between wall and ceiling. These are available in a variety of shapes at any lumberyard and cost less than half as much as frame moldings. Some moldings are shaped in such a way that an angle can be used as the rabbet; others have to be combined so that a rabbet is formed. If you have a power saw, it is easy to cut a rabbet. Figure B shows cross sections of many of the common millwork moldings.

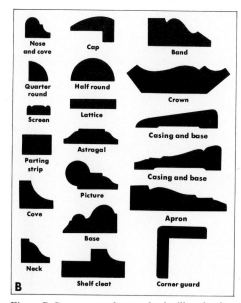

Figure B: Some names for standard millwork trim molding shapes that can be used for framing; they are available at most lumberyards.

Several examples of frames (left) include metal and wood frames that are pre-mitered, or cut to a 45-degree angle at the end. The metal frame has a polished silver-tone finish while the various woods have been painted, stained or simply left natural.

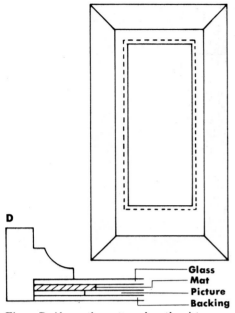

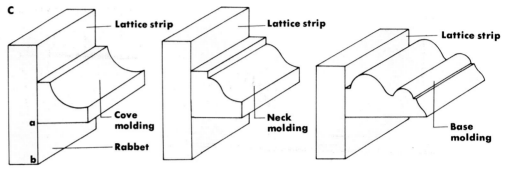

Figure C: Make frame molding with standard millwork trim molding by gluing a lattice strip to the molding to form the rabbet. Measure the combined thickness of the picture, matboard, glass and backing to determine the distance from a to b, which is the depth of the rabbet needed.

Figure D: Above, the mat overlaps the picture at least ¼ inch on all sides. Below, the frame overlaps the mat at least ¼ inch on all sides.

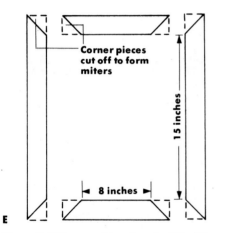

Figure E: If the overall length and width of the matboard (after subtracting twice the rabbet width) is 8 by 15 inches, the minimum amount of 2-inch-wide molding needed is 12 inches for the top and the bottom and 19 inches for each side, or a total for all sides of 62 inches. When buying the molding, allow a little extra for waste.

1: Clamp miter box to work table and use back saw to cut 45-degree angles. Use scrap wood to support rabbet while cutting.

Figure C shows millwork moldings (as shown in Figure B, page 719) in several combinations that create a rabbet.

The first step in making a frame is to decide if you want a mat around the picture (Figure D). To determine mat size, lay your picture on matboard, available at an art supply store, and try placing the molding on the matboard at various distances from the edges of the picture until you have what you feel is a pleasing balance of picture, mat and frame. You can make the mat space equal on all sides of the picture, but it is traditional to use a space one-third larger below the picture. Measure the length and width of the matboard established by your arrangement, and add to it the amount that the molding will overlap the matboard on all sides. This will give you the mat measurements and also those for the cardboard backing and the glass, if you decide to use glass.

The opening in the mat will be the size of the picture minus the mat overlap on the sides. If you are framing a white-bordered photograph, for example, the mat opening should be ¼ to ⅜ inch smaller on each side to cover the white border. Use a square and straight-edge to mark the mat opening in the matboard. Then, using a mat knife or a single-edge razor blade with the straight-edge as a guide, cut out the opening in the mat. If you want a beveled edge, use a heavy metal ruler with a beveled edge, available at art supply stores, and cut the matboard pressing the knife against the slant of the ruler.

Picture glass is thinner and clearer than window glass; you can buy glass cut to size from a glazier. If you cut the glass yourself, make sure the glass is perfectly clean and resting on a flat surface. Use a glass cutter (available in hardware stores) and a hard straight-edge. Hold straight-edge securely and, starting at the far end, draw glass cutter toward you with firm and constant pressure in one straight line. Never go over a cut a second time. To cut the glass after scoring, tap it gently on the reverse side at both ends of the cut (never in the middle) and separate the pieces by bending it slightly downward from the cut.

To determine the amount of frame molding needed, measure the length and width of the matboard (or the picture if you are not using a mat) and subtract twice the width of the rabbet, the amount that the frame overlaps the picture (Figure E). Since the molding is cut at 45-degree angles, you will need more molding than simply the total of all four sides. Add the width of the molding to the side measurement at each corner (Figure E) so the angle can be cut. This will give you the exact amount of molding needed; when ordering, allow a couple of inches extra for saw cuts and waste.

To make the frame in the photograph on page 721, I used cove molding and a lattice strip. When gluing the cove molding to the lattice strip, leave enough space under the cove molding to form the rabbet (at least ¼ to ⅜ inch). To find the exact rabbet depth, measure the combined thickness of the picture, mat, glass and backing. To cut the newly formed molding piece, measure side and top and bottom and cut the ends at 45-degree angles (Figure E). Use a miter box and a back saw to make these cuts (photograph 1). Cut all angles before starting to join. When these molding pieces are joined at the corner, the inside edges should form a right angle. If they don't, minor adjustments can be made by sanding the miters slightly.

2: The finished frame was first painted with red enamel paint. When this red undercoat has dried, the frame is sprayed with gold paint.

3: Then the gold paint, when dry, is rubbed lightly with fine steel wool to let some of the red undercoat show through.

This frame is made with cove molding glued to a lattice strip. The steps in painting the frame are shown in photographs 1 and 2 (left). The warm gold color with a red undercoat showing through harmonizes with the colors in the picture.

When they fit properly, hold both pieces in a vise and attach them with white glue and small brads, two from one side and one from the other. Continue with each corner until all four are joined. Any gaps left in the miters can now be filled with wood putty. Sand the frame and it is ready for paint or other finish. The procedure for applying the red-gold finish that I used is shown in photographs 2 and 3, above.

To assemble, position the picture in the mat opening and secure it all around with masking tape. Put the glass, the mat with the picture, and the cardboard backing in the frame. To hold everything in place, turn the frame on edge and drive tiny brads into the frame's rabbet on the side that is down (or use a brad pusher). Turn the frame and drive brads every 4 inches along each side. Apply masking tape to seal the space between cardboard backing and frame; this will keep out dust. Measure one-third of the distance from the top of the frame down each side, insert tiny screw eyes and attach a light wire between them. When pulled taut, the wire should reach to about 1 inch below the top of the frame.

Furniture and Finishes
Metal frame

$ ▯ 👥 ✈

The modern look of a metal frame is appropriate for photographs, abstract paintings or modern needlework in contemporary room settings. A metal frame is basically the same as a wood frame except that the mitered corners are joined by metal clips rather than being nailed or glued. And the glass, picture and backing are held in place with spring clips instead of brads.

Pre-mitered metal moldings, cut in a variety of lengths in 1-inch intervals, are available in art supply and department stores. They are made of aluminum and come in several finishes: shiny metal, burnished metal, black, white and colors. The moldings also come in wood and plastic finishes, but these may not be as readily available. The moldings are sold in packages containing two pieces of molding of the same length, corner clips and back spring clips. Two packages, one for the sides and one for the top and bottom, are needed to make one frame. The size shown on the package is the inside measurement, the length of the edge which will be next to the mat or picture. Follow the assembly directions on the package.

Metal frame moldings can be sawed to odd sizes. If, for example, you want the inside edge of the molding to be 13½ inches long, buy the next larger size and cut it down, using a miter box and a metal-cutting hacksaw. You can spray paint the frame in any color you choose.

Glass, mat and backing cardboard should be cut to fit inside the frame. They are held in place by spring clips which bridge the corners. Some use screws; others clip into the molding. Metal molding systems include special clips to hold the hanging wire. Use the screws provided to screw these into the groove in the back of the frame and string a wire between them.

The impact of the primary colors of red and blue and the clearly defined shapes of this modern print are enhanced by the straight, thin lines of the metal frame.

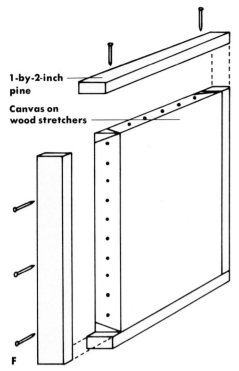

1-by-2-inch pine

Canvas on wood stretchers

F

Figure F: A simple stick frame can be made with wood strips nailed directly to the wooden "stretchers" used to hold the canvas taut.

Furniture and Finishes
Stick frames

$ ⬛ 🚶 🏄

Easily assembled stick frames can be made with simple, unadorned wood strips available at any lumberyard. They are informal, so they go well with casual room settings. Joints are butted instead of mitered, thus calling for much less precision in woodworking. At its simplest, a stick frame is merely a wood border nailed directly to canvas stretchers, the wood supports of an oil painting (Figure F). Or a stick frame can be a combination of lattice and pine as shown in Figure G, and the photograph below. I framed a paper print by first gluing it to a block of ¾-inch-thick plywood. Plywood, tempered hardboard, and pressed wood are good because they resist warping. A color illustration from a magazine can be attached to a piece of plywood several ways. One is the white-glue-and-white-shellac method. Start by cutting the plywood to size with a fine-tooth saw that will not leave a ragged edge. Trim the magazine illustration to the same dimensions as the plywood. Dilute white glue, using two parts glue to one part water and brush onto the back of the illustration. Turn it over carefully and lay it on the plywood, using the palm of your hand to smooth out air bubbles. Leave face up for 20 minutes until the glue dries. You can make the illustration more durable by coating it with shellac. Build up several coats, allowing each to dry before applying the next.

Alternatively, there are several commercial products that you can use. One makes a plastic decal out of printed material by the application of several coats of the liquid. When dry, the paper can be peeled off the plastic and the ink will remain embedded in the plastic. The decal can then be glued to the wood. This works well with art prints, newspapers, magazines, and documents, but cannot be used on glossy photographs, engraved invitations or varnished paper. Another product, a combination adhesive/sealer for decoupage work, combines the gluing and shellacking steps in one procedure.

Another version of a stick frame, made with lattice strips and 1-by-2-inch pine boards, is an inexpensive frame for an illustration from a magazine mounted on ¾-inch plywood. The method of construction is shown in Figure G.

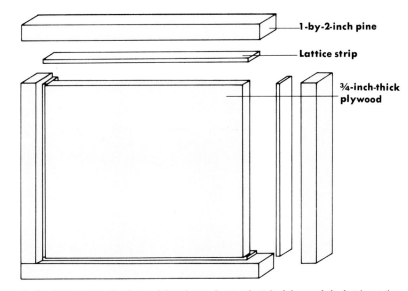

G

Figure G: Mount the lattice strips so the front of the plywood extends ¼ inch beyond the lattice strips. Mount outside 1-by-2-inch pine pieces so they extend ¼ inch in front of the picture.

Once the picture is in place and protected with finish, paint plywood edges a color that will contrast with the color of the frame. In this case white gesso was used. Next, cut ¼-by-1⅛-inch lattice strips to lengths that fit around the plywood rectangle; the vertical pieces match the height of the plywood and the horizontal pieces extend to cover ends of the vertical pieces (Figure G). Nail these pieces to the plywood edges so they are recessed ¼ inch in from the front of the plywood backing on which the picture is mounted. Paint front edges of the lattice strips with white gesso. Then cut the 1-by-2-inch outer frame pine pieces to fit around the recessed frame. Paint inside surfaces of the pine pieces with white gesso. Then nail pine pieces around the lattice frame, with top and bottom pieces overlapping side pieces as shown. Let the front edges protrude ¼ inch in front of the picture surface (Figure G). Paint the front edges and outside faces of the outer pine pieces a color that harmonizes with the picture. Put screw eyes into the plywood back one-third of the way down from the top to hold the hanging wire, and the frame is finished.

A three-dimensional effect is created by placing a ¼-inch-thick spacer between the photograph of a little girl in a garden (which has been mounted on foam core board) and weathered barn siding.

Furniture and Finishes
Barn siding background frame ¢ ☒ 👫 ✈

Using barn siding as a background frame for a photograph as shown above right, provides an interesting blend of colors and materials. The weathered wood, stained or left natural, enhances the feeling of an informal outdoor portrait.

Photographic color prints should be mounted on ¼-inch foam core board. With a single-edge razor blade, cut the mounting board and the photograph at the same time so the edges match and paint the edges of both the print and the mount black. Mount the photograph with special spray adhesive for photographs which is available at art supply stores or camera shops. Spray the back of the photograph and the mount, wait until almost dry and press the photograph in place. Weight the photograph down for 3 minutes until the adhesive is dry. Cut a piece of ¼-inch foam board 1 inch less in each dimension than the photograph to use as a spacer between the mounted photograph and the weathered board. Position the photograph so the background board provides an attractively balanced matboard effect all around the print and mark the position lightly in pencil. Then center the spacer in this marked area and attach it to the siding with glue or small nails (Figure H). Attach the photograph's foam core board to the spacer with white glue and join them to line up with the pencil marks. Leave the assembly face up for several minutes until the glue dries. Then add a screw eye to the center of the wood's top. Such background frames can be used in other ways. A single long board can be hung horizontally or vertically with many photographs mounted on it.

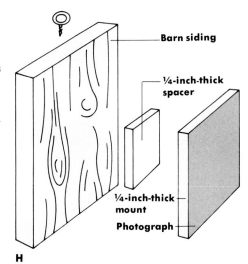

H

Figure H: A spacer, ¼ inch thick and 1 inch smaller in length and width than the foam core board backing for a photograph, is positioned between the photograph and weathered barn siding.

723

A refinished antique typecase is filled with dried beans, pasta, dried flowers, old bottles and buttons, and bits of ribbon and fabric to create a nostalgic box frame.

Furniture and Finishes
A box frame $ ▨ ⚐ ✈

Small three-dimensional objects can be displayed and preserved within a box frame. Such frames are often used to display collections of coins and butterflies. Box frames may be built in two ways. One way uses a molding with a deep rabbet, a spacer between the glass and the background, and some method of holding the samples against the background (Figure I). The other has glass held in place by corner pieces (photograph opposite). As the drawings below show, you can use stock moldings from a lumberyard to frame the display and hold the glass in place.

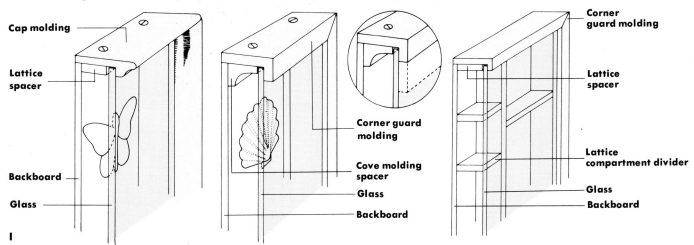

I

Figure I: A box frame can be built with the glass held between a cap molding and spacer strip, as at left. Or you can use a cove molding and corner guard molding to hold glass (center) and trim off one side of corner guard as shown in the inset. A compartmented box frame (right) has an assembly of lattice-strip shelves added to the basic unit.

To make a box frame, cut the moldings first, mitering the corners, and fasten them together with glue and brads. Cut a backboard of plywood so it will fit inside the frame, then set it aside. Have picture glass cut to fit inside frame against the inside rabbet created by the frame molding. Then cut spacer strips to fit inside the box frame against the glass. These can be lattice strips or cove molding. With frame face down, put the glass in place and press the spacers against it to hold it tight. Clamp the spacers in place while you fasten them to the molding frame with two or three screws on each side, turned in from the outside. Drill pilot holes for flat-headed screws and countersink the heads so they are flush; they must be short enough so they do not show inside the box. The backboard may be left exposed or covered with a background material suitable for the objects being displayed. Objects being displayed can be attached to the backboard with pins if you use a glued-on fabric. Or you can use wires through the backboard, or screws driven into the backboard, or simply glue the objects to the board. Use any method that will hold them securely while the box is in a vertical position. To secure the backboard to the frame, place brads flat against the backboard and tap them into the molding.

Box frames need not have only one compartment. For example, an old typecase can be refinished and used to display small objects on a wall, as in the photograph opposite. Here, the compartments are varied in size for a pleasing effect. The pasta and dried beans contrast nicely with the old bottle and buttons. The glass fits on top of compartment dividers and inside the outer frame, where it is held in place by brass corners, purchased at a hardware store.

Or you can build your own compartmented box frame. Use the construction described above, but add lattice strips, nailed and glued together, to make compartment dividers. The shelving should be built as a single assembly that will slip inside the box frame from the rear and rest securely against the glass. Simple butted joints, glued and fastened with wire brads, will do the job. Fill the compartments from the rear, then add the backboard.

FURNITURE REFINISHING
A Restorative Art

John Savage is a versatile craftsman who keeps busy exploring new and rediscovered craft frontiers. He is the author of numerous magazine articles, and of books on subjects ranging from bicycling to furniture repairing and refinishing.

Few workshop satisfactions equal those of uncovering the beauty in old furniture, so often buried under layers of varnish or paint—or even grime. If the original finish is largely intact, restoring it may be easier than you expect. Often a good cleaning—with minimum surface disturbance—is all that is needed to reveal the warm glow of the original piece. At other times, blisters, cracks, or other large mars will obviously call for stripping off the old finish down to the bare wood and applying a new finish.

The expert refinisher avoids over-restoring, which can reduce the value and beauty of a piece. He starts by cleaning the surface, identifying the type of finish, and testing its adhesion. He then determines if burns, chips, gouges and other blemishes can be treated as spot repairs. (See Craftnotes, pages 730 and 731, for techniques for making such repairs.) The tests and inspections reveal how large a job lies ahead. They are simply made. But, as with any operation involving finishing materials and cleaning solvents, do such work in a clean, warm, well-ventilated place, with no sources of flame or sparks nearby, and keep all containers covered when they are not in use.

Cleaning and Testing the Surface

To remove surface wax and dirt, wipe the piece with turpentine, mineral spirits, or a commercial wax remover. Don't use a floor cleaner that might leave a residual wax layer. To find out what kind of finish is under the wax, first rub a clean cloth soaked in denatured (not rubbing) alcohol over an inconspicuous place. Let alcohol remain on surface. If, after five or ten minutes, the finish dissolves enough for the cloth to pick it up readily, it is shellac. If the finish seems little affected, repeat the procedure with lacquer thinner. If the treated surface dissolves readily in five or ten minutes, the finish is lacquer. If the finish is still not affected, it is probably a form of varnish. To determine whether an opaque finish is an oil-base enamel or a lacquer, rub it with lacquer thinner; this will soften lacquer completely but disturb only the surface of enamel.

Because shellac and lacquer can be dissolved, you may be able to repair the surfaces of shellacked or lacquered furniture without stripping them bare. But if the finish is varnish, you may have to strip the piece with varnish remover, as I did the washing stand opposite. Minor blemishes in varnish can be disguised as indicated in the Craftnotes, pages 730 and 731, but extensive surface flaws call for complete refinishing.

How well the old finish adheres may also determine the need for stripping. If the surface seems sound, scrape a large coin across an inconspicuous area while you apply some pressure. If the surface powders but does not chip, you still have a good enough bond to forgo complete refinishing.

Changing the appearance of the piece, or using a different type of finish on it, usually calls for stripping and refinishing. To change the color of the wood, see the section on Staining, page 733. If you are thinking of changing the type of finish, some modern ones such as the penetrating resin oils and the polyurethanes provide tempting alternatives to traditional finishes. Among the latter, it's true that shellac is easy to apply and dries quickly. It is easy to repair (if not old or impure when applied). It adheres well, resists abrasion, rubs to a fine finish, and has excellent clarity. But it is also readily marred by moisture, heat, alkaline solutions, alcohol, nail polishes, and other solvents. And shellac may darken if it is continuously exposed to bright light.

In the last half-century, lacquer largely replaced shellac and traditional oil varnish

Refinishing with a modern penetrating resin-oil finish and no stain worked wonders for a battered old washing stand (inset). The aging mahogany varnish was removed, revealing handsome walnut wood and matched veneer paneling. Missing wood was replaced, new hardware was added, and a marble top was obtained from a local gravestone supplier to complete the stand's rebirth.

as a commercial furniture finish. It provides a hard, clear, reasonably durable surface that resists water and heat and, in some formulations, alcohol and acids. But it is less flexible than other finishes, hence may crack or check more readily. And it dries so quickly that it is harder for the inexperienced to handle.

The common oil varnish gives furniture a tough, durable surface that, when properly applied, emphasizes grain and warms wood colors well. It can be glossy or dull, depending on your preference. But many varnishes must be applied very carefully and, since they dry slowly, they tend to collect dust in the process.

The old natural oil finishes—such as linseed oil—are handsome, but proper application takes a lot of time and rubbing, and the oil does not protect the wood as completely as alternative finishes.

Of the many modern finishes available that let the wood's grain show, two are of particular interest to home furniture refinishers: the new penetrating wood finishes and the clear polyurethanes. Both resist scratches, abrasion, stain, chemicals, water and heat. The penetrating finishes are sometimes called Danish, tung-oil, or resin-oil wood or floor finishes. Neither the penetrating finishes nor the polyurethanes require preliminary sealers. Both may be applied on bare wood (they will darken it slightly) or over certain stains for color tones or to emphasize the grain. The penetrating finishes leave the wood with the non-glossy look characteristic of natural oil finishes used on gunstocks and fine furniture to accent the beauty of the grain. Surface appearance may range from wood that seems unfinished to wood with a soft sheen, depending on the product's application.

In contrast to the penetrating finishes, the clear polyurethanes provide a non-penetrating, on-the-surface finish that ranges from extremely glass-like to a satin sheen, depending on the product selected and how it is applied. The methods of using these two low-maintenance modern finishes—as well as the more traditional finishes—are explained starting on page 738.

Restoring an Old Finish

If inspection has persuaded you that it is feasible to restore rather than replace an old finish, make sure that all the wax and dirt are removed with a turpentine or wax-remover scrub, and repair blemishes, as indicated on pages 730 and 731.

To repair a small flawed area of a shellac or lacquer surface, try dissolving (that is, amalgamating) the flaw into the surrounding area. Keeping the surface of your work horizontal, pour on a little fast-drying solvent (denatured alcohol for shellac, lacquer thinner for lacquer) and use a paint brush to spread it out over the flaw and the adjacent area, as in photograph 1. When the finish softens, brush it out once as though you were applying a new finish. Don't rebrush that same area or overlap brush strokes; the brush marks might show. Let the surface dry completely before you polish it as directed on page 736.

If the surface is varnish and the flaws don't justify stripping and refinishing, remove wax and dirt, repair visible blemishes, and apply a turpentine-linseed oil-new varnish mixture as recommended for scratches and cracks on page 731.

Removing an Old Finish

Even when they are old, shellacs and lacquers can be dissolved with their own solvents and, when softened, can be wiped away with a soft cloth. But you can do a faster job of stripping such surfaces if you use a commercial paint remover. For paint and varnish surfaces, there is no substitute for such a remover. These chemical removers cause the finish to wrinkle and loosen so that it can easily be lifted or wiped off. And they rarely damage the wood's surface, as does blow-torch removal, mechanical scraping or rough-grit power sanding.

The removers come as thin liquids, thick syrupy liquids, or thick pastes. Some contain wax or paraffin to retard evaporation. With some, you can hose away the loosened finish with water after it gets soft. I prefer the paste and thick-liquid forms, since they adhere to the wood without dripping and do not dry quickly so there is less work. With rinse-away removers, the water may damage the wood, lifting the grain or loosening veneers. If the remover contains wax, you will have to wash the stripped wood with turpentine or benzene before you apply the new finish. Some removers are non-flammable, an important plus if you can't avoid working near an area where there might be sparks. So read all labels carefully.

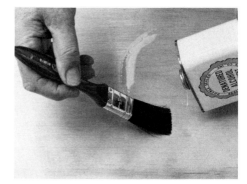

1: To repair flawed shellac or lacquer surface, flow on solvent—denatured alcohol for shellac, lacquer thinner for lacquer—and brush over flawed area. When finish softens, in five or ten minutes, brush it out smoothly and evenly.

Stripping is messy, and has its hazards. Work in a warm, well-lighted area with good cross-ventilation, away from any source of fire or sparks (including a lighted cigarette). Wear plastic gloves and work clothes. Have on hand: old coffee cans that can be covered to hold brushes and remover; several old paint brushes; lots of cheesecloth or burlap rags; newspapers; one narrow and one wide putty knife; wire brush; sharpened popsicle, orange, or Q-tip sticks; old toothbrush; pocket knife; thin twine; coarse to medium-grade steel wool; turpentine or benzene; and, of course, the paint remover. Remove all hinges, door pulls and other hardware from the furniture. Mask off any area (such as a rush-woven seat) you don't want the remover to reach, using masking tape or taped-on newspapers. Place the piece being stripped on spread-out newspapers or a plastic dropcloth.

On a horizontal surface, lay the remover on thickly and gently with a large brush. Brush in one direction only. Do not stroke over the same area twice; doing so breaks the surface membrane that forms almost immediately, letting the working chemicals evaporate. Cover only a few square feet at one time; if the remover dries, you will have to apply more. When the varnish or paint begins to wrinkle and curl (usually after 10 to 20 minutes), test it with a putty knife. If it lifts off easily (as in photograph 2), start removing it. But don't rush the job—let the remover do the work. Clean the putty knife as finish accumulates on the blade by wiping it on an old newspaper. When there are several layers of paint, the remover may not strip all of them with one application. Repeat as needed until all of the old finish has been removed. Spindles can be stripped by using lengths of burlap or cloth with a shoeshine motion (photograph 3). Use a wire brush, toothbrush, pointed stick, twine or steel wool as needed to clean corners and crevices, as in photograph 4. But don't use sharp-edged scrapers or any tool that might easily damage wood.

2: When paint softens enough to lift easily—10 to 20 minutes—scoop the glop off flat surfaces with a putty knife, wipe clean.

3: After finish has wrinkled and loosened, use strips of burlap and a shoeshine-cloth motion to strip the old finish from spindles.

4: Steel wool—2 to 0 grades—can be used to work softened paint out of such crannies as these on the washing stand door panels.

When all the old finish has been removed, neutralize the surface, following directions on the remover-can label. If the wood appears mottled after the neutralizer has dried, apply another coat of remover. Let it work for 10 or 15 minutes, then rub gently with fine steel wool. Give a final rubdown with fine steel wool and lacquer thinner or denatured alcohol. Let the stripped piece dry for at least a day. Make sure all stripped-off finish, remover, and waste rags and papers used for wiping are put in a covered trash container for prompt disposal.

Removing Milk-based Paints
In the 19th century, a type of casein paint made from milk solids was frequently used. These paints are sometimes called "refractory paints," and indeed you will find them to be just that when you try to remove them. Black, brown, red and green were popular colors. If the finish is reasonably sound, you may want to retain it for its antique value. If you decide to remove it, commercial strippers won't work. Instead, use ammonia full strength right from the bottle, working outdoors or in a very well-ventilated room. Pour out a little at a time, soak a pad of fine steel wool in it, and scour away at the surface. Keep the surface wet for 10 minutes. Repeat the scouring. When the paint has been removed, rinse the piece with cold water. If a stain remains, you can bleach it out with the method described for dark stains in the Craftnotes on page 730.

When you make the following repairs, work in a warm, well-ventilated room free of fire hazards, and observe all cautions noted on labels of the products used. If you have an old piece you treasure, don't try to remove all signs of wear and age. Make sure you are removing only truly objectionable mars and stains.

Grease and oil stains

Scrub away animal grease stains with 3/0 steel wool soaked in benzene or a commercial dry-cleaning fluid; for vegetable oil stains, use acetone. Wipe dry. Repeat as needed.

Dents and depressions

Place a folded wet cloth over a depression in wood and apply a hot iron briefly to the pad, as pictured, being careful not to burn the wood. Steam usually will make the compressed wood pores swell back into their original position.

White spots or rings

To erase white marks from shellac or lacquer surfaces, wipe with a soft cloth moistened with the appropriate solvent—denatured alcohol for shellac, lacquer thinner for lacquer. If the spot persists, or the surface is varnished, try using a cloth dipped in household ammonia and wrung dry, then whisked over the spot quickly. Or try a cloth moistened with turpentine, camphor oil, or peppermint oil. Then rub with a dry cloth. For stubborn spots, sprinkle 4/F pumice from a paint store on the spot and rub lightly with 3/0 steel wool dipped in light mineral oil. If that doesn't work, try rottenstone mixed with linseed oil to form a light paste (see page 736). Then wipe with dry cloth. On a high-gloss lacquer surface, use 4/0 steel wool and light mineral oil. To remove a hazy bloom from a varnished surface, wash with a solution of 2 or 3 tablespoons of vinegar in 1 quart of warm water, then wipe dry.

Dark stains and black rings

To remove dark stains, scrub off grease and oil as above, then use a cloth to apply laundry bleach or household ammonia. Let stand for a quarter hour, wash off, and repeat if needed. A solution of oxalic acid (2 tablespoons of powder or 4 of crystals to 1 pint of hot water) may also work. Neutralize this with a solution of borax (1 cup to 1 quart of water), rinse with water, wipe dry. Oxalic acid is a poison: keep it away from children, wear rubber gloves, avoid breathing fumes. Polish the area to match surrounding finish.

Burns

Scrape out dark, charred areas of burns, as pictured. Follow with abrasive paper, or steel wool wrapped around a pointed stick as needed to reach uncharred wood. Wipe away debris. Fill the depression as you would any chipped area (below) or, if it is deep, fill it with melted stick shellac or wood putty of a matching color (as explained below). To erase burns in penetrating finishes, rub them with steel wool and apply more penetrating finish.

Loose veneer

To repair loose veneer, remove glue from joining surfaces between veneer and solid wood by washing with warm water or by sanding lightly. If the veneer is old and brittle, place a damp cloth over the area and let it stay for an hour to restore resiliency to the wood. Let dry. Then coat joining surfaces completely with white glue, applied with a thin stick. Press veneer down to squeeze out excess glue, and wipe away excess. Place wax paper over veneer and use a block and C-clamp or weights to hold it until the glue dries. Allow 24 hours for drying.

Missing veneer

If a spot of veneer is missing or badly damaged, cut a replacement patch from an unexposed area (or buy a piece from a local cabinetmaker) in an irregular shape slightly larger than that area. Lay the patch over the area to be repaired and trace around it. Use a replaceable-blade knife or single-edge razor blade to cut along traced marks as above. Cut away veneer and glue inside the traced area, working down to bare wood. Glue veneer patch in place and clamp. Wipe away excess glue. When dry, sand the patch and refinish the area.

FURNITURE BLEMISHES

Removing old glue from loose joints

To open a loose joint in a piece of furniture, apply hot water to the glued parts with cloth, an eyedropper, or a syringe, depending on the opening available. If the joint does not pull free, try warm vinegar. When joint has been opened, take off the remaining glue with pads soaked in hot water or vinegar, then use sandpaper. If the joint is not too loose, drill a small hole into it and fill it with glue; this may eliminate the need to disassemble the piece.

Refitting loose joints

If you need to tighten a too-loose chair rung or a similar joint, dip toothpicks in glue and drive them into the joint around the rung, then cut the toothpicks off flush with a sharp knife. Of you can glue bits of cloth to the piece that fits into the joint until the fit is tight. Glue the enlarged piece in place, clamp or apply weights, and wipe away excess glue. For greater strength with a bit less beauty, drill a small hole at a right angle through the original joint and drive a small locking dowel, with glue on it, into this small hole. Sink the head of the locking dowel below the surface and fill this recess with wood putty. For some rectangular joints, a thin wedge of wood, driven with a mallet alongside the original tenon, may do the job. (When you refit the legs of a chair, use a rope tourniquet like the one shown above to hold legs in position while the glue dries.)

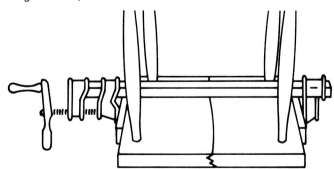

Repairing large cracks

To mend a large crack, work it open by bending the piece slightly and work white glue into it with a thin stick or small brush until the joining edges are covered. Then clamp the pieces together with pipe or bar clamps, as illustrated, wipe off any excess glue, and let dry. If no clamp is available, you can use rope or buckled straps drawn tightly.

Holes, cracks, gouges and chips

To level a major gouge, fill it by heating a small-bladed screwdriver, then holding the hot blade against a matching color of stick shellac or wood putty and letting this molten filler drip into the depression, as pictured. Sand away any excess and smooth with 6/0 abrasive paper and mineral oil. To repair edge damage, tape a thin wood stick against the edge and fill the break with melted stick shellac or wood putty. When this filler hardens, remove the taped-on wood support with a thin-bladed knife. For chips in varnish or paint, feather the edges of the chipped area with a fine abrasive paper, wipe away dust, then brush on matching paint or varnish. Apply several thin layers, allowing 24 to 48 hours of drying time between coats, until the matching thickness is reached. Level the patched area with fine abrasive and oil (page 736). Polish to match old finish.

Shallow scratches and cracks

To conceal minor blemishes in shellac or lacquer surfaces, apply the appropriate solvent to the area (see above). When finish softens, lightly brush it out. On a varnish finish, first try rubbing the scratch with a putty stick of matching color. If that doesn't hide the mar, rub on a mixture of 2 parts new varnish, 2 parts boiled linseed oil, and 1 part turpentine with a soft cloth, using a gentle circular motion. Remove excess with a dry cloth. Reapply if needed. Paste wax will hide fine scratches in natural finishes on unstained wood.

Correcting warping

If a warp in a flat piece of wood is slight, it is best to ignore it. But if it is severe or the piece is valuable, ask a local cabinetmaker about curing it with a professional steam-box or saw-kerf treatment. Some slight warps can be corrected by wetting the convex side thoroughly. Then, when the wood shows signs of flattening, clamp boards across the surface so the pressure is evenly distributed. Apply clamping pressure very gradually to avoid cracking the wood. If the warp disappears, seal and finish the wood on both sides to keep the warp from returning.

Preparing the Wood for a New Finish

With the wood stripped bare, complete any needed repairs before preparing the surface for its new finish. Raise dents, patch veneers, bleach stains and repair loose joints and cracks as detailed in the Craftnotes on page 730-731. The washing stand pictured on page 727 needed special repairs, as shown in photographs 5 to 7.

5: After the finish was stripped off the washing stand shown on page 727, a replacement for the missing drawer piece was cut from matching wood and fitted and glued in place.

6: With the new drawer piece glued in place, drawer pulls were found that were large enough to cover the marks left by missing ones.

7: A local cabinetmaker supplied matching wood to replace sections missing from top and bottom of the washing stand door. The wood was cut to fit.

To be readied for a new finish, the surface must be sanded. Open-coat aluminum-oxide or silicon-carbide papers are preferable for smoothing previously finished furniture surfaces (photograph 8) because they clog less, last longer and do a more effective final sanding job. They come with a wide range of grit sizes and densities and with various backings. For a surface that has previously been finished, start with open-coat No. 120 grit paper (grade 3/0), change to No. 180 (grade 5/0), and finish with No. 220 to 280 (grades 6/0 to 8/0). To leave a minimum of sanding scratches, use the finest grit that will do the job. Select a C-weight backing for a flat surface that you will sand with a sanding block, a more flexible A-weight backing for spindles and other turnings. (Fine abrasive wet-or-dry papers are used for the final rubdown of a new finish.)

8: On previously finished surfaces, avoid flint and garnet papers and use 120- to 220- or 280-grit open-coat aluminum oxide or silicon carbide papers. Check the backs of papers for labels indicating grit size and type backing. Crocus cloth is sometimes used for fine final polishing of finish.

Give the abrasive paper a flexible back-up support—a sanding block surfaced with cork, felt or foam rubber for flat surfaces, rubber-hose sections or padded dowel for curved surfaces. You can buy sanding blocks with flexible coverings at hardware stores, or glue a flexible covering on any scrap of wood. Or use a blackboard eraser. Abrasive paper can be cut to fit into the commercial holder, or you can simply wrap it around an eraser and hold it by hand, as in photograph 9. Use as large a block as you can hold that suits the area you are sanding. It will help level the surface and reduce the risk of gouging or scratching. Never use a disc or oscillating power sander or coarse sandpaper on a previously finished surface; the resulting scratches will be very difficult to remove or conceal.

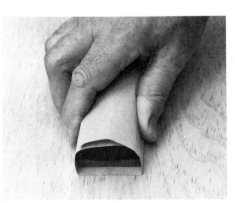

9: Sandpaper wrapped around a felt blackboard eraser (available at variety stores) makes a handy tool. Always sand in the same direction as the grain of the wood.

As you sand, always work back and forth in the direction the grain runs, and use as long a stroke as possible. Keep an even pressure. Never use a circular motion, and you will avoid cross-grain scratches. When the surface seems smooth, wipe it with a slightly damp cloth. The capillary attraction will raise "wood whiskers" (hairlike edges of wood cells) that might spoil the final finish if not removed. Sand these whiskers off with very fine No. 220 grit (6/0) sandpaper. Then remove sanding dust with a brush and tack cloth (see Craftnotes, page 736).

On small turnings or intricate carvings, use steel wool rather than sandpaper to remove old finish and do the final smoothing. It does less damage to the original contours. Steel wool is also good for smoothing the surface between finish coats. (Professionals also use fine-grade emery cloth for cleaning narrow crevices.) Steel wool comes in grades ranging from coarse (designated 3) to superfine (designated 0000 or 4/0). Use somewhat coarser grades to help you remove thick old finishes, as in photograph 4 on page 729, but rub lightly so you do not scratch the wood. Use medium-fine grade (0 to 2/0) with linseed oil to satinize or reduce the gloss on a finish. Use very fine grades (3/0 to 4/0) for polishing the final coat of a finish and for removing any dust mars.

Selecting and Applying the Finish

The new finish you choose will depend on the kind of wood, the result you want, and your time and patience. Some woods need sealing and staining before finishing; some do not. Some finishes will do the job in two applications; some require 20 or more, with in-between hand rubbings. But certain important rules and techniques apply to almost all of the possibilities.

Staining

The first rule governs when you should plan to use a stain or paint. Either can give you the particular color you want, of course. But in more general terms, woods that show very little grain pattern when unfinished are prime candidates for staining or painting. Alder, basswood, gum, hickory, poplar and white pine are good examples of woods with little natural character. Woods that may be given either a natural finish or stained include ash, beech, birch, cherry, chestnut, elm, mahogany, maple, oak, rosewood, teak and walnut (some of these are pictured below). If the wood's color is rich and its grain attractive (as in mahogany, rosewood, teak or cherry), many craftsmen avoid stain and apply a natural finish like one of the penetrating resin/oil wood or floor finishes suggested on page 739. One easy way to test the effect a clear finish will have on the color of wood is simply to touch it with a wet fingertip to see what change occurs. For more information on identifying characteristics of these and other woods, read *Woodworking Technology* (McKnight & McKnight) or *Know Your Woods* (Albert Constantine).

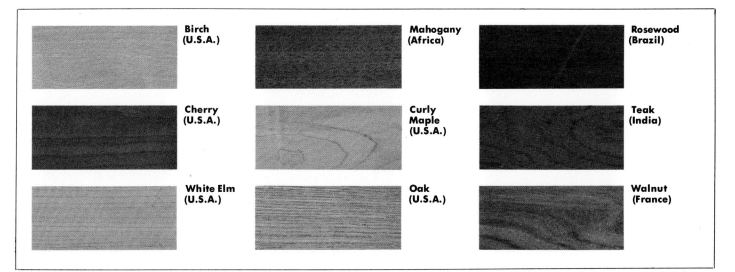

Birch (U.S.A.)   Mahogany (Africa)   Rosewood (Brazil)

Cherry (U.S.A.)   Curly Maple (U.S.A.)   Teak (India)

White Elm (U.S.A.)   Oak (U.S.A.)   Walnut (France)

10: All these woods may be either stained or given a natural finish.

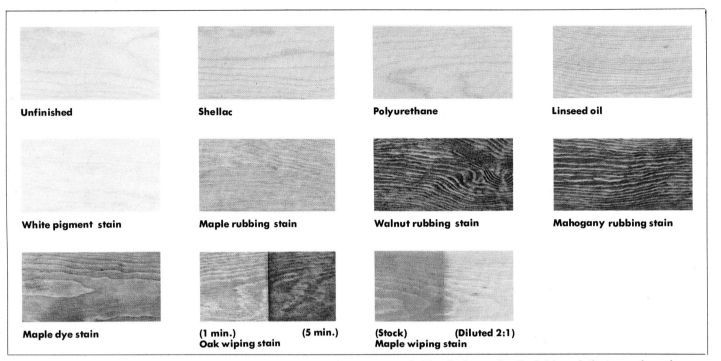

| Unfinished | Shellac | Polyurethane | Linseed oil |

| White pigment stain | Maple rubbing stain | Walnut rubbing stain | Mahogany rubbing stain |

| Maple dye stain | (1 min.)   (5 min.)
Oak wiping stain | (Stock)   (Diluted 2:1)
Maple wiping stain | |

11: You can change the appearance of white pine by varying the finish used, the type, color and concentration of stain, and the time you leave the stain on the wood before you wipe it off.

The color photographs above and opposite show what staining can do for a piece of pedestrian white pine. Note that different types, as well as different colors, of stain were used. Each type has its advantages and disadvantages.

Water stains are aniline dyes that you mix with warm water. They come as liquids or powders. Enough powdered dye to make a half-gallon of stain costs less than a dollar, but you must order powders from a wood-working supply house. Water stains penetrate well, dry fast, do not bleed through varnish or clear lacquer, resist fading in bright light, come in a wide range of colors, and can be mixed to achieve special hues. Because the water content might dissolve glue, they should not be used on veneers. These are not wiping stains; you must thin them and test them on an inconspicuous area, as in photograph 12, to arrive at the right depth of color. Then brush them on quickly with long strokes of a stiff-bristled brush, trying to avoid laps and streaks. Pick up runs quickly. These stains tend to raise the

12: When you think you have found the shade of stain you want, test it on an inconspicuous area, where the wood matches areas that will show. Let dry before you make a final decision.

wood grain. Offset this by first wetting the surface with clear water to raise the grain. Let the water dry. Then sand with 6/0 paper, wipe off and dust with a tack cloth. Either wet end grain with water just before staining or dilute the stain you apply to it so it does not soak up too much stain. Where wood colors differ on the same piece, dilute stains used on darker areas to help unify the color, but test your blend on an inconspicuous area. Two thin coats of a water stain are more likely to give you a uniform color and mask streaks and laps than one heavy coat.

Oil stains are dyes dissolved in oil. They are available in hardware stores as pigment oil stains or, if the label so indicates, penetrating oil stains. The pigment types are best used on close-grain woods, such as maple, cherry, and most soft-woods such as pine. The penetrating types are best on open-grain woods such as oak, mahogany and walnut. Both types dry slowly, do not raise the grain, and do not tend to show streaks or laps. But they may fade. Pigment types penetrate little, the penetrating types enough to make later removal difficult should you change your mind about the color. With either, apply a sealer coat of alcohol-thinned shellac between the stain and any varnish finish to keep the stain from bleeding through. Avoid oil stains if you plan to use clear lacquer. Do not mix different brands of oil stains. After you apply an oil stain and leave it on for several minutes (depending on the depth of color you desire), wipe off excess stain. The color may change somewhat as the stain dries, so test first on an inconspicuous area.

Pigmented wiping stains, like paints, are essentially oil and pigment mixtures. As their labels tell you, stir well before applying. They can be used to help blend woods of different colors, to mask or accent grain (depending on where you apply them), or to enhance signs of aging by accenting defects. Apply freely, let stand for several minutes (depending on the color desired), then wipe excess off.

N.G.R. (non-grain raising) stains are dye stains dissolved in a liquid that does not raise or roughen the grain. They dry quickly, do not bleed through, and can be used under any type of finish. The color is controlled not by wiping but by thinning the stain with its solvent. Because they dry so rapidly, you may need to dilute the stain with an equal amount of solvent to eliminate lap marks.

Sealing stains use a thinned-down finish, like lacquer, shellac or penetrating resin, in which a dye has been dissolved. They can be applied with or without wiping, but check the label carefully. The dye will not penetrate the wood as deeply as it would without the sealer but if final results are not critical, these stains provide one way to stain and seal in one application.

Avoid spirit stains, which bleed through most finishes, and varnish stains, which tend to be cloudy and are not used on good furniture.

After applying a stain, let it dry for 24 hours, then smooth it gently with 3/0 or finer steel wool. Be careful not to cut through the stain, particularly at the edges where it is most vulnerable.

Varying the Color
Turpentine added to an oil stain and water to a water stain will lighten the tone. Mixing light maple stain with walnut stain will produce a browner shade of yellow; mixing mahogany stain will redden the brown. Stains of the same color name but of different brands vary considerably, and they do not always match the color card samples. So experiment on an out-of-sight area until you have the shade you want. You should not, of course, mix oil stains with water stains.

If you want to match furniture to a room decor, use a ready-mixed flat oil paint or tube of oil color. Thin with turpentine to the depth of color desired. Then apply and wipe off so that the grain still shows, as in photograph 13.

Making Wood Lighter
One way to lighten wood is to use a white pigmented wiping stain (photograph 11). This works best on an open-grained wood such as oak, mahogany, elm, and walnut.

The method for bleaching or whitening dark stains described in the Craftnotes on page 730 will also do a fair job of bleaching a larger area. Stronger, commercial-grade bleaches include concentrated hydrogen peroxide and must be applied in a specific sequence. Such bleaches can be tricky and hazardous to use, so follow label instructions carefully.

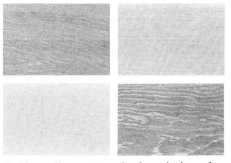

13: Blue, yellow, green and red panels show effects you can achieve by using thinned oil colors as stains on white pine. Apply, then wipe off when the desired intensity of color is reached.

CRAFTNOTES: FINISHING TIPS

Dust control and removal

No matter how much you vacuum beforehand, dust will get on furniture you are refinishing. To remove it from surfaces about to be coated, wipe with a tack rag. You can buy one or make your own as shown above. Dip cheesecloth in warm water and wring out (top left). Soak cloth with turpentine (top right), wring out lightly, apply several drops of varnish over cloth (bottom left) and work in until the cloth is thoroughly tacky. Store cloth in a glass jar with a screw-on lid (bottom right) when not in use.

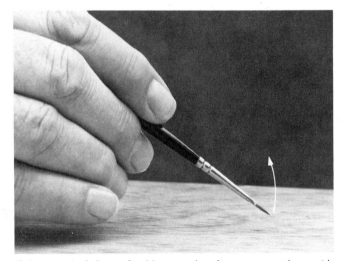

If dust specks fall on a freshly coated surface, remove them with a brush as shown above. Moisten the tip, lower its point carefully toward the speck, use this point to lift the speck straight up and out of the surface film. For an alternate dust remover, make a picking stick by attaching a small piece of tack cloth to the tip of a thin dowel with tape or rubber bands. To use, lower the tip until it touches the dust speck, then lift straight up.

Brushes and brushing techniques

For best results, use a brush with flagged (split or frayed) bristle ends forming a brush tip that tapers to a wedge or chisel shape. Bristles should feel soft and springy when you press them against a surface, and the tip should form an unflared, straight line. Avoid a brush whose bristle edge is blunt or squared-off, or one with big plugs where bristles join the brush; these plugs make the bristles spread out thinly or unevenly when you press them down. Either nylon or natural bristles will do unless the label on the finish specifies type to use. But soft bristles are best for free-flowing shellacs and varnishes.

When applying any finish, dip bristles in finish no deeper than one-third of their length. Tap off excess finish against the inside of the can or wipe the brush across a strike wire (a wire inserted through punched holes across center of can near the top, with the wire ends bent to hold it in place). On wide surfaces, start the brush stroke in the center and work with the grain toward the edges. Work in narrow strips with stroke moving from unfinished area into the wet edge of just-finished area. Keep laps over previous strokes even. With the surface covered, tip off by stroking lightly along the grain from end to end. Use a lightly loaded small brush for corners and crevices to avoid gummy build-ups. Watch for runs and pick them up with the brush before the finish starts to dry.

Rubbing and polishing

Rubbing with 4/F pumice or rottenstone helps produce an evenly polished surface between coats and after the final coat. As the finer abrasive of the two, rottenstone is preferred for the final polishing. Paint stores stock both and techniques for using them are similar. Coat the surface to be rubbed with a thin film of light mineral oil, raw linseed oil or paraffin oil. Sprinkle pumice or rottenstone over the surface and rub with a blackboard eraser, working with the grain as shown above. When the surface sheen satisfies you, wipe off the abrasive-oil mixture with a clean cloth. Wait two days after rubbing the final coat before waxing.

Waxing

If you want a glossy finish, use paste (not liquid) wax on the final coat, applying it with a moistened cloth or rag wrapped in a ball shape. Rub on a thin film of wax. Buff with a felt or lamb's wool polishing pad. Buffing by hand is safer, but you can use a padded reciprocating or orbital power sander with a felt or lamb's wool pad if you keep it moving constantly. Disc-type power buffers may dig into the surface.

Fillers

Wood fillers are sometimes used to level the pores of such open-grained woods as oak, ash, chestnut, mahogany and walnut, if a glass-like final surface is desired. (They are not used under penetrating resin-oil finishes.) Fillers come in standard wood colors, but are often used a shade darker than the finished wood will be to retain the grain contrast. Wood fillers come as pastes that must be thinned, usually with turpentine or naphtha, before applying (check the label).

Twenty-four hours after staining, apply the filler with a stiff brush. Brush with the grain first, then across it to help fill the pores. Use plenty of filler. Then wait until the surface begins to get dull. Use a playing card to scrape across the grain and remove excess filler as in photograph 14. Let dry a little longer, then wipe across the grain with a coarse cloth.

Applying the Final Finish

Whatever final finish you choose, dust will be its worst enemy. Carefully vacuum the area in which you will work; allow stirred dust to settle for an hour or so and then vacuum again. As indicated in the Craftnotes opposite, have a tack rag and picking brush or stick handy and use them frequently.

In addition to the finishes discussed below, you will need a supply of the buffers and polishers described in the Craftnotes opposite.

Shellac

Shellac is a popular finish for pieces that will not be subject to moisture, heat, stains or solvents. Shellac comes in white for light finishes and orange for dark finishes. Different thicknesses—called cuts—are available. A 5-pound cut will have more resin than the 3-pound cut that is most commonly sold. If it is not a 3-pound cut, the can label will probably have directions for diluting with denatured alcohol. Buy only shellac that is dated; do not buy shellac over six months old. It will not dry properly.

Plan to apply at least three coats, and possibly more. Thin the first coat with an equal amount of alcohol. After wetting, sanding and removing dust with a tack cloth as explained previously, brush shellac on freely. Stroke out quickly, avoiding rebrushing. Allow two to four hours for drying. Working with the grain, rub down with No. 280 abrasive paper and padded sanding block. Wipe clean and apply second coat which may be full-strength or slightly diluted for easier application. When it is hard and dry, rub with No. 280 paper on padded block. After the third coat, the surface should be smooth but you can add more coats if you are not satisfied with the sheen.

For a duller, matte finish, rub dried final coat lightly with 3/0 or 4/0 steel wool. Then apply paste (never liquid) wax with cloth and rub briskly. For a highly polished finish, let final coat harden for a week, then rub lightly with rottenstone and mineral oil, as in Craftnotes, page 736. Wipe off and wash down with a solution of equal parts vinegar and water. Then wax.

French polish has long been a favorite shellac finish, prized for its beauty since the days of Chippendale and Hepplewhite. But applying it is a hard, time-consuming procedure, and the results are not always glamorous. If you want to try it, start with a 3-pound cut of shellac, boiled linseed oil, and an apple-sized ball of rags covered with a lint-free cloth. Rub surface with linseed oil on a cloth. Wipe dry and polish hard to remove all traces of oil not absorbed. Let surface dry completely. Thin shellac to water consistency (for a 3-pound cut, dilute with an equal amount of denatured alcohol). Dip cloth ball in thinned shellac. Place two or three drops of boiled linseed oil in the center of the cloth. With a rotating motion that starts before the cloth touches wood, rub the surface as long as the pad continues to coat the wood (photograph 15). Without stopping the motion, rotate the pad off the wood. Then add more shellac and drops of oil and rotate pad back on and off as before. Continue until surface is completely covered. Let dry for 24 hours and repeat. Continue adding coats of shellac this way until the finish is built up into many layers, or until the appearance satisfies you. When you are satisfied with the look, wipe surface with a turpentine-soaked cloth, followed by an equal-parts mixture of vinegar and water. Wipe dry.

14: After applying wood filler with a stiff brush, let dry slightly, then scrape off excess with a playing card. Fillers are put on open-grained woods to level the surface.

15: French polishing technique calls for rotating a pad containing shellac and drops of linseed oil onto, over and off the work repeatedly.

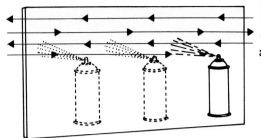

In spraying lacquer, start each stroke beyond the surface being coated, moving across the work and continuing on past it. Keep spray tip same distance from the work as you move. Don't stop to fill in lightly covered spots; do that later. Work in rows with each overlapping the previous one slightly.

Lacquer

Lacquer is the most difficult of all finishes for an amateur to apply, although it is widely used commercially because it dries so quickly. It tends to dissolve stains—and sometimes even the natural colors of wood—and bleed them into the final finish, obscuring the natural wood to some degree. In addition, some lacquers dry so quickly that they don't level after brushing. That is why commercial users almost always spray lacquers on, and why aerosol spray lacquers are easiest for the amateur to use.

The trick in using aerosol sprays is to mist or haze the surface first, without trying to build up a complete finish layer. Start the spray tip moving from beyond the surface and continue past it. Keep the tip the same distance from your work as you move across, though it seems more natural to swing your arm in an arc. Move the tip in rows with each overlapping the last slightly, as shown at left. Do not go over the same area twice with one spray application. The coat will be uneven after the first spraying but you can fill in with subsequent coatings. Allow each coat to dry thoroughly.

Successive coats may be applied without rubbing between each one, but use a tack cloth to remove dust and allow a minimum of four hours for drying between coats. The final coat may be rubbed with pumice or rottenstone in mineral oil (Craftnotes, page 736), wiped off, and then waxed as indicated for shellac above.

Varnishes and the Polyurethanes

The term varnish covers a multitude of confusing selections. For refinishing furniture, your best choice is a modern synthetic resin varnish. It is easier to apply and more durable than the traditional oil-resin varnishes that are getting scarcer and scarcer. Of the synthetics, the oil-modified polyurethanes are perhaps the toughest and have the least tendency to yellow with age. The chair shown below was finished with one of these polyurethanes. After the struggle I had removing the chair's original finish, including a stubborn coat of milk-base paint, I wanted the new finish to be as child-proof and maintenance-free as possible.

Several layers of paint were removed from this chair. They included an undercoat of milk-based paint (see page 729) that had to be scrubbed off with ammonia and a water rinse. The chair was then refinished without staining, as at right, using a polyurethane finish to protect it against anticipated future batterings by active youngsters.

The biggest problem with all varnishes is dust. While many of them set fairly rapidly, they take longer than shellac or lacquer to dry completely. Even the modern synthetic resins have drying times ranging from four to five hours for the fastest ones, to overnight for recoating. (Spar varnish never dries completely—it stays elastic and is not recommended for furniture.) Check labels carefully for information on the type of varnish, and instructions on using.

Work in a dust-free area with good lighting on the work and the work surface held horizontally, if possible. Follow label instructions on thinning and stirring, but do not shake the can or you will get bubbles in the varnish. Flat varnishes will need thorough stirring to distribute the flattening agent, and this is not always indicated on their labels. Apply only on a surface that has been freshly dusted with a tack cloth. The can label may suggest applying with a cloth or lamb's wool pad or a brush. If you use a brush, dip the bristles one-third into the varnish and tap off the excess against the side of the can; this should leave brush full but not dripping. Lay varnish on with long strokes along the grain. Then cross-hatch these strokes by brushing across them in the opposite direction, as in photograph 16. Then quickly brush out again along the grain. Repeat until the surface is covered. The varnish should level itself, obliterating the brush strokes. Use the brush quickly to pick up drips and level out any sags or build-ups. Allow at least 24 hours of drying time before sanding; 48 is safer if humidity is high. (The drying times given on some labels refer to dry-to-touch times, not safe-to-sand times.) Rub with wet-or-dry 400 grit paper or 4/0 steel wool. Wipe off, use tack cloth, and revarnish. Two coats may be enough. If not, repeat. Let dry. Finish with a pumice and mineral oil rub or, for a finer gloss, a rottenstone and mineral oil rub (Craftnotes, page 736). Wipe clean with a cloth. You can apply paste wax if you wish but it is not needed for polyurethane-type varnishes.

16: To insure quick, complete, smooth coverage, some experts lay varnish on with long strokes along the grain, leaving a brush width between strokes. They cross-hatch these with strokes in the opposite direction, then fill the unfinished areas along and across the grain until the surface is completely covered.

Natural Oil and Penetrating Oil Finishes

The traditional early-American natural finish is composed of linseed oil, turpentine and much hand labor. But it is still popular with some patient craftsmen, even though it does require periodic renewal. The penetrating oil-resin finishes are modern cousins of the old oil finishes in the sense that they tend to leave the wood looking natural. But they are far easier to apply and maintain, and they make tough, durable, abrasion-resistant final finishes. This is the type of finish I used on the washing stand shown on page 727. Neither the natural oil nor the penetrating resin-oil finish require a sealer beforehand or a waxing afterward, though wax may be used if you wish.

Traditional Oil Finish

For the traditional natural oil finish, dilute boiled (not raw) linseed oil with an equal amount of turpentine. Use at temperatures of 70 degrees Fahrenheit or warmer. With the piece of furniture ready in a warm room for its final finish, apply the diluted linseed oil. Let it stand until all of it has been absorbed in the wood. Keep adding more until the wood will absorb no more. Usually an entire day of soakings is needed. Then wipe surface dry and rub down vigorously with soft cloth. Allow to dry for two weeks in a warm place; if you rush an oil finish, the surface will get gummy. When this coat is completely dry, repeat the procedure. Allow to dry and buff. Then repeat bi-weekly until you are satisfied with the finish and no dull spots remain. Then recoat once each month for a year. Some craftsmen use 20 or more applications, and then follow with twice-a-year treatments after that.

Penetrating Oil Finish

Your biggest problem with the modern penetrating resin-oil finishes may be finding one amid all the confusing labels. Look for the words "penetrating" and "finish" or "floor finish" on the label. Some brands and names of these finishes you might look for are: Duroseal 500; Watko Danish Oil Finish; Hope's Tung Oil; Tungseal Royal Danish Oil; and Velopar 70 Danish Oil. The thin type sealer/finishes containing varnish (rather than wax) are best for furniture.

   With the surface cleaned and tack-clothed, apply the finish with a cloth pad, lamb's wool, or brush. Allow to soak for the length of time given on the can label (it will vary), but keep the area wet during this period. Then wipe dry with a clean rag. Let dry 24 hours (unless label instructs otherwise) and repeat. If the wood still has dull areas suggesting that it will absorb more, apply a third coat, and wipe off after time specified on label. After 24 hours, buff with dry cloth.

Antiquing and Distressing Furniture

If you want to learn how to achieve special furniture finishing effects —glazing, distressing, striping, feathering, spattering and the like—see the entry "Antiquing Furniture" in Volume One. For other related projects and crafts, see the entries "Boxes," "Caning and Rushing," "Folk Art," "Framing," "Gold Foil and Leafing," "Marquetry," "Tables and Benches," "Upholstery," "Woodworking."

FUR RECYCLING
New Uses for Old Fur

Lee K. Thorpe, an Evanston, Illinois, furrier, teaches fur sewing techniques to amateurs. He is chairman of the Master Furriers Guild of America and a member of the guild's Conservation Committee. Lee is presently writing a book about fur styling.

Old fur garments, too worn to wear but too good to discard, hang idly in many a closet and are forgotten in many an attic trunk. They can also be purchased inexpensively at secondhand clothing stores. There are many new things you can make from a shabby old fur coat. You might shorten it into a jacket and make pillows from the leftover fur. Or you can turn it into one or more fur accessories: matching collar and cuffs; a fluffy, six-foot-long fling; a muff, hat or bag.

You don't need to be an expert seamstress to salvage an old coat for a new use. A novice can make a fine fur pillow. Once you learn the basic differences between working with fur and working with fabric, you will be able to get added mileage out of fur garments that other people might discard as useless.

Fur's unique qualities make it an excellent material to recycle. Unlike fabric, fur can be pieced together so no seams show—since they are hidden by hair. This means you can cut and piece all the good sections from a worn coat and have material that looks like one piece. One important difference between fur and fabric is that fur is sewn without a seam allowance. Seams are butted rather than overlapped, so you cut pattern pieces to their finished size. (Fake fur consists of a face or pile with a knitted or woven back. It requires a seam allowance like any other fabric.) Note, too, that you mark fur on the skin side and cut it with the skin side up. Marking done with a felt-tipped pen will not show through.

Tools and Materials

For all the projects on the following pages you will need: a mat knife or single-edge razor blade; a leather needle with a three-sided wedge-shaped point (sometimes called a three-cornered needle), available at notion counters or craft supply stores; thimble; straight pins; heavy-duty cotton or nylon thread; masking tape; felt-tipped pen. In addition, you will need an adhesive seam binding known as furrier's torsion tape or cold tape, available from furrier's supply companies. You can substitute sewing twill tape or seam binding if you can't find this adhesive, but it will require an extra sewing step (see Craftnotes, page 743). For some projects you will also need cotton batting, grosgrain ribbon, and material for lining. Velvet is recommended for backing the fling on page 749.

Basic Techniques

Testing: Some areas of an old coat may be too worn or too weak to withstand a reconstruction job. To test the strength of an old fur, yank the hair of the fur in several places. If hairs don't pull out easily, the fur is probably usable. Also check the dryness of the skin. To do this, open the lining of the coat along the hemline and pinch the skin side in several places. If it seems powdery or brittle, it is probably too dry to recycle into a new garment, although it might be used as a pillow cover. Another test of suppleness is to moisten a small area of skin and stretch it. If it stretches without tearing, the skin is in good condition. Fur that is still good but has a weak backing can be used, but in that case a lightweight fabric should be sewn in for support.

Stitching: For beginners, it's best to stitch fur seams by hand, so the following projects call for careful hand sewing. A sharp leather needle is recommended because it will pierce the skin more readily than ordinary needles. It is true that furriers use a sewing machine and feed the fur into it edge to edge; your sewing machine might achieve the same effect with a tiny zigzag stitch, using a special needle available at most sewing centers for sewing leather, but with hand sewing you will have more control. This is a good time to get reacquainted with the old-fashioned thimble. It is almost essential for forcing the needle through the tough skin of the fur.

Pillows are a good beginning project involving the use of fur remnants. The designs can be adapted to the size, shape and color of available materials. They are easy to sew and are welcome gifts. Instructions for making the pillow with contrasting triangles begin on page 742.

Needlecrafts
Decorate with fur

Fur-covered pillows like those pictured on the previous page can be made from a single piece of fur, from small scraps sewn together, or from furs of contrasting colors and textures. The fur front is joined to a vinyl, velvet, or suede cloth back, then this pocket is stuffed with a pillow form or loose filling. If you have never worked with fur, you will soon find that it is as easy to use as any other material, once you learn the basic techniques. Making a pillow introduces you to the method of cutting fur and to basic hand stitches.

Begin by experimenting with small pieces of fur, as for the checkerboard pillow or triangle pillow. The size and type of pillow you decide to make depends on the kind and amount of fur you have. The finished triangle pillow (directions below) measures 12 inches on each side. For a larger or smaller pillow, adapt the directions accordingly. Fur can be pieced invisibly, so you can sew small pieces of identical fur together and they will look like one piece so long as the hair all points in one direction. Even if you make a patchwork pillow with different colors and types of fur, your finished piece will be smooth-looking if you stitch carefully when seaming.

Materials: In addition to the basic tools and materials listed on page 740, you will need: a 12-inch square of lightweight cotton stay cloth if you need to support an unevenly worn or fragile skin; four triangles of fur for the pillow front, each with a 12-inch base and 8½-inch sides; a 12-inch square of vinyl, velvet, or suede cloth for the back of the pillow; and a 12-inch square pillow form or enough pillow stuffing to fill the pillow. (A same-size pillow form is used to make sure the cover is taut and the pillow is plump.)

Making the Triangle Pillow
First cut a triangular pattern from heavy cardboard. Make the base 12 inches and each side 8½ inches. Place the pattern on the skin side and anchor it with a weight to keep it from slipping. Then trace the pattern on the skin with a felt-tipped pen. Cut out four fur triangles as shown in Figure A. When cutting, be sure to cut only the skin, not the hair.

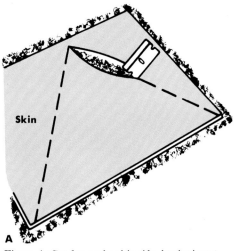

Figure A: Cut fur on the skin side, beginning at one corner of the triangle. Pierce the skin, then cut toward yourself with a drawing motion. Hold the blade at a 45-degree angle from the skin. With your other hand, raise skin as the cutting frees it.

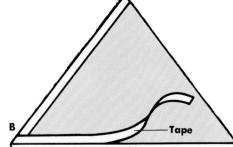

Figure B: To prevent stretching or tearing, tape the cut edges. Apply the torsion tape flush with the edges on the skin side.

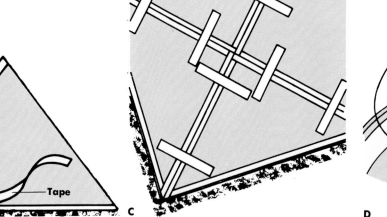

Figure C: Use strips of masking tape (shown in white) to hold fur triangles temporarily in place while you position them properly.

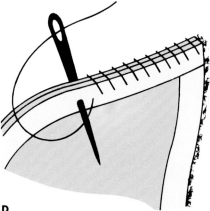

Figure D: With fur sides together, join two triangles by using the simple whipstitch shown. Join all four triangles the same way.

For reinforcement, apply torsion tape (cold tape) flush with the cut edges as in Figure B. Twill tape or seam binding can be substituted (see Craftnotes, opposite). Position the four triangles together and use strips of masking tape to hold the pieces temporarily in place. Starting with two facing pieces, whipstitch all four triangles together (see Figure D). Use masking tape for basting. As you sew, catch the torsion tape in the seam and push stray hairs back to the fur side. Be sure that the four points match at the pillow's center. Remove masking tape as you come to it.

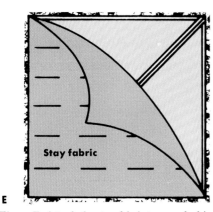

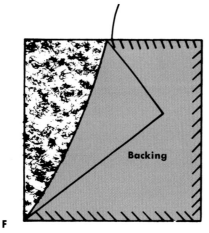

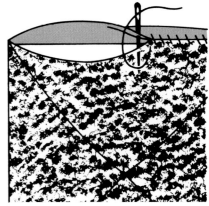

Figure E: Attach the stay fabric to a weak skin with long running stitches in parallel rows two inches or so apart.

Figure F: With the cover inside out, whipstitch vinyl backing to the fur pillow front. Sew around three sides using the whipstitch.

Figure G: Turn the pillow fur side out and insert pillow form or stuffing. Whipstitch the open seam closed with tiny stitches.

If you need a stay fabric to support worn or fragile skin, attach it to the skin side (Figure E) after joining the four fur triangles. Next, join the pillow backing to the front by sewing around three sides (Figure F). Turn the pillow fur side out and stuff it. To finish, whipstitch the remaining seam on the right or fur side. These outside stitches may show slightly on vinyl or other backing but will be hidden by the fur.

CRAFTNOTES: SEWING FUR

Tape is applied to the fur's cut edges to keep them from stretching and to reinforce seams. Furriers use an adhesive tape, called torsion or cold tape. You can also use twill tape or seam binding. Either of these must be sewn in place, but will make the seams more durable; the extra stitching will not weaken the skin.

Apply torsion (cold) tape flush with the skin's cut edge to reinforce it and prevent stretching.

Stitch sewing twill tape or seam binding to a cut fur edge with catchstitches (shown above) or even running stitches (right).

A leather needle's wedge-shaped point (enlarged here) cuts cleanly through skin.

These hand stitches are the basic ones for sewing fur. Most sewing is done on the skin side. Pick up just enough of the skin to make a firm stitch.

Catchstitch: Use this basic basting and tacking stitch for attaching tape or interfacing, and for binding a fur edge with grosgrain ribbon.

Even Running Stitch: Use for sewing on tape and for firm tacking. It is interchangeable with the catchstitch.

Uneven Running Stitch: Use for basting and tacking interfacing. It is also interchangeable with the catchstitch.

Whipstitch: Use to sew two pieces of fur together or to attach fabric to fur. It is interchangeable with the blanket stitch.

Blanket Stitch: For a stronger seam, use this instead of the whipstitch. Insert needle at A and come out at B, with the needle in front of thread loop.

Slipstitch: To make the basic finishing stitch, insert needle at A and come out at B, just catching the under fabric.

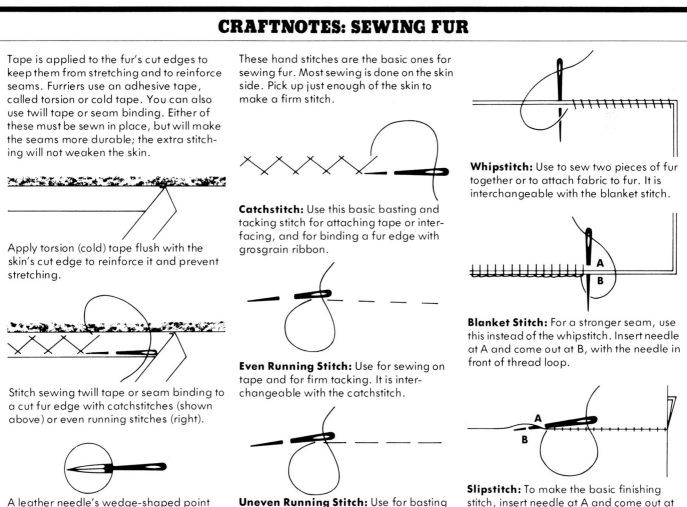

Salvage an old coat by cutting it down to make a finger-tip length jacket; this one is of pieced mink.

Shortening a coat

A new hemline can make a big difference in a garment. Examine any worn coat to see if you can cut it down to jacket length, short or long. Shortening introduces you to the turned-up hem, used at the bottom of fur jackets and coats. A strip of interfacing, cut from sturdy hair canvas or unbleached muslin, for example, is sewn in to give such a hem body, then the fur is turned up and secured in place. Grosgrain ribbon (woven of a firm ribbed fabric) is sewn to the skin edge and serves both to bind the edge and to provide a means of anchoring the finished hem in place.

Materials

In addition to the basic tools for fur work (page 740), you will need ½-inch-wide grosgrain ribbon and a strip of interfacing the length of the hem. This interfacing should be two inches wider than the hem; thus, a 3-inch-wide strip is right for a 1-inch hem.

First, determine the length you want your jacket or coat to be. You will have to use your own judgment here. Ask a friend to help you turn up the old coat before you decide. Using masking tape or safety pins on the skin side, make a temporary hem so you can get an idea of how the garment will look before you cut. Bear in mind that the finished garment will seem slightly longer than the turned-up length because hair will extend beyond the actual hem.

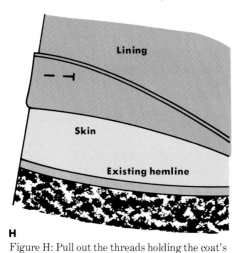

H

Figure H: Pull out the threads holding the coat's lining and pin it up out of the way. Some coats have a second loose lining which should also be pinned back.

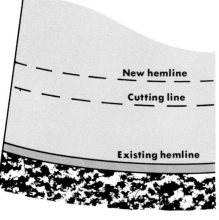

I

Figure I: Measure the amount you want to shorten from the existing hemline and mark the new length with a felt-tipped pen. Draw a line one inch below the new hemline as the cutting line.

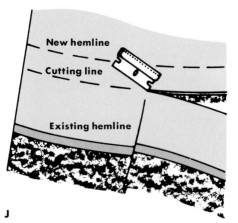

J

Figure J: Pierce the skin and cut toward you along the cutting line, using a drawing motion. Save the fur you remove for another use.

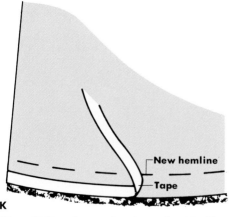

K

Figure K: Tape the new fur edge on the skin side, using torsion tape. This will be whipstitched into the seam when grosgrain ribbon is applied.

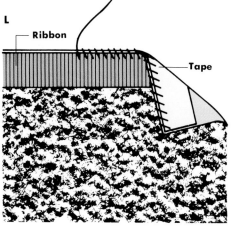

Figure L: Attach grosgrain ribbon on the fur side with an even whipstitch. Sew through all three thicknesses: ribbon, skin, and tape.

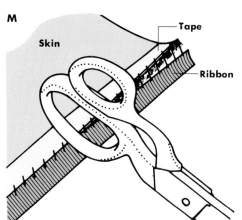

Figure M: Flatten the ribbon seam open by rubbing it with a scissors handle. This is also a good way to flatten seams joining two fur pieces.

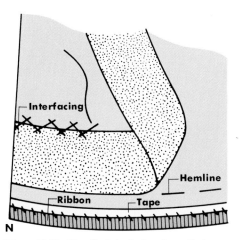

Figure N: Position the interfacing above the hemline and sew the upper edge to the skin with catchstitches. The lower edge need not be sewn.

Figure O: Turn up fur hem and sew the ribbon to the body of the coat through the interfacing. Use a firm catchstitch.

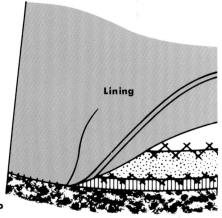

Figure P: Slipstitch lining in place after trimming it and allowing for a ¼-inch hem. The lining should end an inch above the hemline.

Work on a flat surface and use a weight such as an iron or a book to keep the fur from slipping. Pin the lining out of your way (Figure H). Then mark the new hemline and a cutting line on the skin side with a felt-tipped pen (Figure I). A one-inch-wide hem is fine for most furs, but not all. You might want a wider hem if you plan to recycle your fur again at a later date. Consider the weight of the fur and make sure that the hem allowance, if wider than one inch, will not add too much bulk to the hem. The effect you want is a round, smooth look.

Cut off the excess fur (Figure J) and if it is not too worn, save it for another use. Reinforce the new fur edge with tape, applying it flush to the skin side (Figure K). To finish the edge, attach ½-inch-wide grosgrain ribbon, using the whipstitch and working on the fur side (Figure L). Then flatten the ribbon seam open with a scissors handle (Figure M).

Attach a strip of interfacing to the skin side (Figure N). The interfacing gives body to the hem and helps create a smooth, unbroken line. The interfacing should be the length of the hem and two inches wider than the hem allowance. Position it on the new hemline and sew the upper edge to the skin with running or catchstitches.

To hem, turn up the fur to the new hemline and sew the ribbon to the body of the coat using catchstitches (Figure O) or running stitches. The hem should be as smooth as possible.

The final step is to adjust the lining and sew it in place (Figure P). Measure and trim the lining so it falls an inch above the hemline when you have turned it under ¼ inch. Sew the lining to the lower ribbon edge with slipstitches.

A shawl collar can be worn on a jacket, coat or sweater. Here, a wide fox collar adorns a pieced fox jacket. Patterns for a narrower collar and cuffs are at right below.

Needlecrafts
Fur collar and cuffs

A fur collar or a collar and cuffs set can be attached to a jacket, coat or long sweater. Making a collar and cuffs involves one of the trickier problems in fur recycling: laying a pattern so the hair falls properly. When your collar and cuffs are completed, the direction of the hair flow should be uniform for both collar pieces and for both cuffs. If you can, lay out the patterns for the two collar pieces so that the hair flows out and away from the neckline where the two pieces are joined at the center back seam, as the arrow on the pattern indicates. The hair flow for the cuffs should be horizontal—around the cuff. But these are only suggested ways; you may decide to position patterns to achieve hair flow more suitable for the type of fur you are working with.

Try various ways of arranging pattern pieces on the fur so that the direction of the hair for the two collar pieces will be the same and the two cuffs will also be uniform. In most fur coats, the hair runs down. In flat furs, such as broadtail and Persian lamb, the hair twists in all directions. In sheared furs, such as sheared raccoon, nutria, rabbit, mole, beaver and mouton lamb, the texture is uniform and velvety, but you can discover the direction of hair flow by rubbing your hand on the fur to see which way the hair runs flatter. The flatter way is with the hair flow. Furs such as mink, muskrat, and fox have an unmistakable hair flow.

Materials: You will need to make a trial pattern. Use heavy muslin or any heavy fabric. In addition to basic materials (page 740), you will need ¾-inch-wide grosgrain ribbon to bind all outside edges; cotton batting for padding; and satin for lining.

Making the Patterns
Make cardboard or paper patterns for the collar and cuffs by enlarging those shown in Figure Q. Mark arrows on the patterns to indicate the direction of the hair flow. You will have to cut two collar pieces, reversing the pattern for the second piece so the collar curves properly. You may need to adjust the shape and size of the pattern pieces to suit your figure, your coat or sweater, and the fur you have available.

Figure Q: Enlarge the basic shawl collar and cuff patterns right (see Volume One, page 57 for instructions on enlarging a pattern), then adjust them to suit the garment you have selected. Patterns have no seam allowance because fur pieces are joined edge to edge. Arrows suggest the direction of the fur's hair flow. Make a pattern for the left half of the collar, as illustrated, then turn it over and make a pattern for the right half. Cut one pattern piece for each cuff.

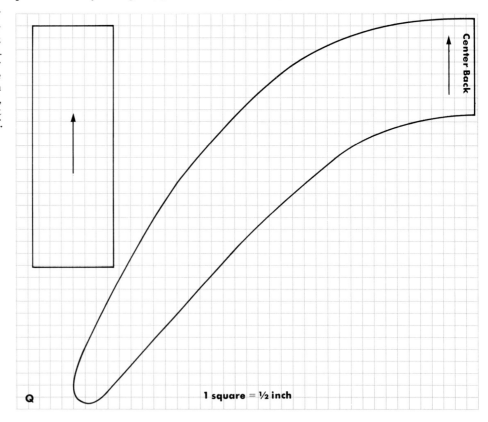

Q   1 square = ½ inch

Center Back

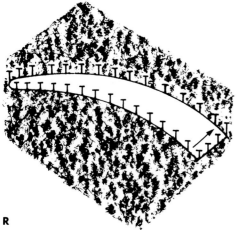

R

Figure R: To assure proper hair flow, first position paper pattern on the fur side. To determine the cutting line, straight pins are pushed through to the skin side all around at 2-inch intervals.

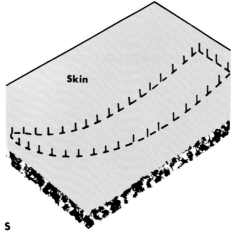

S

Figure S: Turn fur to the skin side and mark pin points with a felt-tipped pen. Then connect the points to indicate the cutting line. Cut each collar and cuff piece separately.

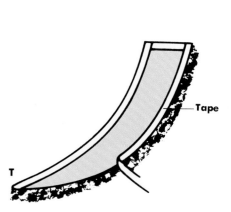

T

Figure T: Tape all cut edges to prevent stretching (see Craftnotes, page 743), after you have cut two collar pieces and one piece for each cuff.

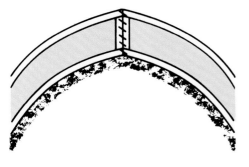

U

Figure U: Join two collar pieces by holding fur sides together and whipstitching the seam. Remember to catch tape with the thread as well. Flatten seam open as in Figure M, page 745.

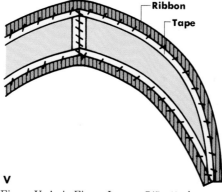

V

Figure V: As in Figure L, page 745, attach grosgrain ribbon to all outside edges and flatten open. This ribbon extension will later be folded over the skin and sewn in place for the hem.

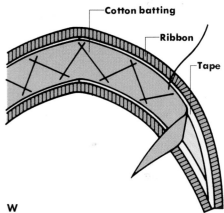

W

Figure W: Cut pieces of cotton batting ¼-inch smaller all around than the fur pieces. Attach the batting to the skin with wide catchstitches.

Cuff widths generally range from three to five inches. Enlarging the cuff pattern in Figure Q will give you a 3½-inch-wide cuff. Using the enlarged paper patterns, cut trial pieces of heavy muslin or similar fabric. Try on the fabric collar and cuffs to see how they look. If any adjustments are necessary, revise the paper patterns before you start to work on the fur.

Assembling the Collar and Cuffs

Lay the fur you are recycling flat and position patterns pieces on the fur side to make sure the hair flows attractively. If you are working with an old coat, pin the lining out of your way. It is not necessary to take the whole coat apart—just free a large enough area of fur. Mark the fur by pushing straight pins through to the skin side at 2-inch intervals along the pattern edges (Figure R). Then turn the fur to the skin side and connect the pin marks with a felt-tipped pen to determine the cutting line. Cut out the fur pieces and tape all the raw edges (see Craftnotes, page 743), including the center back seam edges. Next, using the whipstitch, join the two collar pieces at the center back, catching the tape with the thread. The hair flow should be the same on either side of the seam. With some furs hairs will overlap.

Working on the fur side, attach grosgrain ribbon to all edges, except for the center neck seam where it is unnecessary (Figure V).

Prepare padding by cutting cotton batting ¼-inch smaller all around than the fur collar and cuffs. Then tack it to the skin with catchstitches (Figure W).

FUR CARE CRAFTNOTES

If your old coat is in poor condition, it could be due to improper care, as well as to age. Fur will stay in good condition for many years if it is cared for properly. These tips will help you maintain fur pieces:

Do not leave fur near heat; the fur will dry out and the skin will become brittle.

Hang fur garments on broad-shouldered hangers or padded hangers. Be sure to allow space around the garment for air to circulate.

Never store fur in a plastic bag.

Do not use chemical sprays to moth-proof fur.

If fur gets wet, shake it and hang it to dry in a cool place.

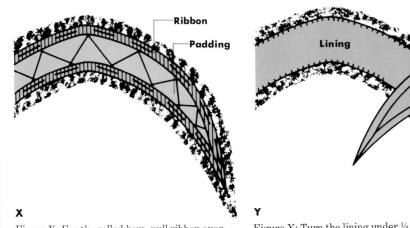

X

Figure X: For the rolled hem, pull ribbon over padding until ¼-inch of fur shows on the underside. Sew ribbon to skin with running stitches.

Y

Figure Y: Turn the lining under ¼ inch all around and sew it in place by slipstitching it to the grosgrain ribbon with tiny stitches.

Rolled hems will add a professional look to the outer edges of the collar and cuffs. To make a rolled hem, pull the grosgrain ribbon so that some of the fur (about ¼ inch) rolls to the underside, and sew the ribbon to the skin at that point (Figure X). Overlap the ribbon at the collar points and the cuff corners so the hem lies smooth and flat.

Cut the satin lining the same size as the fur pieces. Turn under a ¼-inch hem all around and then slipstitch the lining in place (Figure Y).

To finish the cuffs, join the cuff ends with a whipstitch. Match the cuff seam to the sleeve's inner seam if there is one. Pin, then slipstitch the cuffs to the sleeves along both edges to anchor them firmly in place or since the cuffs are lined, you can also attach the upper cuff edge to the lower sleeve edge and have the cuff serve as a sleeve extension.

To attach the collar to a coat or sweater, pin it along the neckline as pictured below. Match the center seam of the collar to the back center seam of the garment if there is one. Pin the inner edge of the collar lining to the inner coat or sweater neckline. Slipstitch along the line of pins. Anchor firmly with extra stitches at the center seam and around lower ends.

To make your collar and cuffs instantly removable when the garment needs cleaning, you can sew snap tape to the inside edge of the garment and to the collar and cuffs. However, a slipstitched set can be removed and sewn on another garment with little difficulty.

Collar and cuffs of racoon fur are pinned to the sweater, then slipstitched in place. Since they are fully lined, they can be sewn on the inside edges only. The set is then easy to detach.

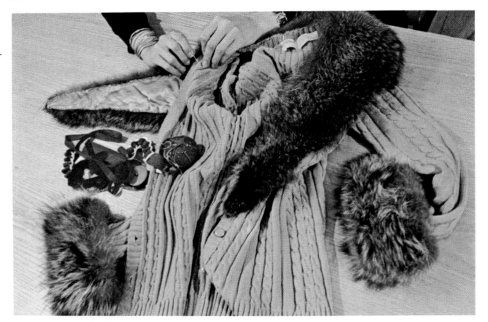

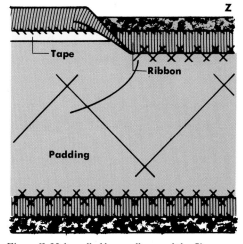

Figure Z: Make rolled hems all around the fling as described for a collar and cuffs (page 748). A small rim of fur shows on the underside.

This six-foot-long fox fling has a velvet lining and rolled hems all around, giving it a soft, rounded look.

Needlecrafts
Have a fling

¢ ☒ ⚐ ⚒

A fling is made with the same techniques used for the collar and cuffs (pages 746 to 748). A worn jacket is likely to have enough usable fur to make a six-foot-long fling. But whatever source of fur you use, you will have to do some piecing.

A fling can be any length, but most are from five to seven feet. A good width is from five to seven inches. The important thing is to make sure the hair flow is uniform for the entire length of the fling. Most flings have a vertical flow.

When cutting an old fur coat or jacket into sections of a fling, try to cut long pieces. Then you will have fewer sections to piece together. Make sure you have the same number of pieces on each side of the center back, so that when you wear the fling it will fall evenly, front and back. For example, if you make a six-foot-long fling, cut four pieces to make a three-foot-long strip, and four pieces for another strip the same length. When the two strips are joined, they will look uniform.

Materials: In addition to basic tools on page 740, you will need cotton batting for padding; ½-inch-wide grosgrain ribbon for all edges; and velvet for backing.

First, study and measure the jacket or coat you're recycling to make sure you have enough usable fur. Then cut and arrange pieces in a line, with uniform hair flow, until you have a piece the desired length. Tape all the edges (see Craftnotes, page 743), and sew the seams as shown in Figure D, page 742. Flatten seams with scissors handle, as shown in Figure M, page 745.

Cut cotton batting an inch smaller than the fur all around. Position the batting on the skin side and tack with wide catchstitches, as in Figure W, page 747. Next, sew grosgrain ribbon to all the outside fur edges as outlined for the collar and cuffs project. Flatten seams.

Make rolled hems following the directions given for the collar and cuffs. At least ¼ inch of fur should show on the underside.

Cut a velvet backing ¼-inch larger than the fur all around. It will be necessary to piece the velvet. You can do this on a sewing machine. Fold the velvet under ½-inch toward the wrong side. You may want to baste this hem so it will be easier to sew to the ribbon. Final finishing involves slipstitching the velvet to the ribbon. Remove the basting stitches and your fling is ready to wear.

For related projects, see "Sewing," and "Sheepskin Coats."

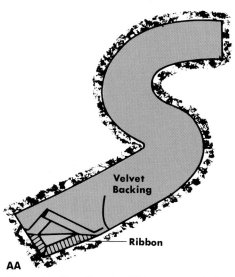

Figure AA: Turn the velvet lining under ½-inch and attach it to the ribbon with small slipstitches. This finishes the fling.

Tracing Your Ancestry

Timothy Field Beard is First Assistant Librarian of the Local History and Genealogy Department at the New York Public Library and serves as New York examiner for the Sons of the Revolution, the Society of Colonial Wars, and several other hereditary and patriotic societies. He has published articles and reviews in genealogical and historical magazines.

When I discovered at an early age that my great-great-great-great-grandfather, for whom I was named, had been a captain in the American Revolutionary War, I became intrigued with the idea of digging further into my past. Throughout my childhood, I continually discovered family mementoes tucked away in scrapbooks and albums, and hidden in attics. Photographs of my ancestors, their clothing, military uniforms, bibles and such, were as exciting to me as buried treasure. Gradually, as I began to fit the pieces together, I saw my family history fall into kaleidoscopic patterns with each ancestral link reflecting the history of the times in a very personal way. I wondered how far back I could go; what were my earliest origins? With no thought at the time of becoming a professional genealogist, I gave in to my curiosity and fascination with the past and began my search. Never did I suspect that my future research would lead me along so many diverse paths, back through 40 generations to Henry VII of England.

Genealogy in History and Today

Whether you are reading the myths of gods and heroes or the histories of former civilizations, or studying the art of primitive cultures, it becomes apparent that genealogy, or the study of ancestry, has always played an important part in religions and in political and social structures. One of the oldest written genealogical records appears in the First Book of Chronicles in the Old Testament, the "begats," in which Adam and Eve are given as the progenitors of all mankind. In ancient times, however, before the invention of writing, family histories were passed on through the oral tradition in the form of epic poems and songs. Genealogy was often a necessity to cultures, especially those ruled by hereditary monarchy or aristocracy, in which whole kingdoms as well as private property were passed on through family lines. Questions of descent could provoke bitter disputes which were often settled on the battlefield. The illuminated family tree at the right indicates the importance of genealogy to European families of the seventeenth century. The coat of arms to the left of the tree illustrates its connection with heraldry, a science which has spoken its own graphic genealogical language since the twelfth century in Europe.

Today, genealogy holds a special appeal for Americans who live in an uprooted and mobile society. Since most of our ancestors emigrated to this country within the past two or three hundred years, it is not surprising that many Americans are interested in discovering their origins.

Genealogy is an ideal hobby for a family to work on together. Your research can be combined with family trips to towns where your first American ancestors settled or the places where they lived abroad. You may discover long-lost relatives and begin corresponding with them, and even meet them.

Getting Started

Although the story of other people's lives is often fascinating, no one is more interesting than yourself when it comes to the genealogical search. When you begin to see your personal history in a larger historical context, you will appreciate the romance of genealogy. By following the procedures I have described here, you will be able to trace your family line back through several generations, perhaps even to your earliest ancestors, without help. How far you go depends upon your own persistence and the accessibility of information. Eventually, however, you may need to employ a professional genealogist to visit distant places or search for obscure data, especially if you decide to pursue your research abroad (see "Professional Help," page 757).

Begin your genealogical research by looking through family records. These notes, written in a family Bible in 1828, record the marriage of the author's maternal great-great-grandparents and the birth of his great-grandfather.

Opposite: an illuminated family tree traces the pedigree of the Bavarian family of Ströhl from the early 1600s to 1836. At the foot of the tree is the first known bearer of the noble name of Ströhl, Jaroslaus, married to Katharina von Kunitz. The background shows a view of the Bavarian town of Straubing on the Danube as it appeared at the time of Jaroslaus von Ströhl.

Stammbaum der Freiherren v. Ströhl zu Straubing in Bayern.

M. Johanna geb. 19./XI. 1750. † 22./VI. 1752.

M. Maximiliana geb. 22./XII. 1751 † 22./XI. 1779.

Joh. Nepomuk Domdechant u. Stadtpfarrer zu Freising geb. 24./IX. 1748.

M. Barbara geb. 3./III. 1754.

Franz Xaver ½ J. alt. † 25./III. 1756.

Franz Xaver Joseph geb. 18./IX. 1756 † 22./VIII. 1757.

M. Franziska geb. 18./VI. 1758.

Alois Joh. N. Generallieutenant geb. 18./VII. 1760 † 9./VII. 1834.

Joseph Max geb. 2./V. 1763.

Maximilian Georg Freiherr von Ströhl. get. 16./V. 1723.

Agnes Felicitas von Werner zu Grafenreuth. verm. 16./XI. 1748.

Franz Anton geb. 7./IV. 1725.

Maria Josepha geb. 5./VIII. 1727.

Maria Barbara geb. 9./XII. 1728.

Joh. Georg get. 24./IX. 1690.

Barbara Hermanna von Edelburg zu Altenweyer. verm. 11./X. 1716.

Joh. Michael get. 20./VII. 1651.

Veronika von Grunau verm. 13./XI. 1674.

Christoph get. 20./VIII. 1624.

Barbara von Staudach zu Freudenthurn verm. 3./VII. 1649.

Jaroslaus von Ströhl.

Katharina von Kunitz.

H. Ströhl.

DEATH OF MRS. BEARD.

Mrs. Philadelphia Stuart Beard, wife of Dr. C. Beard, died last evening at 8:30 o'clock, after a long and painful illness, borne with unexampled patience and fortitude. Mrs. Beard was the daughter of an English gentleman who settled in Canandaigua, New York, where she was born and where a part of her family still reside.

Her eldest brother is the present Sir Stuart Menteth, the owner of the large baronial possessions of the family in Scotland. She married Dr. Beard at a very early age and has since always resided in New Orleans, where she has an extended circle of warm and devoted friends, who will be inexpressibly grieved and shocked to learn of her death. Her eldest daughter married her cousin, Dr. Henry Stuart, surgeon United States navy, and is at present with her husband in Japan, where he is stationed on duty. Three other children—one daughter and two sons—were with her during her last illness.

Mrs. Beard was a woman of the highest qualities of character, of remarkable intellectual and moral force, with the most graceful and refined manners, and the loss to her family is irreparable. "We understand death for the first time when he puts his hand upon one whom we love," and we can well imagine the sadness and gloom which has fallen upon the household of our esteemed friend.

The hearts of all those who know him and value his friendship will go out in warmest sympathy to him and his in their affliction.

DIED.

BEARD—On Tuesday, March 29, 1881, Philadelphia Stuart Menteth, wife of Dr. C. Beard, niece of the late Countess of Mar and Kellie, of Alloa Park, and grand-daughter of the late Sir Charles G. Stuart Menteth, of Closeburn and Mansfield Park, County Dumfries, Scotland, sister to the present baronet, Sir James Stuart Menteth.

Her funeral will take place from No. 380 Prytania street, To-Day, at 3 p. m.

New York and Edinburgh (Scotland) papers please copy.

Tools and Objectives

Your most important tool, an inquiring and selective mind, is free; and you begin by acquiring as much firsthand information as possible. Your primary sources are your relatives, family documents and heirlooms. Then, as you broaden the search, you can investigate old records in out-of-the-way town halls or churches and synagogues, or you can even hunt for your ancestors' gravestones in cemeteries (see page 754). You will accumulate government records of your ancestors' births, marriages, and deaths, and search in libraries and even old newspapers for still more information. Eventually, you may find that you are related to a nobleman, or a horse thief, or both. But don't become side-tracked by trying to prove royalty or rogues in your line. Remember that your objective is to learn something about the people from whom you are descended: who they were, how they lived, what they were like. Trust your detective work to turn up surprises all along the way.

Your Family Tree

Keeping a simple chart, often called a family tree, will facilitate your research. It can be used to record the place of residence and dates of birth, marriage, and death of each ancestor as you trace your family history. Charts such as the one shown on pages 759 and 760 can be purchased from genealogical bookstores or publishers such as Goodspeed's and Charles Tuttle (see Craftnotes, page 755). There are many different formats for charts; some are small enough to put in a typewriter with space for listing three or four generations. Of course, you can always draw your own with a pen and ruler. Just be sure that you leave enough space for clear entry of name, residence, dates of birth, marriage, and death for each ancestor. You can build a series of related charts as you carry your family line back through the generations. List the sources for the information you have found on the back of each chart. Later on, you can transfer your sources to a card file.

Figure B on page 759 illustrates the use of a working chart and shows the ancestral links from one generation to the next. You can see that more research is necessary to fill in the missing names and dates. Chances are, however, that as you gradually discover more about your ancestors and they begin to emerge as real people, you won't settle for just names and dates. Pictures show what they looked like; letters, diaries, newspaper clippings and yearbooks can all tell you something about their personalities and the historical setting in which they lived. Eventually, you can put this kind of documented information into a scrapbook or printed manuscript (see page 761) incorporating your chart, stories, maps, pictures, documents, clippings, and letters.

Talking About the Past

Today, few families remain in one house, or even one region, for several generations. In fact, it has become increasingly rare to find more than two generations living together under the same roof. Children who have grown up without grandparents close at hand to tell them stories about the "old days" often experience a sense of loss about their past as adults. Thus, the first step in the genealogical search, contacting and talking to relatives, might prove to be the most exciting and interesting part of the adventure for many Americans.

It is usually not difficult to get relatives, especially older ones, to reminisce about the family. As your aim is to uncover factual information about your past, you will find yourself listening to old stories with fresh interest. Take notes on everything you hear and pay particular attention to names, dates, places, and incidents that you can verify from other sources. If a relative says your great-aunt was born in 1898, for example, you can write to the town hall of the place where she was born and request a copy of her birth certificate. Ask your relatives to be specific. If they use nicknames, make a note, but try to get them to remember proper names too. If an older relative has trouble recalling an exact date, focus on the approximate year with questions such as, "Was he alive when you were born?" and "How old were you when he died?" Find out what churches your ancestors attended, and in what cemeteries they were buried. Your relatives may recount stories they heard about events that took place before they were born. Make notes of such stories; you may be able to substantiate them later. Write to relatives who live too far away to visit and ask them for information.

Treasures in the Attic

Since public records were not kept until the mid- to late 1880s, family documents are extremely valuable in the genealogical search. While you are questioning relatives, ask if they have any written records, such as family Bibles, that may list births, marriages and deaths. The Bible shown on page 750 was the only record I could find of my great-great-grandparents' marriage and the birth of their son, my great-grandfather. Often, valuable newspaper clippings can be found tucked away in scrapbooks and albums. The obituary notice on the opposite page pays eloquent tribute to my great-grandmother, Mrs. Philadelphia Stuart Beard, who died in 1881, and reveals aspects of her life that I might never have uncovered through other sources. It also relates information about her immediate family, including marriages and property holdings abroad. I discovered a great deal about my great-granduncle, pictured at right, from an obituary notice in the New Orleans *Daily Delta*, dated January 10, 1850. If such pictures do not carry dates, the style of uniform indicates a particular war or an approximate period. You can write to the National Archives for service records.

Though attics are hard to find these days, you may discover family members who have lived in the same house for a long time; and they may have packed away old treasures in an attic trunk. As you search for genealogical clues, don't overlook old jewelry, such as a wedding ring which may be engraved with a marriage date; or a mourning ring, traditionally worn in memory of a loved one, engraved with his name and age and date of death; or even cuff links which may commemorate a special event (see page 760). A wedding quilt, with squares signed and dated by the bride's close friends and relatives, is a valuable find. As you turn up records and heirlooms, continue to ask your relatives more questions. Your discoveries will spark their memories.

A daguerreotype of the author's ancestor George Henry Tobin who served in the Seminole Indian War in the 1830s, was Deputy Sheriff of New Orleans in the early 1840s, a Texas Ranger in the Mexican War (1845–1847) and a war correspondent. He died a forty-niner in California.

Photograph album, below, of the author's family is from the Civil War period. The marriage date is written on the back of the picture of the woman in her wedding dress. Names, dates, and places written on the backs of photographs are all clues in the search.

An obelisk tombstone stands over the grave of the Reverend Timothy Field (1775–1844) in Westminster West, Vermont, near the church where he served as minister for many years. The son of a Revolutionary War captain and a graduate of Yale (1797), the minister was the author's great-great-great-grandfather.

Stones Can Speak

Taking a walk through an old country graveyard can be very interesting even if you don't know any of the names on the gravestones. Imagine the excitement you would feel when visiting the cemetery where your ancestors are buried. By reading the inscriptions on all the tombstones in the family plot, you may discover ancestors you didn't know existed, or you may verify a relationship that had been unclear. Photograph the gravestones, make rubbings with paper and crayon (see entry, "Rubbings"), copy the inscriptions and include the pictures in your scrapbook. If you are unable to visit the cemetery, write to its superintendent for a list of your family's interments.

Church Records

You may find dates of baptisms, marriages, and burial in the records of the church or synagogue your ancestors attended. There may also be a letter of transference which they may have brought from their former parish as an introduction to the church. Such a letter may be your first indication of where your ancestors came from and when they moved.

Library Research

When you have completed your preliminary research and have gathered a good deal of firsthand information, reference books become essential tools in helping you to obtain public records. The library is the next stop as you pursue the family line. The bibliography at right includes general works on genealogy and basic sources for exploring family history in the United States. Also included are sources for birth and death records, marriage and divorce certificates, census records, listings of historical and genealogical societies, and periodicals. The library can also supply you with published references such as town histories, genealogies of your family or related families, abstracts of wills and copies of old newspaper and magazine articles. You may also find pictures of local ancestral homes or businesses in the photographic archives that are sometimes maintained by large libraries.

If you live in or near a large city, the local public library may have a genealogy department or a collection that includes many of these works; if not, the librarian can direct you to the nearest library that does. There may also be a genealogical or historical society with a good library in your vicinity or in the areas where your ancestors lived. The librarians and archivists may provide you with a great deal of valuable guidance. You may also be able to obtain printed data, such as vital records and documents, from these sources. For mailing addresses, consult the *Directory of Historical Societies and Agencies in the United States and Canada* listed in the Craftnotes. If you cannot visit a library, write for information, keeping your inquiry brief and precise, giving specific dates and details. Always remember to enclose a self-addressed stamped envelope for the reply.

The references listed in the bibliography can be found in larger state, university, and public libraries. Catalogs of two book dealers, Goodspeed's Book Shop and Charles Tuttle, are listed because they are extensive enough to serve as references; these are available by mail. You can also send for the inexpensive U.S. Government pamphlets listed with their current prices. If you plan to study overseas, your librarian can direct you to specialized bibliographies for the country in which you are interested.

Public Records and Documents

Public records and official documents will substantiate the facts you have uncovered in your preliminary research and provide further information. For example, if you know nothing about your great-grandfather except his name and date and place of his death, you can get a copy of his death certificate, which will tell the date and place of his birth, the names of his parents, and where they were born. Basic documents used by genealogists include certificates of birth, marriage, and death, church records, wills, deeds, and state and federal census records. Other records may be important, depending upon the specific family. I discovered my ancestor's diploma, shown on page 756, among family papers. An inquiry into school records revealed the place of his birth and parents' marriage. You can send for copies of vital records, but if possible, try to visit the town hall or country

(continued)

GENEALOGY CRAFTNOTES: A SELECTIVE BIBLIOGRAPHY

American Association for State and Local History. **Directory of Historical Societies and Agencies in the United States and Canada, 1973-1974.** Nashville, Tenn. 37230, the Association, 1315 Eighth Avenue South. 378 pages.

American Genealogical-Biographical Index. Middletown, Conn., The Godfrey Memorial Library. First edition, A—Z, 1942-1952, 48 volumes. Revision, A—Hortal, 1952 to date, 83 volumes.

American Society of Genealogists. **Genealogical Research Methods and Sources.** Washington, D.C., the Society, 1960-1971. Two volumes.

Crowther, G. Rodney. **Surname Index to Sixty-five Volumes of Colonial and Revolutionary Pedigrees.** Washington, D.C., National Genealogical Society, 1964. 143 pages. (Special Publication No. 27)

Daughters of the American Revolution. **DAR Patriot Index.** Washington, D.C., NSDAR, 1966. 771 pages, two supplements.

Doane, Gilbert H. **Searching for Your Ancestors: The How and Why of Genealogy.** Fourth edition. Minneapolis, Minn., University of Minnesota Press, 1973. 198 pages.

Everton, George B. **Handy Book for Genealogists.** Sixth edition. Logan, Utah 84321, Everton Publishers, 1971. 297 pages.

Filby, P. William. **American and British Genealogy and Heraldry.** Chicago, Ill., American Library Association, 1970. 184 pages.

Genealogical Society of the Church of Jesus Christ of the Latter-day Saints. **Research Papers.** Salt Lake City, Utah 84111, the Genealogical Society, 50 E. North Temple Street, 1966 to date. (Series A: Great Britain, B: United States, C: Continental Europe, D: Scandinavia, E: Pacific.)

Goodspeed's Book Shop. **Family and Local History Catalogue No. 570.** Boston, Mass. 02108. Goodspeed's Book Shop, Inc., 18 Beacon Street, c. 1971. 136 pages.

Greenwood, Val D. **Researcher's Guide to American Genealogy.** Baltimore, Md., Genealogical Publishing Co., 1973.

Hale, Richard Walden. **Guide to Photocopied Historical Manuscripts in the United States and Canada.** Ithaca, N.Y., Cornell University Press for the American Historical Association, 1961. 241 pages.

Harland, Derek. **Genealogical Research Standards.** Salt Lake City, Utah, Bookcraft for the Genealogical Society, 1963. 404 pages.

Jacobus, Donald Lines. **Index to Genealogical Periodicals.** New Haven, Conn., 1932-1953. Three volumes.

Kirkham, E. Kay. **Survey of American Church Records, Major Denominations before 1880.** Third edition, revised and enlarged. Logan, Utah. Everton Publishers, 1971. 264 pages.

Lancour, Harold. **Bibliography of Ship Passenger Lists 1538-1825; Being a Guide to Published Lists of Early Immigrants to North America.** Third edition, revised and enlarged by Richard J. Wolf. New York, N.Y., New York Public Library, 1963. 137 pages.

McCay, Betty L. **Sources for Genealogical Searching in . . .** (separate volumes for various states). Indianapolis, Ind. 46226. B. L. McCay, 6702 East 46th Street, 1969—.

Munsell, Joel. Index to **American Genealogies with Supplement.** Baltimore, Md., Genealogical Publishing Co., 1967. 352 pages; supplement 107 pages, in one volume. (Originally published 1900-1908.)

National Genealogical Society. **Index of Revolutionary War Pension Applications.** Washington, D.C., the Society, 1966. 1324 pages. (Special Publication No. 32.)

New York Public Library. **Local History and Genealogy Division Catalog.** Boston, Mass., G. K. Hall, projected late 1974.

Order of the Crown of Charlemagne. **Lineage Book Volume 2.** Cottonport, La. 71327, Polyanthos, 1974. (Foreword contains long narrative bibliography of events in the field of genealogy since 1941.)

Peterson, Clarence S. **Consolidated Bibliography of County Histories in Fifty States in 1961.** Second edition. Baltimore, Md., Genealogical Publishing Co., 1963. 186 pages.

Pine, Leslie P. **The Genealogist's Encyclopedia.** Newton Abbot, Devon, England, David and Charles, 1969. 360 pages.

Tuttle, Charles E. **Genealogy and Local History Catalog No. 379.** Rutland, Vt. 05701, Charles E. Tuttle and Co., 1972. 192 pages.

Government Publications

United States Library of Congress. **Genealogies in the Library of Congress.** Edited by Marion J. Kaminkow. Baltimore, Md., Magna Carta Book Co., 1972. Two volumes.

United States National Archives. **Federal Population Censuses, 1790-1880, a Catalog of Microfilm Copies of the Schedules.** Washington, D.C. 20408, National Archives, 1971. 90 pages.

————. **Guide to Genealogical Records in the National Archives.** 1964. 145 pages. (Unfortunately there is no index.)

The following pamphlets are available by writing to the United States Government Printing Office, Washington, D.C. 20402:

First Census 1790, Heads of Families (various states), U.S. Census Office, 1907-1908.

Where to Write for Birth and Death Records, United States and Outlying Areas. Revised, 1972, 9 pages, (DHEW Publications, No. HSM 72-1142) 15 cents.

Where to Write for Birth and Death Records of U.S. Citizens Who Were Born Outside the United States. 1965. 19 pages. (PHS Publication No. 630A-2) 20 cents.

Where to Write for Marriage Records. 1972. 6 pages (DHEW Publication No. HSM 72-1144) 15 cents.

Where to Write for Divorce Records, United States and Outlying Areas. 5 pages. (DHEW Publication No. HSM 72-1445) 15 cents.

Genealogical Magazines

Listed below are a few of the major publications which include query sections to which genealogical problems may be submitted. Consult your library for other regional listings.

The American Genealogist
1232 39th Street
Des Moines, Iowa 50311

The National Genealogical
Society Quarterly
1921 Sunderland Place, N.W.
Washington, D.C. 20036

New England Historical
and Genealogical Register
101 Newbury Street
Boston, Mass. 02116

New York Genealogical &
Biographical Record
122 East 58th Street
New York, N.Y. 10022

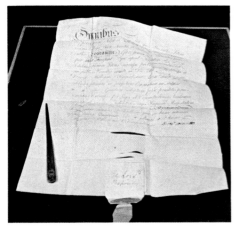

This diploma, dated 1832 from Trinity College, Dublin, belonged to George Tobin (see page 753). School records revealed he was born in the county of Wicklow. After contacting, in person and by mail, virtually every parish in the area, the author located the one where George was baptized and his parents were married.

courthouse in the area where your ancestors lived. Although it is often possible to hire a professional researcher, it is always best to search through the records yourself. Whether you apply for records in person or by mail, you usually have to pay two or three dollars for each copy. When writing for documents of any kind, always ask for particular certificates and be specific about names and dates. A blanket request for information about anyone bearing your family name will probably go unanswered. A typical query might be: "Please send me a full copy of the death certificate of Mary Thompson Warner who died in Jamesville on July 25, 1901. She was my grandmother, and I need this record for genealogical purposes." Enclose a self-addressed stamped envelope for the reply.

Birth, Death and Marriage Certificates
Obtain copies of vital records for all your family members, beginning with your own birth certificate. The place where such records have been kept and the dates from which they are available vary from state to state, but you can probably locate records from the mid- to late 1800s. At one time, such documents were kept in town or county seats; later, the responsibility shifted to the states.

Wills and Deeds
Wills and deeds are generally kept in county courthouses. Look up your ancestors' town in the U.S. Post Office Zip Code Directory: it gives the town's county.

You can locate an ancestor's will if you know his name, where he lived, and the date of his death. Even if he died intestate (without a will) there will be papers relating to the distribution of his estate. Such documents, which are usually indexed and kept in bound volumes, often list heirs, their addresses, and their relationship to the deceased. Ascertain through an inquiry to the county courthouse if the information you are seeking is kept there and if you will be permitted to search through the records.

Examining deeds may turn up more ancestors, for deeds frequently were signed by more than one family member. The earliest deed in your family's name in a given region will help you determine when your ancestors moved to the area and may indicate where they came from. Photostatic copies of wills and deeds can be obtained by mail. Because a white on black negative is the first step in the photostatic process, many government offices send documents in this form. You can obtain a positive print by paying more, but the negative is more legible. Inquire about costs before ordering.

Census Records
The federal census has been taken every ten years since 1790. These records can be a great help in researching your early American ancestors, although, through 1840, only heads of households were listed by name. The 1790 census is available in printed form; others can be studied on microfilm in large libraries. Records of censuses taken after 1900 can be seen only with special permission, because they are considered confidential. Other federal documents, such as land and pension records, may also yield information. To find out what is available, consult *Guide to Genealogical Records in the National Archives* (see Craftnotes, page 755). Write to state archives to find out about the availability of state census records for the region that interests you.

Periodicals
There are more than 900 genealogical magazines published today, many of them specializing in particular regions. A few of the major publications are listed, with their addresses, at the end of Craftnotes on page 755. You can send queries to genealogical magazines or run advertisements in them, asking people with specific information about your ancestors to write you. Frequently, the privilege of placing queries is limited to subscribers, who may do so gratis. The cost of a year's subscription to a genealogical magazine is usually between five and ten dollars. For listings and addresses of other magazines refer to the *Directory of Historical Societies and Agencies in the United States and Canada* and George Everton's *Handy Book for Genealogists* (Craftnotes, page 755). Check local libraries for their own regional magazine listings.

Professional Help

If you decide to seek professional help, it is best to consult the lists of qualified genealogists maintained by large libraries and historical societies. Reputable genealogists work on only one generation at a time and are very careful to establish, with certainty, the identities of all four grandparents before proceeding to the great-grandparents. However, when dealing with "searchers" not listed by a library or an authentic historical society, either by mail or in person, your own judgment is really the only thing you can depend upon in determining their reliability. Unscrupulous "genealogists" have been known to prey upon people with high hopes of finding royalty in their line. Beware of anyone who offers you a prestigious list of ancestors on the basis of your first inquiry and then demands a high fee. Fees usually run from three dollars an hour in rural areas to $12 an hour in major cities like New York.

Back to the Old Country

If you trace your family back far enough, you will discover one or more of the ancestors who emigrated to this country. If you know his name and the approximate date of his migration and can connect him to a town or parish overseas, there is a good chance you can extend your genealogy to his country of origin.

Making the trip to your ancestors' country is, of course, an adventure; and you may even discover relatives who still live there. It is a good idea to gather as much information and establish as many contacts as you can before you start out.

Sources Abroad Vary

The process of tracing your family line in another country is the same as it is here, but the sources are somewhat different (see photograph at right). If you have traced English ancestors to a certain parish, you can write to the rector for records of baptisms, marriages, and burial. If you know in what town French ancestors lived, you can write to the town hall (*hôtel de ville*) for information. Go to a genealogical library and ask the librarian for a list of source books detailing how to look for records and whom to contact in the country in which you are interested. When you write to officials abroad, ask them to send you the name and address of a local "searcher" whom you can employ. Having someone do preliminary research before you arrive is a great help.

Once you are overseas, search for records in local churches and government offices, just as you did here. If any people living in the town have your family name, you may be able to establish their relationship to you. Often they can provide information and family records. Before returning home, you can enlist someone to carry on the research.

If you cannot make a trip abroad, you can always continue your research by mail, possibly with the help of a professional genealogist.

Regional Differences Are Important

The problems you encounter and the sources you use will depend on the religion or nationality of the people you are tracing and the area in which they lived. For example, in this country the North and South had entirely different methods of keeping records. If your ancestors settled in the Northeast, it would be relatively easy to locate old town and church records. In the South, towns and cities did not keep records, so county records are more important, if they still exist. Church records may also be helpful, but many of them have disappeared, as have many southern cemeteries, which were customarily on family property. Therefore, southerners must generally rely on federal census records, while northerners may not have to consult them.

The same differences are reflected farther west, because settlers carried their customs with them. In Michigan, which was settled by northerners, good records date from the 1860s. But in Missouri, settled by southerners, records are scarce.

The problem has been alleviated somewhat by the work of members of the Church of Jesus Christ of Latter-Day Saints, popularly known as Mormons, in whose religion genealogy plays an integral part. The Mormons have collected and preserved an enormous quantity of records, including excellent sources for southern genealogies (see Craftnotes, page 755).

The registration of pedigree, or lineage, of one of the author's ancestors, born in 1769 and created a baronet by Queen Victoria, came from the Lord Lyon's Office, General Register House, Edinburgh, Scotland. When a pedigree was registered, the office verified the individual's ancestry through several preceding generations. Finding the pedigree gave the author access to other valuable information on file.

Black Americans Face Special Problems

Some black Americans have succeeded in tracing their families through the slavery period and back to Africa. Because there are few wills or property records for their ancestors prior to the Civil War, they have generally had to depend on census, birth, and death records. Also, the wills of white slave-owning families sometimes included estate inventories (see photograph below) listing the names of slaves, their ages, and the names of their children. People often passed slaves on from generation to generation, so a study of one family's wills may produce abundant data about a black family's lineage.

Sworn [illegible] Harris Depty. Com'y. of [illegible] County

An Inventory of all and Singular the goods and Chattels of James Martin late of worcester County Gentlemen Deceased taken the 19th. day of May Ann' Dom'. 1748 and appraised at the Instance of Mary Martin Executrix of the Said James by Adam Spence and Robert King of worcester County in Current money in manner following viz.

To 1 negro man called Pompey aged about 40 years a . . . £ 50.. 0.. 0
1 negro Ditto called Mars about Ditto a . . . 40.. 0.. 0
1 negro Ditto called Joe . . . 35.. 0.. 0
1 negro woman called Moll aged about 18 years a Legacey to the deceased Daughter Eliz.a Martin . . . £48..0..0
1 Tartin night gound lined w.th Calaminco and 1 pair of gold buttons a Legacey to Ditto . . . £4..4..0 — 52.. 4.. 0
1 Molatto boy a Slave Called Jethro aged about 5 years a Legacey to the deceased Son William Martin . . . a . . . 16.. 0.. 0
1 Molatto Girl a Called Candis aged about 2 years a Legacey to the deceased Son James Martin . . . a . . . 10.. 0.. 0
1 negro woman called Dinah a . . . 45.. 0.. 0
1 Molatto Girl called Jenney about 4 months old . a . . . 4.. 0.. 0
1 Molatto Woman called Nan old . a . . . 10.. 0.. 0
1 negro man Called Jack past hand labour being very old a . . . 1.. 0.. 0
1 feather Bed and furniture No. 1 . a . . . 9.. 14.. 10
1 feather Bed and furniture . No. 2. a . . . 8.. 15.. 5½
1 feather bed and furniture . No. 3. a . . . 8.. 1.. 6
1 Ditto and Ditto . . . No. 4. a . . . 11.. 4.. 1½
1 Ditto and ditto . . . No. 5 . . a . . . 8.. 3.. 11½
1 Ditto and ditto . . . No. 6 a . . . 4.. 6.. 6½
1 ditto and ditto . . . No. 7 . a . . . 4.. 2.. 10½
1 ditto and ditto . . . No. 8 . a . . . 6.. 17.. 10½
329.. 11.. 0½

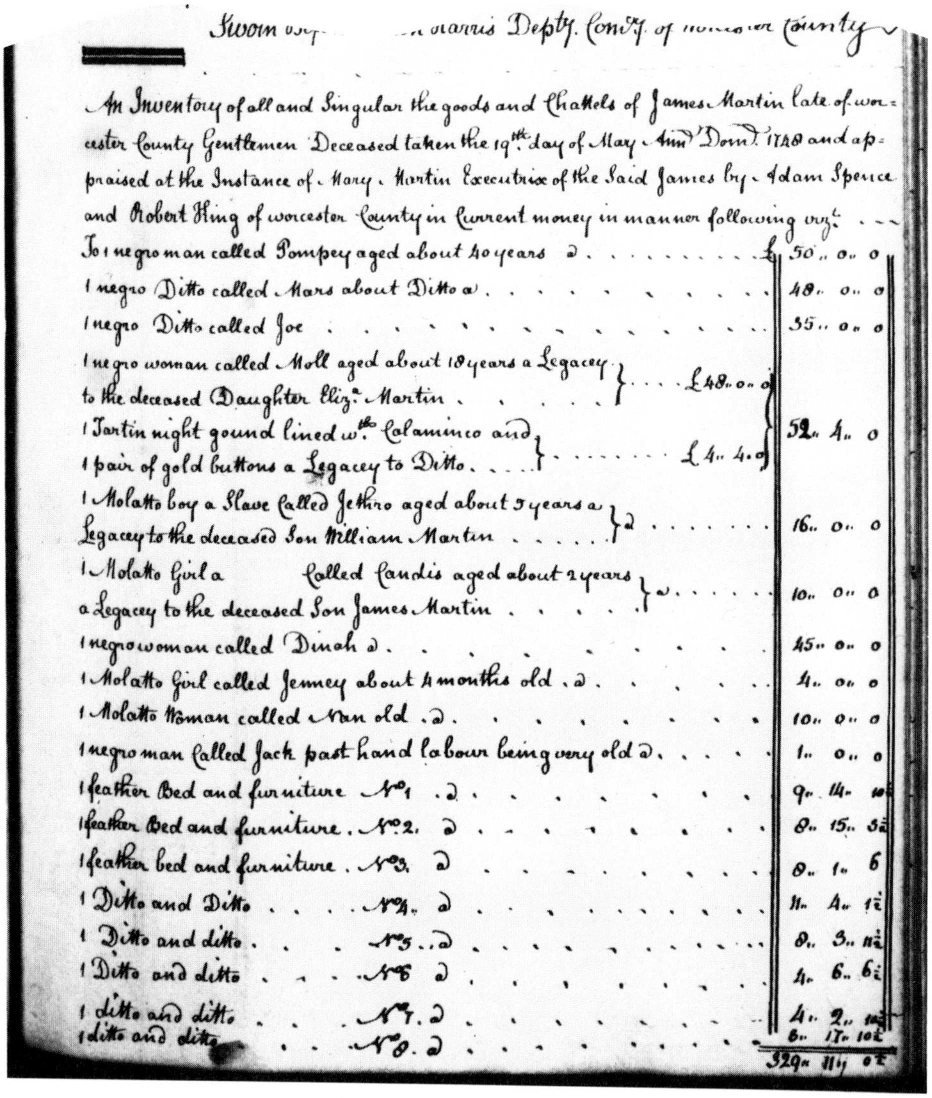

The estate inventory of a deceased Maryland "country gentleman," dated 1748. Among his "goods and chattels" are listed several slaves with their names and ages and often their familial relationships. As slaves were considered inheritable property, their descendants can often trace them back from one generation to another on inventories such as this.

A Case History Blends Many Roots

People whose families have been in the public eye can often trace their ancestors easily. A cursory reconstruction of the genealogy of young Adam Clayton Powell, 3rd, with facts gleaned from newspapers, social registers, and *Who's Who* listings, indicates a variety of ancestors shared by many Americans.

In the chart opposite (Figure A), we see that through his paternal grandfather, the late Congressman Adam Clayton Powell, Jr., his forebears were black Americans; and through his paternal grandmother, musician Hazel Scott, his ancestors were blacks from the Caribbean. Through his maternal grandfather, career dip-

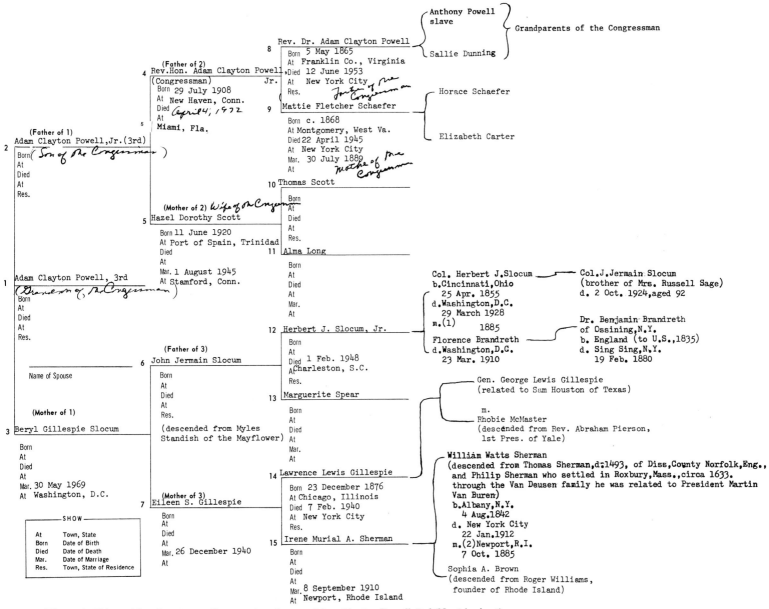

Grandparents of the Congressman

Anthony Powell
slave

Sallie Dunning

Rev. Dr. Adam Clayton Powell
8
Born 5 May 1865
At Franklin Co., Virginia
Died 12 June 1953
At New York City
Res. *Father of the Congressman*

(Father of 2)
4 Rev.Hon. Adam Clayton Powell, Jr.
(Congressman)
Born 29 July 1908
At New Haven, Conn.
Died *April 4, 1972*
At Miami, Fla.

Horace Schaefer

Mattie Fletcher Schaefer
9
Born c. 1868
At Montgomery, West Va.
Died 22 April 1945
At New York City
Mar. 30 July 1889
At *mother of the Congressman*

Elizabeth Carter

(Father of 1)
2 Adam Clayton Powell, Jr.(3rd)
Born (*Son of the Congressman*)
At
Died
At
Res.

10 Thomas Scott
Born
At
Died
At
Res.

(Mother of 2) *Wife of the Congressman*
5 Hazel Dorothy Scott
Born 11 June 1920
At Port of Spain, Trinidad
Died
Mar. 1 August 1945
At Stamford, Conn.

11 Alma Long
Born
At
Died
At
Mar.
At

1 Adam Clayton Powell, 3rd
(*Grandson of the Congressman*)
Born
At
Died
At
Res.

Col. Herbert J. Slocum
b. Cincinnati, Ohio
25 Apr. 1855
d. Washington, D.C.
29 March 1928
m.(1)   1885
Florence Brandreth
d. Washington, D.C.
23 Mar. 1910

Col. J. Jermain Slocum
(brother of Mrs. Russell Sage)
d. 2 Oct. 1924, aged 92

Dr. Benjamin Brandreth
of Ossining, N.Y.
b. England (to U.S.,1835)
d. Sing Sing, N.Y.
19 Feb. 1880

12 Herbert J. Slocum, Jr.
Born
At
Died 1 Feb. 1948
At Charleston, S.C.
Res.

Name of Spouse

(Father of 3)
6 John Jermain Slocum
Born
At
Died
At
Res.
(descended from Myles
Standish of the Mayflower)

13 Marguerite Spear
Born
At
Died
At
Mar.
At

Gen. George Lewis Gillespie
(related to Sam Houston of Texas)

m.

Rhobie McMaster
(descended from Rev. Abraham Pierson,
1st Pres. of Yale)

(Mother of 1)
3 Beryl Gillespie Slocum
Born
At
Died
At
Mar. 30 May 1969
At Washington, D.C.

14 Lawrence Lewis Gillespie
Born 23 December 1876
At Chicago, Illinois
Died 7 Feb. 1940
At New York City
Res.

William Watts Sherman
(descended from Thomas Sherman,d.1493, of Diss,County Norfolk,Eng.,
and Philip Sherman who settled in Roxbury,Mass.,circa 1633.
through the Van Deusen family he was related to President Martin
Van Buren)
b. Albany, N.Y.
4 Aug.1842
d. New York City
22 Jan.1912
m.(2) Newport,R.I.
7 Oct. 1885

(Mother of 3)
7 Eileen S. Gillespie
Born
At
Died
At
Mar. 26 December 1940
At

15 Irene Murial A. Sherman
Born
At
Died
At
Mar. 8 September 1910
At Newport, Rhode Island

Sophia A. Brown
(descended from Roger Williams,
founder of Rhode Island)

─── SHOW ───
At   Town, State
Born   Date of Birth
Died   Date of Death
Mar.   Date of Marriage
Res.   Town, State of Residence

Figure A: This working chart traces the ancestry of young Adam Clayton Powell, 3rd (No. 1 in chart), grandson of the late Congressman Adam Clayton Powell, Jr. (No. 4 in chart). Shown in an incompleted form, it contains only information available in published sources. The chart shows the connection of one generation to the next, and missing names and dates indicate where further research is necessary. The late congressman was known as Adam Clayton Powell, Jr. until the death of his father (No. 8 in chart) in 1953. At that time, the suffix Jr. was adopted by the congressman's son (No. 2 in chart) who had previously been called Adam Clayton Powell, 3rd. Such arbitrary changes and transfers of title are among the problems genealogists sometimes must untangle.

lomat John J. Slocum, he has pioneer white New England ancestry, including Myles Standish, and through his maternal grandmother he is related to Sam Houston of Texas and descended from the Reverend Abraham Pierson, first rector of Yale, Martin Van Buren, President of the United States, and the Reverend Roger Williams, founder of Rhode Island.

All this information was available in public sources. Further details could be obtained by sending for marriage and death certificates, wills and deeds, and by searching family papers and printed local and family histories.

These silver and gold cuff links were presented by the author's great-grandmother, Mrs. Philadelphia Stuart Beard (see pages 752 and 753) to her husband on the occasion of their twenty-fifth wedding anniversary. Intertwined numerals, representing significant dates, form the basis for the design. The date on the right, 1852, is the year of their marriage; the other, 1877, commemorates their anniversary. The backs are engraved "May 10th," the wedding day. The author's grandmother found them years ago at the bottom of her button box.

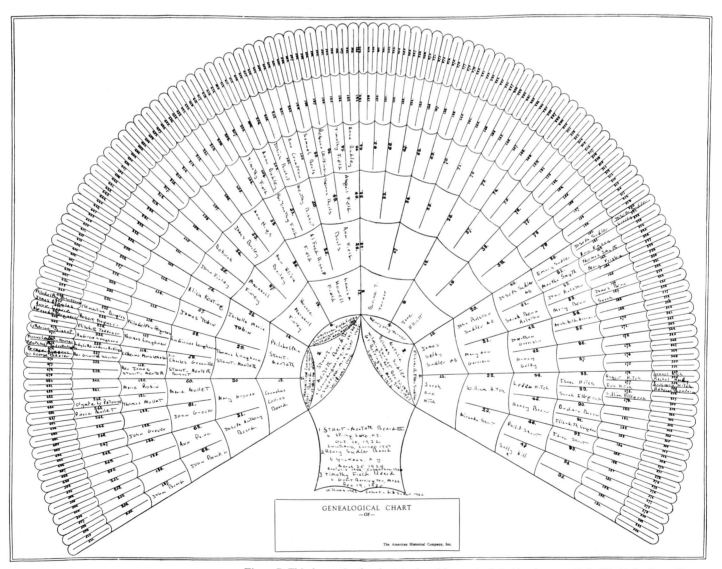

Figure B: This decorative fan chart (reduced from actual size) has been partially filled in by the author as he charted his own genealogy. The photograph opposite shows him at work, transferring information to this chart from documents obtained from sources abroad. Elaborately designed fan charts are available in sizes up to 25 by 35 inches and, when filled in, make excellent wall decorations for libraries, dens, or any room where the family congregates.

To fill out the fan chart shown opposite, the author copies information from a 19th-century death certificate obtained from the Registrar General at St. Catherine's House, London, where all vital records of England and Wales have been housed since 1837. When you come to the end of your genealogical research, names and dates can be transformed into a richly illustrated narrative of your ancestry.

The author's great-grandfather, a southerner, used this forged British passport to pass through Union lines during the siege of New Orleans. Originally, the author knew only that his ancestor had passed enemy lines with the help of an artist friend. When he found, among family keepsakes, some playing cards cut in the shape of the official seal on the passport, he was able to piece the story together: the artist had cut the cards and impressed the seal on the forged document. It is often possible to reconstruct life stories by uncovering such records.

Presenting Your Genealogy

It is easy to expand the chart you have been keeping to include more facts and also to make it attractive enough to display. If you like a flat format and have accumulated daguerreotypes, photographs and signatures of several ancestors, purchase a larger, more decorative chart for a few dollars, one with space for many generations, such as the fan chart shown above and opposite. When you have filled it in, mount reproductions of pictures and signatures around the border (preserve the originals) and frame it.

A scrapbook is also a popular and appealing way to present your family's history. Mount the page-size charts in the front, and fill the rest with written narratives and anecdotes about your family, pictures of your ancestors, photographs of family homes, tombstones, maps, signatures, and letters.

Share Your Work with Others

If you have completed a lot of research and traced your family through several generations, consider putting the results in book form incorporating charts and narratives. Your manuscript can be mimeographed inexpensively, or you can have it typeset and printed. An offset printer can copy and bind your book, or perhaps your relatives will share the cost (roughly $2000 for a few hundred copies of an attractively bound 200-page book) of having it published by one of the many genealogical publishers who do this type of work. Among the best known are Charles E. Tuttle in Vermont (see Craftnotes, page 755); Polyanthos in Cottonport, Louisiana; Genealogical Publishing Co. in Baltimore, Maryland; and Edwards Brothers in Ann Arbor, Michigan. You can give copies to friends and relatives and present or sell them to libraries with genealogical collections. Your local historical or genealogical society or your publisher will advise you on how to organize and distribute your book.

For related crafts and projects, see the entries "Greeting Cards" (Craftnotes. "Preparing Material for the Printer"), "Heraldic Designs," and "Rubbings."

Silhouettes like this were popular in the early to mid-nineteenth century and may be the only available images of ancestors from that period.

GINGERBREAD
A Baker's Art

Born in Switzerand, Albert Hadener developed his baking artistry there and in England and Sweden before coming to the United States in 1957. Gingerbread is only one of the confections he is famous for. His Elk Candy Company is a leading maker of marzipan and chocolates and Mr. Hadener designs and makes his own candy molds, a rare practice today.

Mr. Hadener's Christmas specialties are in such demand that he often makes as many as 50 gingerbread houses at once. This is the first time his recipe has been published.

Gingerbread is made from a spicy dough traditionally sweetened with honey. It was known to the ancient Egyptians who believed that honey had mystical powers. The first recipe for honey-sweetened cake came from Greece, where it reportedly was devised by a baker on the island of Rhodes about 2400 B.C. As with many things Greek, gingerbread was copied by the Romans and spread throughout their empire. Other European cultures developed their own recipes by adding whatever spices were available. During the early Middle Ages, monks refined the recipes, using newly-acquired exotic spices from the Far East. Thus, today we have many different recipes for gingerbread cakes and cookies. Most modern recipes substitute molasses for honey.

In the 14th, 15th, and 16th centuries, elaborate gingerbread creations became almost an art form in many European countries. England's Queen Elizabeth I, for example, had bakers create flattering gingerbread likenesses of lords and ladies in her court. Other royalty handed out their own countenances depicted in gingerbread. Detailed cookies made from handcarved molds became fashionable gifts.

Nowhere was gingerbread more closely mixed with culture than in Germany. The German form of gingerbread, known as *lebkuchen*, is a spicy honey cake, and the kind I used to make the gingerbread house opposite. The art of baking *lebkuchen* was so revered during the 14th and 15th centuries in Germany that contests used to be held among bakers from different towns to produce the finest one. The town of Nuremburg frequently won. Nuremburg's *lebkuchen* is still prized today.

When Grimm wrote *Hansel and Gretel* in the 19th century, the gingerbread house became a German specialty, especially appealing to children.

Kitchen Favorites and Celebrations
Fairy-tale gingerbread house ¢ ◐ 🚶 ✈

An enchanting gingerbread house like the one pictured at right is almost as much fun to make as it is to look at—or eat. First cut out cardboard patterns for the pieces as shown on page 765. Prepare dough ancording to the recipe on page 764, then follow the directions given for cutting and baking. Use the recipe on page 766 to prepare frosting for joining the pieces together and decorating. To give the house its fairy-tale appearance, decorate it with frosting and add commercial hard candies, marzipan, sprinkles, and almonds. I made Hansel, Gretel, and the witch of marzipan, but you can make them of gingerbread if you prefer. Actual-size patterns for these figures are on page 765.

The total working time needed to make this house is about three or four hours but it is necessary to wait between some stages, so you should spread the work over several days. Plan to prepare and chill the dough one day; roll it out, cut and bake it the second day; and assemble and decorate it the third day.

Lebkuchen is remarkably sturdy and long-lasting. It will keep indefinitely if not cooked in a pan greased with fat. The recipe on page 764 requires no fat; you bake the gingerbread on ungreased cookie sheets or tins lined with a layer of aluminum foil. This means that you can make the house long before Christmas, and keep it for several years, so long as you wrap it in plastic and store it in a cool dry place, out of the reach of hungry children.

The recipe on the next page makes one gingerbread house plus Hansel, Gretel, and the witch. If you prefer to make *lebkuchen* cookies, the same recipe yields about 2½ dozen large gingerbread boys.

Fairy-tale gingerbread house, designed by Albert Hadener, is made from *lebkuchen*, a spicy honey-sweetened dough. The decorations are candies, almonds and snow-like white frosting.

Gingerbread House

Recipe ingredients:

2½ cups honey (buckwheat honey,
   if possible)
1 cup sugar
½ cup milk
7 to 8 cups all-purpose flour
1 tablespoon cinnamon
2 teaspoons each of nutmeg, mace,
   ground allspice and salt
1 tablespoon baking soda
2 lemon rinds, chopped

Frosting:

1 pound sifted confectioners' sugar
4 egg whites

Decorations:

almonds
multicolored sprinkles
handful of small candies

What You Will Need

You probably have in your kitchen most of the equipment needed to make the gingerbread house: rolling pin; pastry board or waxed paper for rolling dough on; 2 large cookie sheets (12 inches by 16 inches) or 4 smaller ones; pastry wheel or paring knife; candy thermometer; pastry bag with a No. 5 tube opening (or similar opening to make a line of frosting about ¼-inch wide); large mixing bowl; heavy 2-quart saucepan; measuring cups; measuring spoons. Ingredients (left) are available in any supermarket. To prepare patterns you will need cardboard and scissors.

Making Cardboard Patterns

Patterns in Figure A on the opposite page are half their actual size. On stiff cardboard, scale up the patterns to the dimensions given and cut them out. Dotted lines on the front pattern show where to cut the front window and door *after* this front section is cut from dough. Dotted lines on the sides show where to place shutters after baking. Those on the chimney pattern show where to cut an angle that fits the slope of the roof. This is done on the chimney front and back *after* baking. Make separate patterns for the front door, window shutters, and for Hansel, Gretel, and the witch (shown actual size in Figure A).

Preparing the Dough

Combine honey, sugar, and milk in a saucepan and heat until the mixture registers 140–150 degrees Fahrenheit on a candy thermometer. While the mixture is heating, mix flour, spices, baking soda and lemon rind in a large bowl.

Pour the hot mixture into the dry ingredients and mix thoroughly. The dough should leave the sides of the bowl and you should be able to shape it into a smooth ball. If it is too wet and sticks, mix in more flour. Chill the dough for two or three hours or overnight in the refrigerator.

1: Cut each piece by laying the cardboard pattern on top of the dough and tracing around it with a pastry wheel or paring knife.

2: Place cut pieces on cookie sheets. You can line cookie sheets with aluminum foil or bake on ungreased sheets. Be sure to leave room between pieces for spreading.

3: After the front piece is trimmed, cut the witch's window and front door (see Figure A). Pictured is a round cutter the size of the door opening, but a sharp knife is fine to use.

Rolling and Cutting Dough

Remove dough from the refrigerator and let it stand until it is soft enough to roll out. (It is easier to divide the dough in fourths and work with one fourth at a time.) Using a lightly floured rolling pin, roll out the dough on a lightly floured board until it is ¼-inch thick. (You may need to work in more flour.)

Lay cardboard patterns on the dough and cut around them with a pastry wheel or paring knife. Cut a front, a back, two sides, two roof pieces, a base, three chimney pieces and a chimney roof, a front door, and two pairs of shutters. Also cut out Hansel, Gretel, and the witch.

After the front section is cut, follow the dotted lines and cut out the front window and door openings. Cut round windows for both sides. Decorate the archway over the front door by pressing a few almonds into the dough (see photograph, page 763). Press an almond into the front door.

Place cut pieces on ungreased or aluminum foil-lined cookie sheets. If you don't have enough cookie sheets to accommodate all the pieces, bake several batches. Pieces should be placed about an inch apart to allow them to spread.

Continue rolling dough and cutting until you have all the pieces you need.

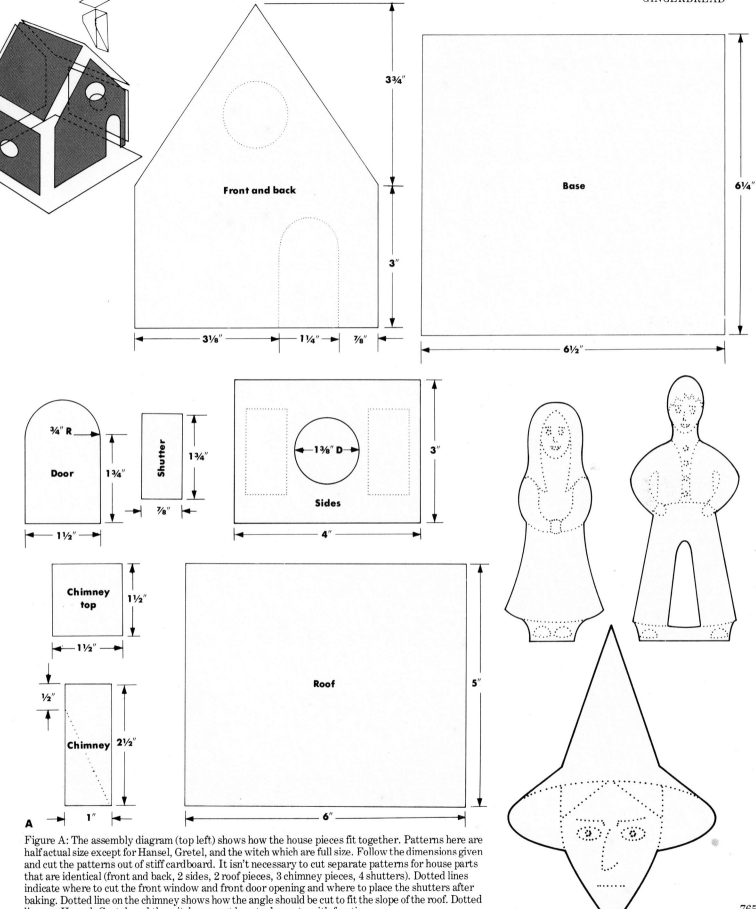

Front and back

3¾"

3"

3⅛" 1¼" ⅞"

Base

6¼"

6½"

Door

¾" R

1¾"

1¾"

1½"

Shutter

1¾"

⅞"

Sides

1⅜" D

3"

4"

Chimney top

1½"

1½"

Chimney

½"

2½"

1"

Roof

5"

6"

A

Figure A: The assembly diagram (top left) shows how the house pieces fit together. Patterns here are half actual size except for Hansel, Gretel, and the witch which are full size. Follow the dimensions given and cut the patterns out of stiff cardboard. It isn't necessary to cut separate patterns for house parts that are identical (front and back, 2 sides, 2 roof pieces, 3 chimney pieces, 4 shutters). Dotted lines indicate where to cut the front window and front door opening and where to place the shutters after baking. Dotted line on the chimney shows how the angle should be cut to fit the slope of the roof. Dotted lines on Hansel, Gretel, and the witch suggest how to decorate with frosting.

765

Baking

Preheat oven to 350 degrees Fahrenheit. Bake for 8 to 10 minutes. Remove gingerbread from the oven and leave on cookie sheets until it cools. If you are reusing the cookie sheets for additional baking, make sure the sheets cool before starting the next batch. This will prevent dough from spreading.

Frosting and Assembling

In a large bowl, make the frosting by beating 1 pound of sifted confectioners' sugar and 4 egg whites until the mixture forms stiff peaks. Place several heaping spoonfuls of frosting in a pastry bag fitted with a No. 5 tube opening. (Keep the rest of the frosting covered with a damp towel or plastic wrap so it won't dry out.)

Apply a line of frosting to the lower outside edge of the back of the house and spread it with a knife to make an inch-wide band. Dip frosted area in colored sprinkles. Apply a line of frosting to the bottom edge (photograph 4). Set the back on the base about an inch in from the base edge. Hold in place for several minutes until the frosting sets.

Frost the shutters with green frosting (or any color you choose). To do this, mix a few spoonfuls of white frosting with food coloring in a separate bowl and apply with a knife to cover the shutters. Using frosting as an adhesive, attach the shutters beside each side window.

Apply frosting and sprinkles to the lower outside edges of the sides and dip them in sprinkles. Frost the sides in place and hold until set.

4: Put a band of sprinkles on the back piece, then apply a line of frosting to the bottom so you can affix the back to the base.

5: Reinforce the house corners from inside with an extra line of frosting. Then position the witch inside the front window with frosting.

6: Gently place joined roof halves on the frosted top edges of the house and hold them in place until they set—about five minutes.

7: Attach the chimney and frost the roof generously. Then place candy decorations in the frosting before it hardens. Use the photograph on page 763 as a guide.

Frost and fit the front in place the same way. Then reinforce the joined parts of the house from inside with frosting (photograph 5).

With dots of frosting, make eyes for the witch. Put some frosting on her hat so that you can frost her in place inside the front window. The front door is frosted in place after the house is completely assembled.

Take great care when you set the roof on the house so that it doesn't slip. First, allow front, back, and sides to set undisturbed on the base for about two hours. Meanwhile, frost the roof halves together. To attach the roof, apply frosting to the exposed edges of the front, back, and sides. Gently place the roof on the house so it rests evenly (photograph 6). Hold the roof in place and allow it to set.

Final Decorating

The base of the chimney is cut on the angle shown by the dotted line in Figure A, page 765, so that it will fit the slope of the roof. Cut, then frost the three chimney pieces together and let them set for five minutes. Then frost the chimney to the house. Set the top on the chimney and frost it as well.

Frost the roof with a spatula, using light sweeps to cover the surface liberally (photograph 7). Then position decorations on the roof by pressing them gently into the frosting. I used nuts, wrapped candies, marzipan and a foil-wrapped Santa.

You may want to decorate Hansel and Gretel with colored rather than white frosting. Make it by adding food coloring to the remaining white frosting. Decorate Hansel and Gretel to your liking and then frost them in place. Finally, frost the front door in place so it stands ajar.

Kitchen Favorites and Celebrations

For young cooks

¢ ▯ ⚇ ⚒

Gingerbread cookies of all shapes and sizes are a good-tasting Christmas treat. The cookies below were made with traditional cookie cutters. Such cutters are available in kitchen shops and department stores. The smaller figures—the girl with blue skirt (top right) and the two small boys—are traditional European designs. The three large figures—all gingerbread boys—use a popular American design. If you don't want to buy cookie cutters, there are patterns you can enlarge given in Figure B, page 768. Cut cardboard patterns, then trace around them on rolled-out dough with a paring knife.

The recipe for these cookies calls for molasses, but I used treacle instead; it gives cookies a rich, dark tone. Treacle is imported from England or Scotland and is available in gourmet food shops. Molasses, of course, is fine to use.

After cookies are baked and decorated, wrap them in bright-colored tissue paper and place them in baskets or tins. The recipe makes about two dozen cookies.

Lisa Bosboom's love of traditional European foods can be traced to her Dutch father and Hungarian grandfather who operate H. Roth, Lekvar-by-the-Barrel, a store in New York City that has been importing delicacies since Lisa's great-grandfather founded it 60 years ago.

Lisa, 13, learned to bake gingerbread cookies at the cooking school run by her family's store. At Christmas she makes a variety of cookies and packs them in baskets as gifts for her friends. Lisa also bakes delicious Dutch speculaas, *traditional holiday sugar cookies formed in wooden molds.*

Holiday Cookies

Ingredients:
½ cup butter or margarine
½ cup sugar
¼ teaspoon salt
1 egg
½ cup molasses or treacle
1 tablespoon white vinegar
3 cups all-purpose flour
1 teaspoon baking soda
2 teaspoons ground ginger
½ teaspoon each of cinnamon,
   nutmeg, and cloves

Basic Frosting
2½ cups sifted confectioners' sugar
¼ teaspoon cream of tartar
2 egg whites

These cookies were decorated using a pastry bag and three tube openings: No. 3, which produces a thin line, for eyes and small details; No. 5, for a thick line such as for the large boy's lattice top (top left), and thick trims; No. 46, for a fine stripe such as for pink apron trim (top right). The same frosting can be used for decorating and as a glaze. For elaborate effects, use frosting along with sprinkles and small bits of candy. Buttons and boy's mouth are heart-shaped cinnamon candies.

How to Make Gingerbread Cookies

Cream the butter, sugar and salt in a large bowl. Stir in egg, molasses and vinegar and mix well. In another bowl, sift together flour, baking soda, and spices. Add the dry ingredients to the molasses mixture a little at a time and mix thoroughly. Shape the dough into a ball and chill in the refrigerator at least three hours or overnight.

Remove dough from the refrigerator and let it soften. Preheat the oven to 375 degrees Fahrenheit. Using a lightly floured rolling pin, roll out the dough on a lightly floured board until it is ¼-inch thick. You may need to add more flour to keep the dough from sticking.

Use cookie cutters to cut out cookies or place cardboard patterns on the dough and trace around them with a paring knife. Place cookies on lightly greased cookie sheets. Bake the cookies for about 10 minutes. Cool on wire racks for at least a half hour before frosting.

8: Roll out the dough on a lightly floured board using a smooth, firm motion until it is ¼ inch thick. Add more flour if dough sticks.

9: Cut out cookie shapes. Save scraps to reroll to make additional cookies. Excess flour is brushed off before baking.

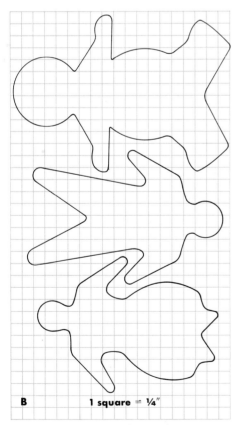

B   1 square = ¼"

Figure B: To make cardboard cookie patterns, enlarge these patterns onto cardboard, as described on page 57, Volume One.

Each colorful cookie is given an individual look with frosting tinted with food coloring. Other combinations of colors and patterns are shown on page 767.

Fun With Frosting

To make frosting, beat 2½ cups confectioners' sugar, ¼ teaspoon cream of tartar and 2 egg whites until the mixture is so stiff that a knife drawn through it leaves a clean path. You may have to add more sugar to achieve the right consistency. To make colored frosting (photograph, page 767), mix in small amounts of food coloring. Use a separate bowl for each color.

To use frosting as a glaze, thin with a drop or two of hot water. Glaze cookies first, spreading with a knife. Let glaze harden before adding frosting details. Then spot-decorate, using a pastry bag and various tube openings. Experiment with different openings for different effects. For the cookies on page 767 I used three openings, No. 3, No. 5, and No. 46. Other decorating tips are given in the entry, "Birthday Celebrations."

For related entries, see "Bread Sculpture" and "Christmas Celebrations."